"This book is a delectable immersion course in noodles and the boundless possibilities of street food in Thailand. With a bowl of broth, laden with herbs and chewy noodles, Andy Ricker transports me to an endlessly tasty place and makes me want to put on my apron and start cooking!"

ALEX GUARNASCHELLI, chef at Butter and The Darby

"When I think of Andy, I see him in a tattoo form, sitting low, eating noodles. It's how I always imagine him. So it made perfect sense that he wrote a book about noodles. Now reality just caught up to imagination. I cannot wait to learn from his book and from the people who have become his family in Thailand."

ROY CHOI, chef and author of *L.A. Son*

"Andy Ricker's newest gem is an homage to the foods he loves most dearly, and is one of the best books ever written on the most mystifying and crave-able piece of the Thai culinary canon, the noodle! This masterpiece is ideal for even the most casual home cook, inspiring anyone to get into the kitchen and make the Thai noodle dishes we all love so much."

ANDREW ZIMMERN, host of *Bizarre Foods*

"Andy Ricker is a true authority on Thai cookery. There has never been a book that covers Thai noodles as thoughtfully as *Pok Pok Noodles*. This book completes a trilogy that tells the story of Thai food, ingredients, and people."

JET TILA, chef at the Food Network

"There was a time when I used to consult my grandma when I wanted to know how things were 'in the old country.' These days, I mostly turn to Andy. In his latest book, we learn everything there is to know about his greatest love, noodles. We benefit from Andy's decades of experience pounding the pavement, chatting up shop owners, and delving deep into Thai culinary history so that we don't have to. Buy Andy's book, cook from it, thank me later."

KRIS YENBAMROONG, chef at Night+Market

"I was first drawn to Andy Ricker because of his strong, manly name. It turns out that he also knows a lot about Thai food. His new book, *Pok Pok Noodles*, is so effing gorgeous that I almost feel dirty looking at it. Even the table of contents, which is basically a list of noodle dishes and their descriptions, is legitimately thrilling. And it's beautifully written, which doesn't even seem necessary. Devour this book!"

ANDY RICHTER, actor

"I love noodles in all forms and guises. One of the greatest joys of walking in Bangkok is to survey the markets and street stalls in all their glory. My eyes usually always fall to the noodles, glistening, inviting and enticing. I find them irresistible. Reading Andy's book is as good as a stroll in Bangkok. The wide-ranging choice of noodles is arresting. I read his book in one sitting, imagining myself eating every dish with relish. His book is an essential entrée into my favorite world, the noodles of Thailand."

DAVID THOMPSON, author of *Thai Food* and *Thai Street*

pokpok
NOODLES

ANDY RICKER
WITH JJ GOODE

PHOTOGRAPHS BY AUSTIN BUSH

RECIPES FROM THAILAND AND BEYOND

pokpok
NOODLES

10
TEN SPEED PRESS
California | New York

Contents

Khanom Jiin
THAILAND'S INDIGENOUS NOODLE

Kuaytiaw Naam
NOODLE SOUPS

Kuaytiaw Phat
FRIED NOODLES

Kuaytiaw Sut Eun Eun
OTHER NOODLE DISHES

NOT NOODLES

Suan Phasom Eun Eun
SUNDRIES

Luuk Chin Muu / Neua / Plaa   214
PORK / BEEF / FISH BALLS

Muu Daeng   218
CHINESE-STYLE BBQ PORK

Muu Krob   220
CRISPY PORK BELLY

Naem   222
FERMENTED PORK SAUSAGE

Muu Sap Sawng Khreuang   224
MINCED-PORK BALLS

Khaep Muu   225
PORK CRACKLINGS

Naam Man Muu   226
RENDERED PORK FAT

Khruang Nai   227
OFFAL

Phat Muu Sap   228
STIR-FRIED GROUND PORK

Muu Sap Luak   228
POACHED GROUND PORK

Neua Kai Chiik   229
SHREDDED POACHED CHICKEN

Sambal Belacan   229
SPICY SHRIMP PASTE

Khai Tom   230
BOILED EGGS

Khai Khem   231
SALTED DUCK EGGS

Naam Phrik Phao   232
CHILE JAM

Naam Phrik Phao   233
ROASTED-CHILE PASTE

Naam Jim Kai   234
SWEET CHILE SAUCE

Naam Jim Si Ew Dam Phrik Sot   234
BLACK SOY-CHILE DIPPING SAUCE

Phrik Phao Naam Som   235
GRILLED-CHILE VINEGAR

Phrik Naam Som   235
VINEGAR-SOAKED CHILES

Phrik Naam Plaa   236
FISH SAUCE-SOAKED CHILES

Naam Man Hom Jiaw   236
FRIED SHALLOTS IN SHALLOT OIL

Naam Man Krathiam Jiaw   237
FRIED GARLIC IN GARLIC OIL

Naam Makham Piak   238
TAMARIND WATER

Kapi Kung   238
HOMEMADE SHRIMP PASTE

Naam Taan Piip   239
SOFTENED PALM SUGAR

Naam Cheuam   239
SIMPLE SYRUP

Naam Cheuam Naam Taan Piip   240
PALM SUGAR SIMPLE SYRUP

Phrik Pon Khua   240
TOASTED-CHILE POWDER

Kung Haeng Khua   242
DRY-FRIED DRIED SHRIMP

Phrik Haeng Thawt   242
DRIED THAI CHILES FRIED IN OIL

Phrik Haeng Khua   243
PAN-TOASTED DRIED THAI CHILES

Kiaw Thawt   243
FRIED WONTON SKINS

Khao Hom Mali   244
JASMINE RICE

Khao Niaw   245
STICKY RICE

Naam Jim Seafood   246
SPICY, TART DIPPING SAUCE FOR SEAFOOD

Phak Dong   247
PICKLED MUSTARD GREENS

Khreuang Deum
DRINKS

Introduction

When you go to Thailand as a tourist, the food thrills you and confounds you. The streets teem with vendors manning carts, presiding over screaming-hot woks, and hawking unfamiliar fruit. Food is everywhere. It's on every corner and down every alley. Your options seem infinite, until you remember your limitations: You can't speak the language. You can't read the signs. You can hardly identify what's on offer, since it all looks so different from the Thai food back home.

That's how it was for me early on. Back in the early '90s, I was walking the streets of Bangkok, wide-eyed and hunting for lunch. And like so many travelers before and after me, I took comfort in noodles.

I spotted a typical operation: a cluster of folding tables and plastic stools colonizing a street corner, with umbrellas set up for relief from the sun. I approached the guy in charge, who stood beside a steaming vat of broth and behind a sort of rickety display case, inside of which a few cooked chickens were hung. A pile of clear plastic bags contained noodles of various shapes and sizes. I ordered by pointing, sat down on one of the stools, and, in no time, was staring down at a bowl of *kuaytiaw naam kai*—essentially, chicken noodle soup.

Of course, this wasn't the chicken noodle soup I'd grown up eating. Instead, I was confronted with a clean, mild broth infused with ginger, green onion, and cilantro; a tangle of slightly chewy rice noodles; and a dose of chopped Chinese celery, fried garlic, and bean sprouts. Although I didn't realize it yet, as I sat on that street corner, plowing through my bowl and watching the city rush by, I had hit upon the formula that would later make my restaurant Pok Pok a success. This bowl of noodles occupied that sweet spot between familiar and novel. Give diners food that both satisfies and thrills, and they will come.

Since then, my travels in Thailand have revealed an entire world of noodles that I didn't know existed. I ate brothless bowls of fresh, wide rice noodles topped with stewed beef at roadside restaurants outside of Chiang Mai. I wandered alleys in Bangkok's Chinatown in search of *kuay chap*, peppery broth filled with tubular noodles and pork offal, and *kuaytiaw khua kai*, fresh rice noodles fried in a wok with chicken and pickled cuttlefish. I sampled the finest *kuaytiaw sukothai* in all of Sukothai and the best *kuaytiaw reua* (boat noodles) in Ayutthaya, where it was once sold by hawkers from vessels floating in the canals that lead down the Chao Phraya River to Bangkok.

As I tucked into bowls, I dug into history as well. I learned that most noodle dishes in Thailand are of Chinese origin, popularized by people who are Thai in nationality but ethnically Chinese. Around the ends of the seventeenth and nineteenth centuries, two major influxes of are emigrants from southern China, specifically the Teochew and Hokkien peoples, brought people with an affection for noodles. And so these new residents began serving them within their communities and later outside of them. By the turn of the twentieth century, the audience expanded, particularly in rapidly modernizing urban centers such as Bangkok, where the pace of life forced working folks to seek meals away from the traditional home kitchen.

Gradually, Thai cooks tweaked these dishes to appeal to local palates until they became, more or less, Thai, crossing the illusory lines that separate the vast web of cultures into discrete pieces. And so noodles joined the litany of foreign influences and ingredients—from the technique of stir-frying (also from China) to chiles (from the New World via Portuguese missionaries) to dried spices such as coriander and cumin (from India)— that Thai cooks have integrated into the country's culinary repertoire. Those adaptations might be as simple as adding ingredients such as galangal and lemongrass to pots of pork, simmering, in Chinese fashion, with star anise and rock sugar, and using the resulting stew to crown bowls of rice noodles. Or it could be serving a clay pot of glass noodles, shrimp, and pork belly with a tart, fiery chile dipping sauce.

I also found out that Thailand has an indigenous noodle called *khanom jiin* (see page 44). I visited village factories that produce the thin, slightly sour strands made from fermented rice-flour batter that are sold in skeins, like yarn. I frequented market stalls that serve them topped with curries and sauces.

As I ate, read, and inquired, I began to understand the place of noodles within Thai cuisine. Although many Thai foods are mistakenly equated with street food, noodles are indeed the quintessential example. They are the stuff of curbside vendors operating with little more than a wok or pair of pots, even if those cooks often eventually move on to brick-and-mortar locations.

These enterprises usually specialize in a certain dish, a laserlike focus born mostly of kitchen constraints: If your shop has only two pots, one for bubbling broth and one for boiling water, you're probably not going to serve both boat noodles and curried noodles. If you have just one wok and limited storage, you probably wouldn't offer both *phat si ew* and *kuaytiaw khua kai*. (You might, however, offer *lat na*, since it shares main ingredients with the former.) Specialization often breeds expertise. The best boat-noodle vendors are so good in part because they have made one thing and one thing only for decades.

Sadly, as the pressure of modern life impinges on vendors in Thailand, the old way of making noodle dishes is slowly dying. Buying a franchise—and, yes, many of the carts you see lining the streets of Thailand are actually franchises—offers a proven recipe, brand recognition, and a built-in customer base that guarantees at least a modicum of business as long as the location is decent. Purchasing ready-made broth, premade pork balls, and seasonings from food conglomerates saves both money and time. The more vendors take this route, the more the tastes of their customers change, especially those of the younger generation, their appetites bending toward franchise recipes and processed foods. Luckily, some decades- or generations-old vendors still carry on their familial traditions and show no signs of changing. Their places are the ones I seek out, give my custom to, and champion however possible. The recipes in this book pay homage to these dedicated heritage cooks and food makers.

About This Book

In these pages, you'll find recipes for the noodle dishes with which I'm most familiar. Most of them are common in Thailand, but a few that I couldn't resist including come from elsewhere. In addition, you'll find recipes for a handful of dishes that don't contain noodles but might appear on a noodle-shop menu.

As in my previous cookbooks, the goal of each recipe is to replicate my favorite version of the dish in question, typically one made by a vendor who eschews concessions to convenience, like purchased fish balls and premade broths, in order to make something extraordinary. My ambition requires that the lists of ingredients and instructions be more precise and comprehensive than those in a manual of, say, Italian pasta, where the typical brown-and-braise and dice-the-carrots culinary instincts of the West can fill in most blanks. Don't let this deter you. You'll be pleased by the rewards of patience and extra effort. I should say, too, that most of the portions in this book are a bit larger than you typically see in Thailand—another bonus of making the food yourself.

Because some of the particulars of enjoying noodles are also foreign, each recipe indicates the preferred accompaniments, with which guests adjust the seasonings themselves, and the recommended eating utensils—my gentle rebuke to the persistent assumption of chopsticks. Amid all this prescription is a tribute to the flexibility of the noodle genre, where customers can tailor nearly every aspect of a dish, from the amount of broth to the type of noodle to, paradoxically, whether there are noodles at all.

A final note to acknowledge a quirk of this book: These recipes originate from restaurants. In adapting them for the home cook, I have made some modifications, yet there are certain essential techniques that cannot be altered or compromised. It would be expedient, for example, if noodles cooked in a wok were made to serve the cookbook-standard four people. But to accommodate that convention, you'd be forced to overload the cooking vessel, and the food would suffer immeasurably. In the same vein, it would be more convenient to apply the principles of spaghetti to noodle soups, boiling *sen lek* or *ba mii* by the pound and then dividing the noodles among bowls. Instead, to achieve a worthy result, you must make and assemble bowls one by one, whether you mean to make two portions or ten.

For these reasons, many recipes in this book yield one portion. Note that making more is as easy as doubling, tripling, or quadrupling the ingredients listed—since it's impossible to purchase just 1 tablespoon of fish sauce or make just 1 cup of broth, you'll likely have plenty of each ingredient on hand already—and cooking each portion separately. I find this more helpful than the conventional recipe—assuming, of course, you don't socialize exclusively in groups of four.

For boiled noodle dishes, scaling up is especially simple. You need just one large pot of water. Each portion takes mere minutes to assemble. Make the first bowl (or the first *and* second, if you have two long-handled noodle baskets), serve, then get to work on the next one—just as a vendor would. For stir-fries and other dishes made in a wok, make the portions in batches, cleaning the wok after each one.

The exceptions are those dishes that require a recipe-specific broth, stew, or curry. In those cases, I instruct you to make a reasonable amount of said component, then use it to make as many bowls of noodles as makes sense.

A Note on Weight and Volume

In a book full of unfamiliar ingredients, techniques, and flavors, where the culinary instincts that might otherwise offset a lack of rigor don't apply, precision is of particular importance.

Weight is the preferred measurement for the solid ingredients in this book. For curry pastes and other preparations for which solid ingredients are pulverized, I have provided *only* weights—in grams and without volume equivalents. That's because in these cases, precision is vital. Cramming slices of a knobby rhizome into a tablespoon measure or rounding up to achieve a neat fraction of an ounce will have a profound effect on the outcome of a dish. It may sound fussy to call for 17 grams of galangal. So be it.

Those instances aside, I have also provided the approximate volume for solid ingredients when the finished product won't suffer dramatically from fudging in one direction or another. I've used volume for liquid ingredients and those that are grated, minced, in powder form, or otherwise fine enough for volume to be an accurate measure. I've added weight measures in case you'd rather not have to switch between tablespoons and cups and the digital scale.

A good digital scale that toggles between US units of measurement (ounces and pounds) and metric units (grams and kilograms) is inexpensive. Weighing ingredients is really easy. Once you start, you'll be hooked.

Ingredients

Fear not: You can, with just a little effort, find all the ingredients listed in this book. In fact, the task has never been easier. Nowadays, big-city supermarkets often stock Thai chiles, lemongrass, and even fresh turmeric root, which has developed a reputation as a health food and, lucky us, is also common in Thai cooking. In general, however, your best bet is a supermarket that serves Southeast Asian customers, as it will typically have aisles devoted to Thai products such as fish sauce, black soy sauce, and coconut milk. Markets with a Chinese focus often have much of the produce and noodles you need because of overlap in the pantries of the two countries. Locating some products requires ingenuity. For example, sawtooth herb is common in Thailand, but in the US, it's more readily available at Vietnamese or Latin American grocery stores. And of course, if ever your search should fail, there's always the internet.

Banana

BANANA BLOSSOM (HUA BLII)

The purplish red, tightly closed buds of the banana tree are used in many Thai dishes. They're difficult but not impossible to find in the US, typically at Southeast Asian markets.

In this book, fresh blossoms are served raw and sliced to accompany *phat thai* (see pages 137 to 141) and *phat mii khorat* (see page 133). They're mild in flavor and produce the mouth-drying sensation known as *faht* (tannic), a welcome way to balance the rich, sweet noodle stir-fries. Do not substitute frozen, jarred, or dried.

To prepare banana blossoms, fill a large bowl with water and stir in ¼ cup or so distilled white vinegar. Peel off and discard the tough petals, discarding any long, thin flowers (essentially, infant bananas) between the petals, until you reach the off-white, tender ones. Cut off the stem, halve the blossom lengthwise, and cut lengthwise into ½-inch wedges. Transfer the wedges to the vinegar water to prevent them from browning, and top with a plate to keep them submerged. Right before you're ready to serve, drain really well and pat dry.

BANANA LEAF (BAI YOK)

Primarily used to wrap ingredients before grilling or steaming, banana leaves impart a subtle tannic flavor and aroma. They're occasionally available fresh but are more typically sold frozen in Chinese, Southeast Asian, and Latin American markets (where they go by *hojas de platano*).

Basil

HOLY BASIL (BAI KAPHRAO)

Also known as hot basil, holy basil, has a peppery flavor and intense, distinctive aroma. Your best bet for finding it is in a Thai-focused market (ask for "by ga-PROW"). Beware, however, as I've seen the label "holy basil" attached to purple-stemmed Thai basil (see below). The two are not interchangeable.

LEMON BASIL (BAI MENGLAK)

This variety of basil has a lemony, minty quality. It's available at some Southeast Asian markets (those serving Thai and Hmong people, in particular) and at farmers' markets.

THAI BASIL (BAI HORAPHA)

This licorice-scented variety, sometimes called sweet basil, makes an aromatic addition to soups and curries. Look for it at Chinese and Southeast Asian grocery stores and at farmers' markets. Thai basil has distinctive purple stems, which, along with its fragrance, make it easy to identify, even if the herb is labeled simply "basil."

Bean sprouts (thua ngok)

Look for bean sprouts in the refrigerated section of Asian markets, where they're often sold from bins or in bags. For the recipes in this book, you want to use mung bean sprouts, which have slender yellow tops, not soybean sprouts, which have bulbous yellow tops.

Bitter melon (mara)

Also called bitter gourd, there are several varieties of this aggressively bitter fruit. The type you find in Chinese and Southeast Asian markets—long, pale green, and slightly bumpy, with ridges running the length of the fruit—is ideal for the purposes of this book. The more jagged kinds you see at South Asian markets will work, too.

Blood

RAW BLOOD (LEUAT)

Used to enrich dishes such as boat noodles (see page 81), raw pig's (and, less often, cow's) blood can be found in the freezer at Korean, Chinese, and Southeast Asian markets, some Latin American markets, or at butcher shops that work closely with local farms and allow special orders. Defrosted, the blood will have a liquid or gelatinous texture.

STEAMED BLOOD (LEUAT KAWN)

The butcher cases at Korean, Chinese, and Southeast Asian markets often display large chocolate-brown blocks of steamed coagulated pig's blood. It is sometimes labeled "blood tofu" or "blood curd" but is often labeled simply "pig blood." In Thailand, chicken blood is preferred for its mild flavor and silky texture, but in the U.S.A., it's considered a toxic substance by the USDA and is thus unfortunately unavailable.

Candlenuts

Toasted, ground, and used to provide texture to some curries in Indonesia and Malaysia, candlenuts are available in bags in Southeast Asian and Chinese markets. They are slightly toxic when raw, so don't eat them without cooking them first. Macadamia nuts make a passable substitute.

Cardamom

BLACK CARDAMOM (CHAOKO)

These seedpods are a species of black cardamom, though they shouldn't be confused with what is frequently sold as black cardamom in South Asian markets. Instead, look in Chinese markets for bags labeled *tsao-ko* or a different transliteration, such as *cha koh* or *cao guo*.

WHITE CARDAMOM (LUUK KRAWAN)

These round, beige pods, a cousin of the more familiar green cardamom, are the preferred variety among Thai cooks making *khao soi* (see pages 175 and 181). The two types are not interchangeable. Look for bags in Thai and Chinese markets and some specialty spice shops.

Chiles

PUYA, DRIED

This Mexican chile mimics the size and flavor of *phrik kaeng*, a medium-size dried chile used in Thailand. Puya chiles are available in Mexican and Latin American markets, the "Latin foods" section of some supermarkets, and online. If the chiles are particularly supple, leaving them uncovered for a day will make them brittle and easier for novices to pound as instructed in the recipes.

SERRANO, FRESH

These fresh chiles stand in for a moderately spicy green variety that cooks in Thailand would use. Common in Latin American markets, farmers' markets, and many supermarkets, serrano chiles resemble long, slender jalapeños, though for the purposes of this book, the two are not interchangeable.

THAI, DRIED (PHRIK HAENG OR PHRIK JINDA)

Pounded into pastes or added whole to stir-fries and salads, these chiles are available online and in Southeast Asian–focused grocery stores. Look for red chiles that are 2 to 3 inches long in bags that specify "from Thailand." If you fail to find them, the small dried chiles available in most Asian markets will do.

THAI, FRESH (PHRIK KHII NUU)

You will find these small (about 2-inch-long), fiery chiles at Asian and Southeast Asian markets as well as some big-city markets, where they might be labeled "bird chile," "bird's eye chile," or occasionally "finger chile." Frozen ones are fine (they actually tend to have a more consistent heat level). Some recipes specifically call for green Thai chiles and some for red Thai chiles. In general, the colors have slightly different flavor profiles and heat levels, with red being hotter and slightly sweeter, as well as different aromas—a quality of particular importance in Thai cooking. In other words, do your darndest to use the color indicated in the recipe.

Chinese broccoli (phak khanaa)

Almost every market with a wide selection of Chinese products and some farmers' markets carry this leafy vegetable (*gai lan* in Chinese, which is often the language transliterated on signs). Unless otherwise instructed, use the more common mature Chinese broccoli, which has long, fat stems.

Chinese celery (kheun chai)

A common ingredient in stir-fries and soups, this variety is leafier and has much thinner stems than the celery ubiquitous in supermarkets in the States. Look for it in the produce section of Chinese and Southeast Asian markets.

Chinese keys (krachai)

In the United States, you'll likely only find this rhizome frozen, which works well for the recipes in this book. Look for it, whole or shredded, in Chinese and Southeast Asian markets, where it might also be labeled *krachai* or *grachai*. It's sometimes referred to as "lesser galangal," "finger root," or simply "rhizome." Avoid canned or jarred *krachai*.

Cilantro root (rak phak chii)

In the United States, cilantro (or coriander) is typically sold without its root attached. When you see roots-on bunches at farmers' markets and Southeast Asian grocery stores, buy them. The root adds the herb's punchy flavor without the *men khiaw* (the strong green quality that some call "soapiness") of the leaves. Roots vary widely in size, so measuring by weight is of particular importance.

Before you use them, rinse the roots under running water, rubbing them with your fingers. Clean them thoroughly, but don't bother peeling for the recipes in this book, then freeze them.

Cinnamon (op choei)

There are two main types of cinnamon. For the recipes in this book, use common cinnamon, which comes in sturdy sticks and is technically cassia, rather than the so-called true cinnamon, which is also known as Ceylon cinnamon and canela and comes in flaky, relatively delicate sticks.

Coconut milk and cream (kati)

There is no substitute for the freshly pressed coconut milk and cream you can get in Thailand, which is made by squeezing the grated flesh of mature coconuts. Home cooks in the States, however, are stuck with the packaged stuff. In my experience, boxed UHT (ultra heat treated) is preferable to canned, not least because it's typically 100 percent coconut milk or cream without preservatives or thickeners. If the fat in the box has solidified and separated from the liquid, empty the contents into a saucepan and gently warm over low heat, stirring occasionally, until it's all liquid.

For recipes that require "cracking" coconut cream (heating the cream in order to separate the water from the fat), using a boxed UHT variety is close to essential. If you can't find it, be aware that the cream might take longer to crack (or might not crack at all). That said, I have had good luck cracking the Savoy brand canned product. Regardless of the packaging, make sure you buy the unsweetened kind, both cream and milk.

Coriander seeds (met phak chii)

Those eager to go the extra mile will use coriander seeds sold at Chinese or Southeast Asian grocery stores rather than the ones available at your local supermarket. The Asian seeds have a nutty, spicy quality, while the Western ones call to mind hot dogs a bit too vividly for my taste.

Cuttlefish (plaa meuk)

Sometimes referred to as "sepia," cuttlefish are cephalopods like squid and octopus. It resembles large squid in appearance and flavor and somewhat in texture, since its body is thicker than that of squid. Look for it at specialty fish markets or, better yet, Chinese fish markets.

Daikon radish (huay chai thao)

This large, long, white-skinned radish has a relatively mild flavor compared to many other radishes. It's sold at Chinese markets and some farmers' markets.

Dried shrimp (kung haeng)

Chinese, Korean, and Southeast Asian grocery stores stock dried shrimp loose or in bags. The shrimp come in different sizes. Look for medium-size (sometimes you'll just see the letter *M* on the bag) for the purposes of this book.

Fish sauce (naam plaa)

Look for bottles of this intensely salty seasoning and condiment, made from salted, fermented fish, on shelves in Chinese and Southeast Asian markets. For the purpose of this book, buy Thai fish sauce. The Squid and Tiparos brands are solid (avoid the common Thai Kitchen brand) and Megachef is best. Vietnamese fish sauce tends to be mild and sweet in comparison.

Galangal (khaa)

This knobby rhizome looks like fat, pale-skinned ginger but tastes citrusy, earthy, and much less sharp than its kin. Find it fresh in Thai and some Chinese grocery stores in the refrigerated section or near the produce and frozen in the freezer section.

Garlic chives (kuay chai)

Look for bunches of these flat blades, not to be confused with the chives with yellowish buds at the tips at Chinese and Southeast Asian markets.

Lemongrass (takrai)

Lemongrass has become fairly common in big-city markets, Asian and not. Note that the flavor begins to deteriorate after a few days in the fridge. Some recipes call for the tender part of the stalk. The size and freshness of the lemongrass will affect the yield of thinly sliced tender parts, though you can figure on about 7 grams / 1 tablespoon for every large stalk. Save the trimmings for stock.

To access the tender parts, remove about 1 inch from the bottom and about 9 inches from the top of the stalk. Next, peel off the fibrous layers.

After about five layers, you should have reached the tender portion. Start slicing at the bottom, discarding any parts that give a sharp knife pause.

Lime

The limes you find in Thailand are closest in size and flavor to Key limes. The recipes all work with regular (aka Persian) lime juice, but I urge you to look for Key limes, which are available in many major supermarkets, or to add a squeeze of Meyer lemon juice to regular lime juice. The goal is a more fragrant and less bitter juice. Choose limes with smooth, shiny (not dull, rugged) skin. These tend to have thinner skins and contain more juice.

MAKRUT LIME (LUUK MAKRUT)

The fruit of the same tree that gives us makrut lime leaves (see following entry), these limes are used primarily for their bumpy, fragrant skin. They are sold fresh and frozen at some Thai markets.

MAKRUT LIME LEAVES (BAI MAKRUT)

The fragrant leaves of the makrut lime tree are available fresh (typically in the refrigerated section) or frozen in some Thai, Indian, and Chinese grocery stores. Do not use dried leaves. If you don't use fresh leaves within a couple of days of purchasing them, freeze them for up to 3 months.

Limestone paste (naam boon sai)

Sometimes labeled "lime paste," this product is slaked lime, also known as calcium hydroxide. It is a pantry staple in the Thai kitchen, where it's mixed with water and used to make batters that fry exceptionally crisp. It's also part of the concoction of betel nuts and leaves that old-timers chew as a stimulant. In this book, it is used to keep mustard greens firm after pickling (see page 247).

Long beans (thua fak yao)

You'll find these at most Chinese and Southeast Asian markets that sell produce. They're occasionally called yard-long beans or snake beans, but you won't need a label to identify them, as they look like very long green beans. If you have a choice, choose the thinner, darker variety, which is the one preferred by most Thai cooks.

Malaysian fermented shrimp paste (belacan)

Different in flavor from the Thai shrimp paste called *kapi* (see page 238), *belacan*, sometimes labeled "dried shrimp paste," is also made from salted, fermented shrimp. Look for Malaysian brands, which are typically sold in blocks (and wrapped in a way that make them look a bit like bars of soap) on shelves at Southeast Asian and Chinese markets.

MSG (phong chuu roht)

Monosodium glutamate, or MSG, is an unfairly maligned ingredient (see page 22) used frequently in the preparation of noodle soups in Thailand, as well as some other dishes. It generally comes as white flakes sold in bags, often under the Japanese Ajinomoto brand, but sometimes, especially in Western stores, in cylindrical containers under the name Accent.

Oyster sauce (naam man hoi)

A common bottled seasoning in Thai cooking, oyster sauce should have a salty, briny flavor along with a mellow sweetness, not just an intense saltiness. To achieve the right flavor for the recipes in this book, buy a Thai brand, such as Maekrua or Megachef, which you'll find at Southeast Asian and Chinese markets.

Pandan leaf (bai toei)

The fresh leaves (sometimes called pandanus) of a variety of screwpine are hard but not impossible to come by in the US. You're more likely, however, to find these long leaves in bags in the freezer section of Southeast Asian and Chinese grocery stores.

Pennywort (bai boa bok)

This medicinal herb has serrated, fan-shaped leaves and a green, slightly bitter flavor. It goes by *gotu kola* in Sri Lankan, *brahmi* in Hindi, *rau má* in Vietnamese, and sometimes centella (from *Centella asiatica*, its scientific name) in English. Look for it at Southeast Asian and South Asian markets.

Pickled garlic (krathiam dong)

Look for Thai brands of pickled garlic, such as Cock or Pantainorasingh, in jars in Southeast Asian markets or the relevant section in Chinese supermarkets. The garlic heads are pickled whole in a sweet vinegar solution. Some recipes call for peeled cloves and some for whole heads. Follow the instructions in the each recipe.

Pickled mustard greens (phak dong)

The committed among you will make these yourself (see page 247). Otherwise, look for Cock or other Thai brands sold in bags on shelves.

Pressed tofu (taohu khaeng)

Phat thai requires this especially firm tofu that's often labeled "pressed" and is a few degrees more dense than the more common "extra-firm" tofu. Look for the unflavored or plain kind in the refrigerated case at Chinese supermarkets and some health food stores. It's often sold in vacuum-sealed packs.

Red fermented bean curd (taohu yii)

This pungent Chinese jarred product is bean curd (aka tofu) that's been fermented and then soaked in a brine of, among other ingredients, vinegar, rice wine, and red-yeast rice, which imparts a vivid color. Look for it at Chinese and Southeast Asian markets.

Salt (kleua)

Most instances of salt in these recipes are kosher salt. The weight-to-volume conversions have been calculated using the popular Diamond Crystal brand. If you use Morton kosher salt, be aware that the volume measurements will differ significantly from those given.

Salted radish (hua chai po)

You'll find this pale-brown product, also labeled "preserved radish," on shelves at Chinese and Southeast Asian markets. Look for a Thai brand sold in a bag, and opt for shredded or "stripped," not minced. If you can find only whole salted radish, cut it into 1 by ⅛ by ⅛-inch strips.

Sawtooth herb (phak chii farang)

This long, serrated leaf is used to finish many of the dishes in this book. A better bet than Thai markets in the US are Latin American ones, where the herb goes by *culantro* and *recao*, and Vietnamese ones, where it goes by *ngò gai*.

Seasoning sauce (sauce phrung roht)

Yes, it's labeled "seasoning sauce." In Thai, it's *sauce phrung roht* ("sauce to adjust flavor"). Made from fermented soybeans, salt, sugar, and other ingredients, it provides Worcestershire sauce–like flavor enhancement but without the dried-spice component. Look for Thai-brand bottles, such as Golden Mountain and Healthy Boy, which almost always have a green cap, at Chinese and Southeast Asian markets.

Shallots, Asian (hom daeng)

For shallots that are to be pounded into pastes for stir-fries, soups, stews, and so on, my preference is for the small, round variety sold at Chinese and Southeast Asian markets, which have a more appropriate size and flavor and lower water content than torpedo-shaped French shallots. For salads and fried shallots, you can comfortably use either type.

Shaoxing wine (lao jiin)

This Chinese wine made from glutinous (sticky) rice is occasionally used in Thai dishes, including a few in this book. Buy it at Chinese and Southeast Asian markets, where different brands may have labels with various phonetic transliterations.

Soy sauce

BLACK SOY SAUCE (SI EW DAM)

One of three types of soy sauce common in Thai cooking, black soy has a strong, molasses-like character and tastes markedly sweeter than thin soy sauce. Seek out Thai brands, such as Kwong Hung Seng (look for the dragonfly on the label), Healthy Boy, or Maekrua, at Chinese and Southeast Asian markets.

SWEET SOY SAUCE (SI EW WAAN)

Sweet soy is very sweet compared to the molasses-like sweetness of black soy. Seek out Thai brands, such as Kwong Hung Seng (look for the dragonfly on the label), Healthy Boy, or Maekrua, at Chinese and Southeast Asian markets.

THIN SOY SAUCE (SI EW KHAO)

Thin soy is salty without a particularly intense flavor. Seek out Thai brands, such as Kwong Hung Seng (look for the dragonfly on the label), Healthy Boy, or Maekrua, at Chinese and Southeast Asian markets. Do not substitute Japanese soy sauce.

Sriracha sauce

In Thailand there's a town called Sri Racha that's famous for its eponymous hot sauce. This sauce, not the "rooster brand" Sriracha, made by the California-based Vietnamese-American company Huy Fong Foods, that has conquered America, is what you want for the recipes in this book. Look for Shark brand; if that fails, select another Thai brand and welcome a different Sriracha into your pantry.

Sugar

PALM SUGAR (NAAM TAAN)

If you're lucky, you'll find soft palm sugar (*naam taan piip*) sold in small plastic containers at Thai markets. A gentle squeeze will tell you if it's hardened from improper storage. If it has, opt for palm sugar in hard disk form (*naam taan beuk*) and approximate the soft stuff in the microwave (see page 239). Either way, look for brands that sell 100 percent palm sugar from Thailand, such as Golden Chef or Cock. Vietnamese palm sugar and Indian jaggery are acceptable substitutes. Brown and white sugars are not.

ROCK SUGAR, CHINESE

This type of crystallized sugar is sometimes labeled "rock candy." For this book, you can use either the large, craggy chunks or smaller, smoother pebbles sold in bags in most Chinese or Southeast Asian markets. Just make sure you opt for the brownish kind, referred to on some labels as "yellow." The large chunks make volume measurements particularly unreliable, so if you use those, using a scale to measure is especially important.

Sweet potato starch (baeng man)

Not technically made from sweet potatoes, and not to be confused with sweet potato flour, this powder is derived from cassava. Chinese and Southeast Asian markets stock the right stuff. Buy an Asian brand and you're good.

Tamarind paste (makham piak)

Sometimes labeled as "paste" or even just "tamarind," the tart, seedless pulp is sold in bagged blocks at Chinese and Southeast Asian markets and in some supermarkets. Buy Vietnamese or Thai brands, such as Cock. Liquid tamarind concentrate is not right for the recipes in this book.

Tapioca starch (baeng man sampalang)

Used as a thickener, tapioca starch is a powder sold in bags at most markets, Western and not. At Asian markets, you might have a choice between products that are fine, granular, and in chunks. Opt for fine powder and, if you can, a Thai brand.

Thai eggplants (makheua praw)

Southeast Asian and Chinese markets and some farmers' markets stock these firm, round, golf ball–size eggplants. They're typically green with white streaks near the base and have a crunchy texture even when cooked, as well as a pleasantly bitter flavor.

Tofu puffs (taohu thawt)

Also labeled "soy puffs" and "fried soybean cake," these prefried cubes of tofu are stocked in bags in the refrigerated case at Chinese and Southeast Asian supermarkets.

Turmeric root, yellow (khamin)

Nowadays, you'll find fresh yellow turmeric in high-end supermarkets and health food stores. It's also stocked in Indian, West Indian, and some Thai grocery stores and in the freezer section of many Chinese or Southeast Asian supermarkets. Unlike its white cousin (see Note, page 59), it's not slivered and eaten raw but rather pounded into pastes for curries, soups, and the like, particularly in Northern Thailand and elsewhere in Southeast Asia.

Vietnamese mint (phak phai)

Look for this herb in Southeast Asian markets, where it also goes by "laksa leaf" and "Vietnamese coriander" in English, *daun kesum* in Malay, or *rau răm* in Vietnamese.

Vietnamese pork roll (muu yaw)

This slightly spongy, cold cut–like pork product is sold at Vietnamese and other Southeast Asian markets, typically in the refrigerated section. Most likely, it will be labeled *chả lụa* or *giò lạu*.

Water spinach (phak buung)

Sold in generous bunches in Chinese and Southeast Asian markets, this green vegetable, also called Chinese spinach, is best identified by its hollow stems and narrow, pointed leaves. Depending on the market, it goes by *ong choy* or *on choy* in Cantonese, *kangkong* in Malaysia, or *kangkung* in Indonesia.

White pepper (phrik thai khao)

To my taste, the white pepper sold under Asian, and especially Thai, brands has a much milder, more pleasant flavor than the stuff on offer at Western markets.

Yellow bean sauce (tao jiaw)

This bottled sauce is made from fermented yellow soybeans blended with salt, sugar, and other ingredients. It's often labeled "soybean paste." Look for Thai brands, such as Healthy Boy in Chinese and Southeast Asian markets.

Yellow beans, salted (tao jiaw)

Unlike yellow bean sauce, this product is just soybeans, more or less intact, in a salt brine. To make matters as confusing as possible, salted yellow beans are often labeled "yellow bean sauce." To identify the right product, look for squat jars, rather than tall bottles, that contain large chunks of beans, not a coarse, saucey mixture, and whose ingredients don't include sugar. Choose a Thai brand, such as Pantainorasingh from Chinese and Southeast Asian markets.

Yu choy (phak kat)

Similar in appearance to Chinese broccoli, this Asian green has a slightly different flavor and can typically be identified by its tiny yellow flowers. It's available in Chinese and Southeast Asian markets.

A Note on MSG

We have come a long way from the days when MSG was considered toxic. The panic began in the late 1960s with a letter to the *New England Journal of Medicine* in which a physician described some unpleasant symptoms he experienced after eating at American Chinese restaurants and casually wondered whether monosodium glutamate was the culprit. His anecdotal observations morphed into a kind of gospel, the transformation no doubt made possible by both ignorance of and prejudice against Chinese food and, by extension, Chinese people. Restaurants fearful of losing customers banished MSG from their menus. Mine essentially do as well. When you run businesses that support your family and employ about two hundred people, you choose your battles.

Mercifully, the consensus has changed, especially in the past decade or so. This is due in part to chefs such as Momofuku's David Chang championing both the science confirming the safety of the amino acid glutamate and its role in making food taste good. Practically every cuisine has its preferred source. Japanese food leans on kombu and miso, Italian cooks look to Parmesan and tomatoes, and Thais employ fish sauce and shrimp paste, to name just two. These products have a mouth-watering quality and general deliciousness that Japanese chemist Kikunae Ikeda dubbed *umami* and most everyone now recognizes as the fifth taste, along with sweet, salty, sour, and bitter. At this point, with chefs regularly tinkering with fermentation and ingredients known to boost umami, you can find monosodium glutamate or other sources of free glutamates in most modern professional kitchens.

MSG is a bit different than the glutamates you find in Parmesan and shrimp paste. Sold as flaky crystals, it is an isolated form of the amino acid, a by-product of the bacterial fermentation of things like sugar beets, sugarcane, and tapioca that has been stabilized with salt (the "sodium" in monosodium glutamate). MSG is in the same family as ingredients such as hydrolyzed soy protein and autolyzed yeast, which you find in many processed foods and are essentially MSG by another name. All of them have been deemed safe by the World Health Organization and the FDA. Research suggests that our bodies process them in the same way as they do naturally occurring forms of glutamate.

In many Asian countries, MSG is not only an industrial food additive, but also a pantry staple. In Thailand, for instance, it is a common addition, in homes and restaurants, to everything from grilled meats to papaya salad to noodles dishes in general and noodle soups in particular. (In Laos, MSG is often treated as a condiment, set out on tables to be added to your dish like sugar or fish sauce.) Known in Thai as *phong chuu roht* (basically, "make flavor better powder"), MSG is a crucial ingredient for anyone committed to making food that tastes like it does in Thailand (at least nowadays). For the few purchasers of this volume who still fear MSG, don't worry. For the recipes in this book, it's recommended, but optional. By adding a bit of MSG to a dish, you can back off on the addition of salty *and* sweet ingredients during cooking.

Recognizing that the reasonable application of MSG won't harm your health doesn't mean you shouldn't be skeptical of its widespread use. Its power corrupts. The temptation to rely on MSG, rather than technique, has proven too much for some cooks to resist. Without a solid bedrock of flavor to boost, food made with MSG as the primary seasoning is unfulfilling, somehow flavorful but not delicious, like bouillon compared to real chicken stock. MSG can't fill a void. When added judiciously, however, its presence is hard to detect unless you're practiced. All you know is that whatever you're eating tastes better than it did before—the flavors a little more vivid, more intense.

Noodles

Here are the types of noodles you'll need to make the recipes in this book and where to find them.

Khanom jiin (fresh rice vermicelli)

In this book, dried thin rice noodles stand in for this fresh, slightly fermented noodle common in Thailand but not available in the West. For information on Thailand's indigenous noodle as well as shopping guidance and preparation instructions, see page 44.

Sen lek (thin, flat rice noodles), aka rice sticks

A relatively narrow, flat noodle made from rice and (sometimes) tapioca flours, *sen lek* is often sold fresh in Thailand. In the West, it comes in two forms, semidried (slightly pliable and kept in the refrigerated section of Chinese and Southeast Asian markets) and fully dried (brittle and kept on shelves). I prefer the semidried product, but you can successfully imitate the semidried kind by soaking the fully dried noodles in lukewarm (about 100°F) water until pliable but not fully hydrated, about 10 minutes.

There are two varieties of this noodle. One is flat and narrow (similar in shape to linguine) and often labeled *bánh phở*, its Vietnamese name. The second is flat and slightly wider (similar in shape to fettuccine) and often labeled *pad thai*.

Sen mii (very thin rice noodles)

Not to be confused with the thin rice vermicelli used for making *khanom jiin* (see page 44) and Vietnamese *bun*, which have a slightly different composition, *sen mii* are very thin, opaque, round rice noodles usually sold dried in bags in the West. Look for a Thai brand, such as Wai Wai, near other dried noodles on shelves at Asian markets.

Sen yai (fresh wide rice noodles), aka chow fun in Cantonese

Made from a runny batter of water, rice flour, and tapioca flour then coated liberally with vegetable oil, these slippery, chewy fresh noodles are steamed in sheets and then cut to size.

The task of cooking will be easier and the food better if you seek out a shop that stocks *sen yai* made that day, either in-house or delivered from another operation, and stored at room temperature. Buying them in sheets, as they're often sold, and cutting them yourself lets you control the width of the noodles. Buying them precut, often ¾ inch wide, is just fine. Use them as soon as possible after purchase, and if you must, store covered in a cool, dry place for up to 12 hours.

Otherwise, settle for what are sometimes sold in the refrigerated section of Chinese and Southeast Asian markets. Because these will be slightly brittle and difficult to work with, soften them for a few seconds in the microwave or in boiling water. Before proceeding with the recipe, carefully separate the noodles, trying your best to keep them intact.

Ba mii (fresh thin wheat noodles), aka wonton noodles

For the purposes of this book, there are two varieties of this fresh, typically yellowish wheat noodle that often contains eggs. One is thin (similar in shape to angel hair or spaghetti) and suitable for *Ba Mii Bak Kut Teh* (see page 107) and *Ba Mii Tom Yam Haeng Muu* (see page 187); the other is wide and flat (similar in shape to linguine) and suitable for Khao Soi Neua (page 175). You'll find both in the refrigerated section of Chinese and other large Asian markets. They're sometimes labeled "wonton noodles." Mercurial labeling, however, can make identifying the proper noodle difficult, but as long as you find uncooked fresh, thin yellow Chinese wheat noodles, you're in good shape.

Ba mii yok (jade noodles)

These noodles, which are used in Ba Mii Yok Haeng (page 165), are essentially the same as *ba mii* (see above) but are dyed green with food coloring. They are typically found in the same section of the store.

Kuay chap (bean sheet noodles)

Thin sheets of this Chinese noodle made of mung bean flour and other starches (depending on the manufacturer), are cut into 2-inch squares and dried. Before cooking, the squares are typically soaked in water until they curl into a tubular shape. Once cooked, they're soft with a springy chew. In this book, they're used for *Kuay Chap Naam Sai* (see page 97) and *Yam Kuay Chap* (see page 159). Look for a Thai brand, such as Double Dragon, in bags on shelves near the other dried noodles at Chinese and Southeast Asian markets.

MAMA (instant ramen noodles)

Instant noodles may not be the healthiest option (they're mostly palm oil and wheat flour) but they're probably the most popular form of noodle in Thailand, where they're even eaten raw as a crunchy snack.

Look for Thai brands, such as Yum Yum, Wai Wai, or MAMA (a brand so popular that all instant noodles are called MAMA, the way some people call tissues "Kleenex"). Any flavor will do for Yam MAMA (page 157), since the seasoning packet plays no role. But for MAMA Naam (page 87), seek out the *tom yum* flavor. Find them in bags on shelves near the other dried noodles at Chinese and Southeast Asian markets.

Wun sen (glass noodles), aka bean thread or cellophane noodles

Made from mung bean flour, these thin noodles usually come dried and in little bundles. Typically, the noodles require soaking in warm water to rehydrate before cooking. Once cooked, they become almost crystal clear and have a slightly chewy texture. Alone they have little flavor, but they hold sauce very well. You'll find them in cellophane bags on shelves at Chinese and Southeast Asian markets near other dried noodles.

Boiling Noodles

In this book, boiling noodles differs slightly from the dominant Western way—that is, the cooking of pasta—and therefore deserves brief elaboration. Decades of al dente have complicated the straightforward instruction of boiling noodles. So, here it is: Unless otherwise noted, noodles should be boiled *not* to the intentionally underdone specs of spaghetti or, it should go without saying, for so long that they turn to mush. Instead, they should be boiled until they're cooked through but still retain their distinctive texture.

Because noodles differ by brand and maker, cooking times differ accordingly. For noodles, fresh and dried, the package instructions offer a useful estimate. Still, tasting is the best way to assess doneness. Simply lift the noodle basket from the water and use chopsticks to pull out a strand to taste.

Like pasta, they should be boiled in plenty of water; enough by volume that adding the noodles won't stop the boil and enough in depth that the noodles will be submerged in the noodle basket (a near-essential tool for the purpose)—but not so much that the basket will be submerged when set on the rim of the pot, thereby surrendering the basket's contents to the water. Unlike regular pasta, however, these noodles should be cooked in unsalted water.

Equipment

If you plan to cook the recipes in this book, you might need to purchase some inexpensive equipment. Here you'll find two lists of what you need—"Many Recipes Require" is for cooks who want to cook the most recipes with the least stuff, and "Some Recipes Require" is a supplementary list for anyone committed to making every recipe in this book. Each item includes a brief explanation of why you need it. Besides the large pot, digital scale, and charcoal grill, which you can buy just about anywhere, your best bets for shopping are Thai and other Asian markets, restaurant supply stores, and online.

Many Recipes Require

Cooking chopsticks Many noodle-soup recipes require stirring the noodles as they are boiling in a basket. The best tool for that is a pair of long, sturdy heatproof chopsticks (I use wooden), so you don't scald your fingers in the process.

Digital scale To get the best results from this book, embrace precision and measure ingredients with an inexpensive digital scale, that can toggle between metric (grams and kilograms) and US customary units (ounces and pounds).

Large, tall pot For making stock and boiling noodles, you'll want a tall pot with a 6- to 8-quart capacity.

Noodle basket A basket attached to a long handle, this instrument is essential to noodle operations throughout Asia. The basket holds noodles and other ingredients destined for boiling water, and the end of the handle hooks onto the rim of the pot to keep the basket upright. The baskets are sized to make one portion at a time. If you own more than one, making multiple bowls is that much more efficient.

Thai granite mortar and pestle This sturdy, squat stone mortar and matching pestle is useful for bruising and crushing ingredients for soups, stir-fries, and salads and is essential for pounding smooth pastes for curries and soups. Look for them at Asian markets, especially those with a Thai focus, cookware stores, and online. Choose a mortar with an opening of about 6 inches in diameter. For guidance on using the mortar and pestle, see below.

Wok The recipes in this book that require stir-frying call for a thin, flat-bottomed wok that's anywhere from 11 to 14 inches in diameter. If you have a gas stove, look for an aluminum, stainless-steel, or carbon-steel wok. For home use, I like the one made by Vollrath. If you have an electric stove, consider moving—or opt for a cast-iron wok. Keep in mind that the cooking times in this book were determined using a wok made of thin metal.

Using the Mortar and Pestle

To properly pound curry pastes, bruise aromatics for broths, and crush garlic and chiles for stir-fries and salads, a granite mortar and pestle are indispensable. To bruise and crush, you can get away with using a sturdy, blunt object, such as the flat side of a knife blade or a pan bottom. To make curry pastes, however, there is no substitute, no more convenient way from which your food will not suffer.

Because using a mortar for pounding curry pastes is unfamiliar to most Western cooks, the technique requires elaboration. Before you begin, set the mortar on a folded towel to steady the base and minimize the impact of the pounding on the work surface. If you can, position the mortar over the leg of the table on which you are working to transfer the energy of the pestle to the floor rather than the unsupported center of the table. Or do as Thais do and cut out the middleman, putting the mortar on the floor and sitting while you pound.

Put the prescribed ingredient (say, dried chile or sliced galangal) in the mortar and pound

with force, keeping your wrist fairly loose and letting the weight of the pestle do most of the work. When you first add the ingredient, pound firmly to flatten, crush, or otherwise begin to break it down. After 10 seconds or so, change your task slightly. Pound firmly but now aim to strike so the pestle drives the material down the wall of the mortar (in contrast to pummeling ingredients in the base from overhead). This action, repeated many times, creates the friction you need to turn the ingredient into a powder or paste. Only after the ingredient is completely pulverized should you add the next in the list.

As you add more ingredients, it'll take more time to incorporate each new addition. The paste will be more voluminous and slightly slick as you pound in softer, wetter ingredients. Once the paste takes on this new character, plan to pound the ingredients less and to crush and scrape them against the walls of the mortar more. Stir the mixture occasionally to make sure nothing has escaped the pestle's wrath.

Wok spatula This implement, which looks like a small, long-handled shovel, is used to stir, flip, and occasionally break up ingredients in a wok. Buy a metal one, unless you have a nonstick wok, in which case buy a wooden one to avoid scratching the surface.

Some Recipes Require

Charcoal grill Cooking over charcoal imparts a smoky flavor to meats that gas grills can't match. A simple kettle grill is all you need.

Clay pot Needed in this book exclusively for Buu Op Wun Sen (page 163), look for this stoneware pot with an unglazed exterior and a glazed interior, often bound with wire on the outside and always sold with a lid of the same construction, in Asian markets or online. Choose one with a 1-quart capacity.

Rice cooker There's no easier way to cook rice than in an electric rice cooker, no bells or whistles required.

Spider This large-holed, fairly flat-bottomed strainer is useful for scooping ingredients (fish balls and wonton skins, for example) from hot liquids (water or oil, say). Find one online or at most cookware shops.

Sticky-rice steamer set Just one recipe in this noodle-focused book calls for cooked sticky rice. Still, to make it properly, you'll need this duo, typically sold as a set: a cone-shaped bamboo basket and a pot with a narrow opening and wide, flared lip perfect for holding the basket. Find it online and in Southeast Asian–focused markets.

Tao thaan (charcoal stove) Only Buu Op Wun Sen (page 163) employs this bucket-shaped clay cooking device. The mouth of the *tao* cradles the clay pot, and the heat from the charcoal, which is fed into the opening in its base, envelops the sides of the pot, almost baking the dish. The stove is available at Thai markets or online for around thirty dollars. It can also be used as a charcoal grill, so double your pleasure if you do get one.

Wide, aluminum Chinese steamer I recommend this kind of three-tiered steamer to properly cook the banana leaf packets for Khao Kan Jin (see page 49). Surely some of you will attempt to steam them using a Western steamer. Do so at your food's peril. A 9- or 12-inch aluminum steamer will do just fine.

Cham Tra Kai

THE CHICKEN BOWL

When I first came to Thailand, I saw that many noodle vendors served their wares in a particular kind of bowl. It was ceramic and adorned with an image of a rooster rendered with just a few paintbrush strokes, the head and body in red, the tail in black. Before experience taught me how to identify a quality place to eat, I used the presence of these bowls as an imperfect guide to good noodles.

Today, you see bowls emblazoned with the iconic rooster all over Thailand, as well as in Singapore and Malaysia, made by various factories throughout the continent. In Thailand, however, you often come across specimens of a certain quality. These are most likely made at Dhanabadesakul, a factory in Lampang Province and the first outfit in Thailand to make these bowls.

The operation was founded by the late E Simyo Saechin, a ceramicist and immigrant from Guangdong Province (once known as Canton), China, soon after he arrived in Lampang and struck gold—or, more accurately, clay. In 1955, he discovered major deposits of kaolin, a high-quality clay ideal for ceramics, then he built a *tao mangkawn* (or "dragon kiln," named for its long shape) and began producing bowls with the same rooster design as those made at the factory where he had worked in Guangdong.

The same lack of copyright protections that helped give him his break means that his family, who now run the factory, currently sees plenty of competition in the form of cheap knockoffs. I've even seen chicken bowls made of light, unbreakable melamine. In other words, the factory's fortunes have fluctuated over time. Still, Saechin's factory honors the old ways, making hand-spun, twice-fired, hand-painted bowls. Just as some of my favorite noodle vendors sometimes try to adapt by diversifying their menus, the company has taken steps to compete without conceding quality. In 2013, the family opened the Dhanabadee Ceramic Museum, an addendum to the factory. Today, you can purchase not only bowls but also plates, mugs, and saltshakers. I won't knock the hustle. But for me, the classic form will always be the humble noodle bowl.

HAENG: DRY STYLE

KHRUK KHRIK: A LITTLE BIT OF BROTH

NAAM: SOUP STYLE

KAO LAO: NO NOODLES!

How to Eat Noodles in Thailand

When it comes to eating, the only right way is the way that pleases. That said, it's worth explaining how noodles are typically eaten in Thailand, because there is often wisdom in custom.

Utensils

If you're in Thailand, there's a nearly foolproof trick for selecting the proper utensils for eating noodles: use whatever is on the table. Unless you're at a place that caters to *farang* (foreigners), the establishment will provide the implements that Thai people use, whether out of tradition or practicality, to deliver the dish in question from plate to mouth. It deserves special note that despite the widespread assumption, the implement of choice is not always chopsticks.

When the utensils are a spoon and fork—as they are for, to name a few, Phat Si Ew Wun Sen (page 125), Kuaytiaw Lat Na (page 169), and all preparations of *khanom jiin* (see pages 47 and 53 to 61)—note that the spoon is there to eat from and the fork is there to transfer food to the spoon.

At home, of course, you can eat with whatever utensil you want—even a butter knife, for all I care. That said, for each recipe in this book, I offer the preferred eating implements.

Customizing: It's Up to You

Like so many Thai foods assembled at the last minute—papaya salad, for example, or nearly anything from the many stalls that traffic in *aahaan tham sang* ("food made to order")—noodle dishes can be tailored to your taste preferences. I'm not just talking about the seasoning, which I address later, but the rudiments, too.

At shops selling noodle soups, you have not technically completed your order until you have specified whether you'd like, say, *ba mii* (thin, yellow strands made from wheat), *sen yai* (fresh, wide noodles made from rice), *sen lek* (narrower rice noodles), or MAMA (essentially, instant ramen). Some dishes do have a preferred noodle, though even they aren't sacrosanct. Fresh, wide rice noodles, for instance, are commonplace for *phat si ew*, the soy sauce–spiked stir-fry particularly popular in the US, but the dish is also great made with glass noodles (see page 125).

Some modifications involve addition. You might order *tom yam* noodles in *naam sai* (clear broth) or *naam khon* (opaque broth from a dose of coconut cream or evaporated milk). You might decide to take your pork or beef noodles *naam tok* (with blood) for a richer flavor. Others involve subtraction. You can order your favorite noodle soup *kruk khrik* (with only a little broth) or *haeng* ("dry," without any broth). You might even order it *kao lao*, if you want a bowl without the noodles, just the toppings and broth. No component is off-limits.

You can occasionally choose the serving size as well. In Thailand, a regular order (*thamadaa*) will usually come in a prudent portion, not the bathtub-size bowls of broth or hills of stir-fried noodles we see in the US. You might order one, then later another. Or you might order *phiseht* (special) and get a larger bowl, closer to what comes automatically in the West.

The recipes in this book often reflect my partialities. For instance, I enjoy *sen lek* in noodle soups, with few exceptions, and prefer the "dry" *sukii haeng* (see page 147) to the brothy version. They also reflect my desire to demonstrate how fluid the food can be and how far from the "traditional" it strays. That's one reason you'll find, for instance, two recipes for *phat thai*, one made with the familiar rice noodle and another with glass noodles. The other reason is that both are killer.

In general, you can use whatever noodle you please as long as you account for the difference in cooking time. This is easy enough, and for soups, it's particularly simple if you separate the noodles from any ingredients they're boiled with—yet another reason to own multiple long-handled noodle baskets.

Adjusting Flavor: Khruang Phrung and Accompaniments

Most noodle dishes in Thailand often arrive tamely seasoned, with the understanding that the customer will season them to his or her liking. Tweaking food so it tastes the way you want it to isn't a foreign concept to Westerners—people put mustard and sauerkraut on hot dogs and lime and salsa on tacos without hesitation. Yet it often eludes people who are new to the food of Thailand.

Most restaurants there, no matter what's on offer, provide condiments called *khruang phrung* to adjust the flavors (*phrung roht*) of your food. At spots selling *jok* (rice porridge), those might be a bottle of soy sauce or Maggi and a shaker of white pepper. At noodle shops, you'll typically find a tabletop caddy of *khruang phrung*—namely, sugar to add sweetness; hot *phrik khii nuu* chiles drowned in fish sauce for a boost of salt, umami, and heat; distilled vinegar with milder chiles to provide tartness and floral-spicy notes; and *phrik pon khua* (toasted-chile powder) for smoky heat—each in a small jar with a spoon for you to dose your food as you see fit.

While the customer can do what he or she pleases, certain *khruang phrung* are informally but closely linked to certain dishes. For instance, those fish sauce–soaked chiles go especially well with MAMA Phat (page 131), while people tend to apply vinegar-soaked chiles and coarse chile powder to Kuaytiaw Tom Yam Muu Naam (page 79). To guide you toward the way noodles are eaten in Thailand, each recipe in this book provides suggestions for my preferred *khruang phrung*. Of course, no one's looking over your shoulder, so do what you will.

Many recipes also come with another set of ingredients (in the recipes these are referred to as, for lack of a better term, "accompaniments") that are important to the experience of eating the dish. Essentially, while *khruang phrung* are meant to adjust elemental seasonings (salty, sour, spicy, sweet), accompaniments often add flavor and texture.

The purpose of the accompaniments varies. *Khanom jiin* (see pages 47 and 53 to 61) typically comes with bean sprouts, thinly sliced cabbage, and boiled eggs that you add to your bowl after seasoning and before mixing the contents. *Phat thai* (see pages 137 and 141) often arrives with a plate bearing pennywort leaves and sliced banana blossom for eating between bites of the rich noodle dish. *Buu op wun sen* (see page 163) comes with a fiery, tart sauce in which you dip bites of crab.

The line between accompaniments and the *khruang phrung* might be blurry for those new to eating in Thailand. A lime wedge, for example, is an accompaniment in this book, while vinegar with chiles is *khruang phrung*, because lime delivers flavor and vinegar adds more elemental acidity. The most important thing to understand about *khruang phrung* and accompaniments, however, is not the distinction between them but rather that both are not to be skipped when preparing the recipes in this book.

Stir Before You Eat

Noodles are often thrown together, with remarkable speed and efficiency, by busy vendors. For soups, they combine noodles and broth with seasonings, proteins, vegetables, and herbs. For fried noodles, they plate the starchy strands and then add components such as herbs, bits of fried garlic or pork skin, chiles, bean sprouts, and the occasional fried egg, any of which are often just plopped on top. Each dish hits the table ASAP, the elements unevenly distributed and the flavors barely combined. For this reason, I advise that before you dig in to boat noodles or *phat thai* or *kuaytiaw tom yam*, you stir to loosen the noodles, which may be in a clump in the bottom of the bowl, and make sure that whatever seasonings and herbs and whatnot that have been quickly dashed into the bowl have mingled. Only then does it make sense to taste and adjust the flavor.

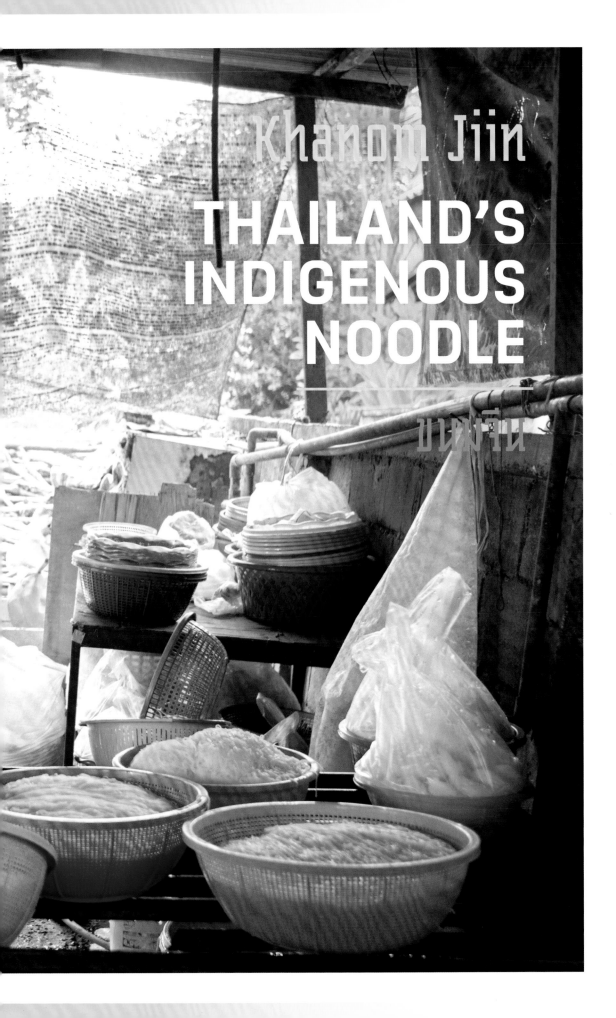

Khanom Jiin

THAILAND'S INDIGENOUS NOODLE

ขนมจีน

How Khanom Jiin is Made

I was in Chiang Mai, almost three decades ago, when I realized that everything I thought I knew about Thai food was wrong. I'd come to the northern capital to visit my friend Chris and his wife, Lakhana, who had grown up nearby. A seasoned backpacker, I had eaten plenty of *phat thai*, coconut curry, and banana pancakes abroad. But the meals to which Lakhana guided me were unlike anything I'd imagined eating in Thailand, let alone like what I'd eaten before. Among the revelations were coils of thin, slightly sour noodles in a brothy curry served at a market stall. I didn't know it at the time, but I was eating *khanom jiin*, which, in a country enamored of all manner of noodles, has the distinction of being the only variety indigenous to Thailand.

While most of the noodles we associate with contemporary Thai food came to the country with Chinese immigrants, *khanom jiin* likely has roots with the Mon, an ethnic group who lived in what is now Thailand (and brought Buddhism to the country). Before mechanization turned these noodles into a food of the people, making them was a laborious process, cooks put together a dough of rice flour and water, fermented it, cooked half of it, combined the cooked and uncooked halves, and pounded the mixture by hand using enormous pestles until the dough was very smooth. After thinning this dough with water, they used a handheld press made of brass to extrude long strands directly into boiling water. Finally, they cooled the noodles in room-temperature water and formed skeins. No wonder the thin, slightly sour strands were typically reserved for the wealthy or exalted—those with staff to perform the labor. Today, however, they're ubiquitous and inexpensive, sold in skeins, like yarn, at markets throughout Thailand, though they're particularly popular in the northern and southern regions of the country. As far as I can tell, sour *khanom jiin* are becoming harder to find, the step of fermenting the dough sacrificed to the demands of modernity.

1

Rice flour is mixed with water to make a dough (which is sometimes fermented for a few days to make it sour) and then boiled in its bag until the outer layer of the dough is cooked. The inner layer remains uncooked.

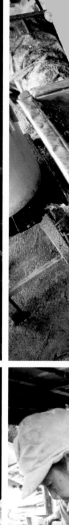

4

The batter is then transferred to another hopper and pumped through a nozzle that looks like a dish-rinsing sprayer to form long, thin strands that go directly into a huge boiling water bath, where they cook for a few minutes.

2 The half-cooked dough is put into a hopper with mixer hooks (often controlled with an old manual transmission repurposed from a car!). As it mixes, small amounts of water are added until it forms a silky batter.

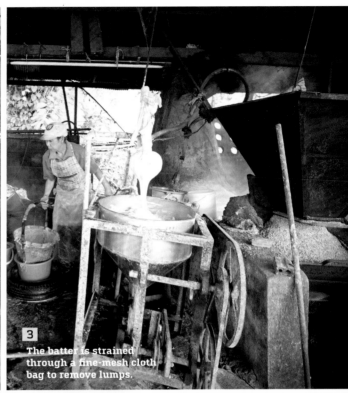

3 The batter is strained through a fine-mesh cloth bag to remove lumps.

5 The cooked noodles are pulled from the boiling water with bamboo or plastic baskets, cooled in a large cold water bath, and rinsed.

6 & 7 The freshly made *khanom jiin* is quickly and expertly coiled into skeins by hand, then stacked in plastic-lined baskets for sale on the spot or for transport to the local market.

Replicating Khanom Jiin

This chapter is devoted to the remarkable roster of sauces regularly served with *khanom jiin* at the stalls, restaurants, and all operations in between devoted to the noodle. To do them justice, you must produce a reasonable replica of *khanom jiin*, which is next to impossible to find in the US. (Unless, that is, you're lucky enough to live near a large Vietnamese community, like in L.A. Then you can skip these instructions and purchase fresh *bun*, the cultural equivalent to *khanom jiin*, in some Southeast Asian markets.)

First, you must buy the correct dried noodles, in this case dried thin, round rice noodles (about the thickness of angel hair pasta and sometimes labeled "fine") that are straight rather than wavy. Due to mercurial labeling, the proper noodles may be called "rice vermicelli" or "rice stick" and often have the words "Jiang Xi" or "Guilin" on the label. If you can, buy the Three Ladies brand.

Next, you must boil the noodles, rinse them to remove excess starch, and then form them into coils, the latter an easy though optional step that gets you that much closer to the real thing. The noodles are best served at what I like to think of as Thai room temperature—call it 90°F, give or take—so either leave them by a warm oven for 10 minutes or so before serving or nuke them briefly in the microwave on low power. Don't store them in the fridge.

Makes 24 oz / 12 coils (enough for about 4 servings); the recipe can be easily doubled

1

2

10½ oz dried thin,
round rice noodles

Bring a large pot of unsalted water to a boil over high heat. Add the noodles, immediately stir and toss with tongs to prevent clumping, and cook, stirring frequently and separating any clumps, until they're fully soft—you're not shooting for al dente—but not cooked so long that they turn to mush. The timing varies by brand, but expect 7 to 9 minutes.

Meanwhile, fill a large bowl with cold water and ice cubes and a second large bowl with enough lukewarm (about 100°F) water to submerge the cooked noodles. Set a colander, metal cooling rack, or a similar perforated surface over a tray or sheet pan.

When the noodles are cooked, drain them in a large colander, then rinse well under lukewarm running water, gently stirring and tossing, for about 1 minute to wash off the starch. Shake the colander to drain the noodles well, then transfer the colander with the noodles to the bowl of ice water. Gently stir the noodles with your hand until they have fully cooled. Drain well and transfer the noodles to the bowl of lukewarm water to hold them as you make the coils.

Grab a loose handful of noodles (about 2 oz; weigh it the first few times, then eyeball thereafter), making sure they aren't tangled together. **1**

Wrap them around the middle three fingers of your other hand, starting at the base of your fingers and working toward your fingertips. (If instead you start at the tip of your fingers, the coil will unravel later.) **2 & 3**

Transfer the coil to the prepared surface, letting it slide off your fingers. Repeat with the remaining noodles, overlapping the coils if necessary. **4**

Let them drain at room temperature until they're dry to the touch, at least 20 minutes or up to several hours, before using in another recipe.

3

4

Khanom Jiin Naam Ngiaw

RICE VERMICELLI WITH NORTHERN THAI CURRY

ขนมจีนน้ำเงี้ยว

When I lived in Chiang Mai proper, I spent many mornings at the Santitham location of Akha Ama, my friend Lee Ayu Chuepa's café that brews top-notch coffee from beans grown in Maejantai, the rural village where he was raised. Cappuccinos imbibed and resident cats petted, I'd often amble up the *soi* (side street) to a neighborhood joint popular for late breakfast or early lunch with the café's workers and the local folks who live nearby. There is no French toast here, but there are coils of the thin fermented rice noodles topped with brothy curry. This is *khanom jiin naam ngiaw*, the curry tart from tomatoes; fragrant from a paste of dried chiles, galangal, and turmeric; and bobbing with a few pork ribs and a shitload of steamed blood cake. It's one of my favorite renditions. The other is sold from a no-name nook on the sidewalk in Kat Luang, the city's oldest wholesale market, where Khun Waraporn has been selling her meaty version of the dish—along with a very nice rendition of *naam yaa*, its vegetarian counterpart (see page 53)—for more than twenty years.

The dish likely originated with the Tai Yai people (also known as the Shan), an ethnic minority from the land that's now Northern Thailand and Burma. It's a common sight up north. You'll see it at operations like these, as well as at truck stops, market stalls, and other establishments specializing in either *khanom jiin* or *aahaan meuang* (the food of Northern Thailand). I've even enjoyed a bowl from an outfit comprising a few stools and a pot outside of a barbershop near the village where I now live when I'm in the country. You'd be hard pressed, however, to find the dish in Bangkok, let alone abroad. It just hasn't caught on like *phat thai*, drunken noodles, and, more recently, *khao soi*.

So if you're outside of *khanom jiin naam ngiaw* range, you must make it yourself, which you can without much fuss. The paste is relatively rudimentary, the cooking process as straightforward as that of American chili or rustic French stew. All the ingredients in the dish are readily accessible, save for the dried flower called *dawk ngiaw*, which tints the broth a shade or two darker and adds a bit of flavor and a chewy texture when you eat one. It takes some work to find, so call around to Thai-focused markets or start Googling (try "dried red cotton flower"). If you must, you can omit it with only little ill effect.

Makes 6 bowls (6 servings)

Note

A kindly butcher will saw standard racks of ribs through the bone into the roughly 2-inch slabs you need for this recipe and for Ba Mii Bak Kut Teh (Noodles with Pork Bone Tea; page 107). Most Chinese and Southeast Asian markets offer them already cut in the butcher case.

FLAVOR PROFILE

Umami-rich, tart

SUGGESTED KHRUANG PHRUNG

Thai fish sauce

SUGGESTED UTENSILS

»

THE PASTE

7 g stemmed dried puya chiles, split open and seeded

1 g kosher salt

6 g cilantro roots

7 g thinly sliced lemongrass, tender parts only (from about 1 large stalk)

9 g peeled fresh or thawed frozen galangal, thinly sliced against the grain

10 g peeled fresh or thawed frozen yellow turmeric root, thinly sliced against the grain

18 g Kapi Kung (Homemade Shrimp Paste; page 238)

THE CURRY

1 lb pork spare ribs, cut lengthwise through the bone into 2-inch-wide racks, then cut into individual ribs

6 g / 12 dried red cotton flowers (dawk ngiaw; optional)

5 g / 1½ tsp kosher salt

4½ cups water

1½ tbsp Thai fish sauce

1½ tsp Thai thin soy sauce

½ tsp yellow bean sauce

7 g / 1½ tsp granulated sugar

12 oz lean ground beef

8 oz / 16 cherry tomatoes, halved

4 oz steamed blood (see page 11), cut into ¾-inch cubes

36 oz / 18 coils cooked khanom jiin (see page 44)

ACCOMPANIMENTS

Bean sprouts, blanched

Drained, chopped (½ inch) Phak Dong (Pickled Mustard Greens; page 247; if store-bought, soak in cold water for 10 minutes, then drain well), at room temperature

Cilantro sprigs or chopped cilantro

Sliced (¼ inch) green onions

Phrik Haeng Khua (Pan-Toasted Dried Thai Chiles; page 243)

Khao Kan Jin (Tai Yai "Dirty Rice"; facing page)

Suggested khruang phrung

Make the Paste

In a mortar, combine the dried chiles and salt and pound firmly, scraping the mortar and stirring the mixture after about 3 minutes, until you have a fairly fine powder, about 5 minutes. Add the cilantro roots and pound, occasionally stopping to scrape down the sides of the mortar, until you have a fairly smooth, slightly fibrous paste, about 2 minutes. Do the same with the lemongrass, then the galangal, then the turmeric, fully pounding each ingredient before moving on to the next. Pound in the shrimp paste until it's fully incorporated, about 1 minute. Use the paste right away, or store it in an airtight container in the fridge for up to 1 week or in the freezer for up to 6 months.

Make the Curry

Rinse the pork ribs, then combine them, the dried flowers, salt, and water in a medium pot. Cover the pot, set it over high heat, and bring the water to a simmer, then lower the heat to maintain a steady simmer, skimming off any scum from the surface. After 30 minutes, stir in all of the paste, the fish sauce, thin soy sauce, yellow bean sauce, and sugar. Crumble in the beef and stir well to keep it from clumping. Keep cooking until the pork is tender but still chewy (you'll be able to pull the meat from the bone with a fork but with some resistance), about 15 minutes more.

Add the tomatoes and blood cubes and cook until they're both hot through, about 5 minutes more. Turn off the heat and let the curry cool to warm or, even better, just above room temperature. Taste and consider adding more fish sauce, keeping in mind that the mixture should be highly seasoned, since it'll be served with relatively bland noodles.

Divide the noodles among six bowls, then spoon in the curry. Serve with the accompaniments and khruang phrung alongside. Tell guests to add these ingredients to their bowls to taste and to stir well before eating.

Khao Kan Jin

ข้าวกั้นจิ้น

On paper, Khanom Jiin Naam Ngiaw (page 47)—with its noodles, pork ribs, and blood cubes—sounds like a gut bomb. It's not. A bowl brings mostly light, lean broth with a little protein, and a relatively small portion at that. So I often order its customary partner, *khao kan jin*, as well. A rich counterpoint to the soupy curry, *khao kan jin* is like a Tai Yai dirty rice, made by tossing steamed grains with blood, ground pork belly, and garlic-infused oil, then steaming the mixture in banana leaf-wrapped bundles. You're meant to eat it between bites of curry, which I mention to forestall the Western temptation to dump the rice into the bowl or drag spoonfuls of it through the broth. But hey, do what you will.

Makes 10 servings

Note

The signature shape of *khao kan jin* packages is a pyramid, the edges stapled in place, but at home, most methods of wrapping work, as long as the rice is completely sealed in the banana leaf, and toothpicks will do for fastening.

FLAVOR PROFILE

Umami-rich, salty

SUGGESTED UTENSILS

2½ oz / 2 large stalks lemongrass (outer layer, bottom 1 inch, and top 9 inches removed), bruised and cut into 3-inch pieces

½ cup fresh or thawed frozen raw pig's blood

1¼ lb / 4 cups freshly cooked Khao Hom Mali (Jasmine Rice; page 244), at room temperature

8 oz skinless, boneless pork belly, finely chopped or ground twice through ¼-inch die

Naam Man Krathiam Jiaw (Fried Garlic in Garlic Oil; page 237), 3 tbsp oil, plus solids and oil for seasoning

7 g / 2 tsp kosher salt

5 g / 1 tsp granulated sugar

5 g / 1 tsp MSG (optional)

20 (9 by 7-inch) pieces fresh or thawed frozen banana leaves

Very roughly chopped cilantro (thin stems and leaves)

Sliced (¼ inch) green onions

Phrik Haeng Khua (Pan-Toasted Dried Thai Chiles; page 243)

In a small bowl, combine the lemongrass and blood and use your hand to squeeze and squish them together for a few minutes. You're helping to release the oils in the lemongrass, which tones down the flavor of the blood. Strain the blood through a fine-mesh strainer into a large bowl, stirring and pressing to extract as much blood as possible.

Add the jasmine rice, pork, 3 tbsp garlic oil, salt, sugar, and MSG to the bowl with the strained blood and mix well with your hands, breaking up any clumps of pork, until the ingredients are evenly distributed, about 45 seconds.

Trim any stems from the banana leaves. Pass both sides very briefly over a gas flame to make the leaves more pliable and less likely to break when you fold them. Use scissors to snip off the four corners of each piece, cutting perpendicular to and about 1½ inches from the corner.

Put one piece of banana leaf, shiny side down, so that the ridges run horizontally. Fit a second piece directly on top, shiny side up. Scoop about ½ cup of the rice mixture in a tidy pile onto the center. Lift the long sides of the banana leaves so they just about meet in the center to form what looks like a large taco. Hold it in place with one hand. With the other, fold one of the short ends toward the center, guiding the edges toward the center to form a rough half-pyramid. Secure it with one hand and use your free hand to fold the other short end in the same manner to form a pyramid that fully encloses the rice mixture. Staple the peak (or use a wet toothpick) to secure the leaves. Repeat with the remaining rice mixture and banana leaves. Put the packets, in a single layer, into each tier of a wide aluminum Chinese steamer.

Pour about 3 inches of water into the steamer, insert the tiers, cover, and bring the water to a boil over high heat. Lower the heat slightly to maintain a strong simmer. Cover and cook until the contents of the packets are firm and springy to the touch, 15 to 20 minutes.

Let guests open their own packet at the table. Add a little fried garlic in garlic oil over each one. Add a pinch of cilantro and green onions. Serve the pan-toasted dried Thai chiles on the side for anyone who wants a little heat.

Khanom Jiin Naam Yaa Kati Jay

RICE VERMICELLI WITH MUSHROOM, KRACHAI, AND COCONUT CURRY

ขนมจีนน้ำยากะทิเจ

A classic Central Thai-style gravy served over coils of *khanom jiin*, *naam yaa* gets its flavor from galangal; *krachai* (aka Chinese keys), a spindly rhizome with an earthier character than galangal or ginger; lemongrass; and, in most versions I've had, fish, which is blended along with the aromatic ingredients to provide body as well. For Westerners raised on red and green curries, a bite of this dish expands the mind while also hitting most of the notes that most diners associate with the cuisine in the first place: the heat of chiles, the richness of coconut milk, the fun of noodles.

This version adds another element of appeal to a specific group: it's vegetarian. When you run restaurants in the States, you're often on the prowl for dishes that satisfy customers set on avoiding meat and fish or, in this case, those that can be rendered vegetarian without sacrificing the pleasures of the dish.

While I've never seen *naam yaa* made with mushrooms instead of fish in the wild, I decided to make the unconventional leap with tradition in mind. In Thailand, where the vast majority of the population is Buddhist, abstaining from eating animals is commonplace either all day every day or during certain holidays, depending on the believer. Hence, there's a long-standing practice of taking dishes cooked with animal flesh or seasoned with shrimp paste and making them *jay* (vegetarian). I use mushrooms here, a no-brainer since in the north of Thailand and beyond they frequently stand in for flesh, mimicking its texture and replacing some of the umami lost when fish sauce and other fermented sea creatures are left out of the equation. This tweak aside, the dish is more or less the same as the classic and a delight to eat with its standard fixings: shredded cabbage and bean sprouts for crunch, pickled mustard greens and lime for tang, and sprigs of lemon basil (*bai menglak*) for herbaceousness. Thai basil is a suitable proxy. Sweet basil is not.

Makes 8 bowls (8 servings)

FLAVOR PROFILE

Herbaceous, earthy, rich

SUGGESTED KHRUANG PHRUNG

Thai thin soy sauce

SUGGESTED UTENSILS

»

THE SAUCE

2 cups water

4½ oz small Asian shallots, peeled and halved

35 g shredded fresh or thawed frozen Chinese keys (page 13)

28 g drained salted yellow beans, rinsed

25 g garlic cloves, peeled

20 g thinly sliced lemongrass, tender parts only (from about 3 large stalks)

10 g peeled fresh or thawed frozen galangal, thinly sliced against the grain

8 g stemmed dried puya chiles, split open and seeded

2 g stemmed dried Thai chiles, split open and seeded

1¼ lb king oyster mushrooms, halved lengthwise, then sliced crosswise ½ inch thick

2 cups unsweetened coconut milk (preferably boxed)

¼ cup Thai thin soy sauce, plus about 2 tbsp

6 g kosher salt

THE DISH

48 oz / 24 coils cooked khanom jiin (see page 44)

1½ cups unsweetened coconut cream (preferably boxed), warmed

ACCOMPANIMENTS

Bean sprouts, blanched

Sliced (¼ inch) long beans, blanched

Very thinly sliced green cabbage

Drained, chopped (½ inch) Phak Dong (Pickled Mustard Greens; page 247; if store-bought, soak in cold water for 10 minutes, then drain well)

Lemon basil sprigs

Phrik Haeng Khua (Pan-Toasted Dried Thai Chiles; page 243)

Suggested khruang phrung

Make the Sauce

In a small pot, combine the water, shallots, Chinese keys, yellow beans, garlic, lemongrass, galangal, puya chiles, and Thai chiles, then cover and bring to a boil over high heat. Boil, covered and stirring occasionally, until all the ingredients, including the shallots and galangal, are tender, about 20 minutes.

Meanwhile, put the mushrooms in a medium pot with about 4 cups water, just enough to cover. Cover the pot, bring to a boil over high heat, and then turn off the heat. Drain the mushrooms, reserving 3 cups of the cooking liquid and discarding the rest.

In a medium pot, combine the drained mushrooms, reserved cooking liquid, shallot mixture, coconut milk, ¼ cup thin soy sauce, and salt. Bring to a simmer over high heat, lower the heat to maintain a steady simmer, and cook, uncovered, until thickened slightly, about 15 minutes. Transfer to a blender in batches and blend (use caution when blending hot liquids) just until fairly smooth (there should no longer be chunks, but you're not looking for a super-smooth Western puree), about 2 minutes per batch.

Return the mixture to the pot and let it cool to warm or, even better, just above room temperature. (Fully cooled, it can be stored in an airtight container in the fridge for up to 5 days.) Taste and consider adding about 2 tbsp more soy sauce, keeping in mind that the curry should be highly seasoned, since it'll be diluted slightly with coconut cream and served with relatively bland noodles.

Serve the Dish

Divide the noodles among eight shallow bowls. Spoon on about 1 cup of the sauce and then 3 tbsp of the coconut cream into each bowl. Serve with the accompaniments and khruang phrung alongside. Tell guests to add these ingredients to their bowls to taste and to stir well before eating.

Khanom Jiin Kaeng Khiaw Waan Luuk Chin Plaa

RICE VERMICELLI WITH GREEN CURRY AND FISH BALLS

ขนมจีนแกงเขียวหวานลูกชิ้นปลา

One of the best-known Thai dishes in the US, green curry is served differently across the pond, at least outside of the tourist ghettos. Instead of strips of chicken breast, canned baby corn, and bell peppers, you're more likely to see fish balls and crunchy Thai pea or apple eggplants. While jasmine rice is still a common partner in Thailand, I'd wager you'd just as soon find the curry spooned over coils of *khanom jiin*. This is the way I had the dish years ago at a meal hosted by my old friends Chris and Lakhana at Hong Taew Restaurant in Chiang Mai. There, it came with a plate of salted duck eggs, fried tiny fish, and pickled garlic. It's a practice I have adopted and recommend highly.

The classic Central Thai-style curry itself will be familiar in form and flavor to American diners. Rich with coconut cream and milk and fairly sweet by design (the word *waan* in the dish's name means "sweet"), its flavor comes from a paste of galangal and lemongrass, garlic and shallot, and the fresh green chile. Pounding the paste yourself gives the curry an even more complex character and aroma. Fashion the fish balls, too, which is easier than you'd think, and you'll swap the cheap thrills of store-bought orbs for the delicate texture and fish-forward flavor of the homemade kind.

Makes 4 bowls (4 servings)

»

Notes

To be sure the coconut cream will "crack," which is essential to properly frying the curry paste, skip the canned stuff and go for boxed. The fat and liquid in canned coconut cream don't separate as reliably.

To fry the anchovies, rinse, drain, and pat them very dry with paper towels. Fry in about 2 inches of neutral oil at 325°F until crispy, about 2 minutes.

FLAVOR PROFILE

Hot, full-flavored, rich, a little sweet

SUGGESTED KHRUANG PHRUNG

Thai fish sauce

SUGGESTED UTENSILS

THE PASTE

4 g coriander seeds, preferably Asian

1 g cumin seeds

2 g yellow mustard seeds

1 g black peppercorns

6 g cilantro roots

7 g kosher salt

28 g thinly sliced lemongrass, tender parts only (from about 4 large stalks)

28 g thinly sliced (1/8 inch; against the grain) peeled fresh or thawed frozen galangal

2 g finely grated makrut lime zest, from fresh or thawed frozen limes (optional)

3 oz fresh serrano chiles, stemmed, halved lengthwise, and seeded

55 g garlic cloves, peeled and halved lengthwise

3 oz small Asian shallots, peeled and thinly sliced against the grain

25 g Kapi Kung (Homemade Shrimp Paste; page 238)

THE DISH

1 cup unsweetened boxed coconut cream (see page 13)

3 cups unsweetened coconut milk (preferably boxed)

16 fresh or thawed frozen Luuk Chin Plaa (Fish Balls; page 216 or store-bought), at room temperature

10 oz / 8 Thai apple eggplants (green and golf ball size), stemmed

1/4 cup Thai fish sauce, plus more as needed

3 oz / 1/4 cup packed Naam Taan Piip (Softened Palm Sugar; page 239; preferably Thai)

10 to 15 g / 8 to 12 fresh or thawed frozen green Thai chiles, smashed to split slightly

12 g / 16 large fresh or frozen makrut lime leaves

28 g / 1 cup packed Thai basil leaves

24 oz / 12 coils cooked khanom jiin (see page 44)

ACCOMPANIMENTS

Fried tiny (about 2 inch long) dried anchovies

Khai Khem (Salted Duck Eggs; page 231; cooked 8 minutes) or Khai Tom (Boiled Eggs; page 230), peeled and cut into small wedges

Drained, peeled pickled garlic cloves

Phrik Haeng Thawt (Dried Thai Chiles Fried in Oil; page 242)

Suggested khruang phrung

Make the Paste

In a small pan, combine the coriander, cumin, and mustard seeds, set over medium-low heat, and cook, stirring often, until the spices are very fragrant, 6 to 8 minutes. Let the spices cool slightly and then pound them, along with the pepper, in a mortar (or grind them in a spice grinder) to a fine powder. Scoop the powder into a small bowl and set aside.

Pound the cilantro roots and salt in the mortar to a fibrous paste, about 30 seconds. Add the lemongrass and pound to a fibrous paste, about 1 minute. Do the same with the galangal (1 minute), then the lime zest (1 minute), then the chiles (4 minutes), then the garlic (4 minutes), then the shallots (4 minutes), then the shrimp paste (1 minute) to make a smooth paste, fully pounding each ingredient before moving on to the next and stirring occasionally with a spoon. Finally, pound the spice powder into the paste until it's well incorporated, about 30 seconds. You'll have 10 oz / generous 1 cup paste. Reserve 4 3/4 oz / 1/2 cup for this dish. The remaining paste will keep in an airtight container in the fridge for up to 1 week or in the freezer for up to 6 months.

Make the Dish

Pour the coconut cream into a medium nonstick flat-bottomed wok or skillet, set it over medium-high heat, and bring to a boil. Cook, stirring occasionally, until the cream has reduced by about half and "cracks;" that is, the water has evaporated and you're left with mostly translucent fat plus some white solids (it'll look like curdled milk). This will take anywhere from 3 to 10 minutes, depending on the brand of coconut cream. Add the 4 3/4 oz / 1/2 cup curry paste and cook, stirring constantly, until very fragrant, 2 to 3 minutes.

Stir in the coconut milk and fish balls. Quarter the eggplants (if you do it earlier, they'll turn brown) and add them to the pot along with the fish sauce and palm sugar. Let the liquid come to a simmer and cook, stirring occasionally, until the eggplants are tender but still crunchy, about 3 minutes. Add the smashed chiles, then twist the lime leaves (to bruise them slightly) and add them, too. Cook for 1 minute more, turn off the heat, and stir in the basil leaves.

Taste and consider adding more fish sauce, keeping in mind that the curry should be highly seasoned, since it'll be served with relatively bland noodles.

Put 3 coils of noodles in each of four shallow bowls, then divide the curry among the bowls. Serve with the accompaniments and khruang phrung alongside. Tell guests to add these ingredients to their bowls to taste and to stir well before eating.

Khanom Jiin Sao Naam

RICE VERMICELLI WITH COCONUT CREAM, PINEAPPLE, GREEN MANGO, FISH BALLS, AND LIME

ขนมจีนชาวน้ำ

Props where props are due. This preparation of *khanom jiin* came to my attention by way of David Thompson, an Australian expat chef who has authored several indispensable Thai cookbooks. According to Thompson, the dish arose during the mid-nineteenth century as a hot-season offering to monks attending special occasions, like housewarmings. It's delicious; the noodles are dressed with turmeric coconut cream and fish balls, sugar, and lime juice and decked out with slivers of green mango and young ginger, bits of pineapple, sliced fresh red chiles, and dried shrimp pounded to a fluffy powder.

The dish, which is served at room temperature, is both refreshing and rich, a scrum of sweet and tart, astringent and salty, and a little spicy. It's also tough to find these days, the kind of treat you'll occasionally come across at old-school restaurants or in homes, in hi-so precincts of Bangkok or down south in pineapple-plantation country. My most memorable bowl was at Thompson's former Bangkok restaurant, Nahm, where the coconut cream sported a yellow hue from turmeric, and fish balls joined the fun.

Makes 4 bowls (4 servings)

Note

Khanom jiin sao naam requires three ingredients you may need help finding. **White turmeric** (botanical name *Curcuma amada*) is readily available in Thailand, though your best bet for locating it stateside is online or at an Indian market, where it may be labeled "mango ginger," "mango turmeric," or *amba haldi*. **Young, or "new," ginger** is sold at Chinese and Southeast Asian markets and is distinguished from the more common mature ginger by its light, shiny skin. You might also spot some pink skin and shoots. **Green mango**, available at both Southeast Asian and South Asian markets, is not just firm and unripe but has skin that is actually green—not mottled or greenish. A mandoline makes julienning the lot of them significantly easier.

»

THE DRESSING

1/2 cup water

3 1/4 oz / 1/4 cup packed Naam Taan Piip (Softened Palm Sugar; page 239; preferably Thai)

3 tbsp fresh lime juice (preferably from Key limes or from regular [Persian] limes with a squeeze of Meyer lemon juice)

2 tbsp Thai fish sauce

2 g / 3/4 tsp kosher salt

THE COCONUT CREAM

1 cup unsweetened coconut cream (preferably boxed)

3 g / 1 tsp kosher salt

1/4 tsp turmeric powder, or 1 g / 1/2 tsp pounded (to a smooth paste) peeled fresh or thawed frozen yellow turmeric root

THE BOWLS

12 fresh or thawed frozen Luuk Chin Plaa (Fish Balls; page 216; or store-bought), at room temperature

24 oz / 12 coils cooked khanom jiin (see page 44)

11 oz / 2 cups matchstick-cut (1 by 1/4 inch) peeled ripe pineapple

4 oz / 1 cup julienned (2 by 1/8 inch) peeled green mango

20 g / 1/4 cup finely julienned (2 by 1/16 inch) peeled young ginger

2 oz / 1/2 cup finely julienned (2 by 1/16 inch) peeled white turmeric

8 g / 4 tsp very thinly sliced peeled garlic

20 g / 1/4 cup shrimp floss (recipe follows)

8 g / 4 tsp thinly sliced fresh or frozen red Thai chiles

28 g / 2 cups lemon basil leaves

4 Key limes, halved, or 8 small wedges regular (Persian) lime

Suggested khruang phrung

Make the Dressing

In a small saucepan, combine the water, palm sugar, lime juice, fish sauce, and salt and bring to a simmer over medium-high heat, stirring to help the palm sugar dissolve. Turn off the heat. Let cool to room temperature. The dressing will keep in an airtight container in the fridge for up to 3 days.

Make the Coconut Cream

In a small saucepan or flat-bottomed wok, combine the coconut cream, salt, and turmeric and bring to a simmer over medium-high heat. Lower the heat to maintain a gentle simmer and cook, stirring occasionally, until slightly reduced, about 10 minutes. Set aside.

Assemble the Bowls

Just before you're ready to serve the dish, bring the coconut cream mixture to a simmer, turn off the heat, and add the fish balls. Stir and let them sit until warmed through, about 2 minutes.

Divide the noodles among four shallow bowls. Top each bowl with the following, in this order: about 2 3/4 oz / 1/2 cup pineapple, 1 oz / 1/4 cup green mango, 5 g / 1 tbsp ginger, 1/2 oz / 2 tbsp white turmeric, and 2 g / 1 tsp garlic. Pour 1/4 cup of the dressing over each bowl. Spoon 3 fish balls and 1/4 cup coconut cream into one side of each bowl. Top each bowl with 5 g / 1 tbsp shrimp floss, 2 g / 1 tsp Thai chiles, and 7 g / 1/2 cup lemon basil. Serve with the lime wedges and khruang phrung alongside. Tell guests to stir their bowl well before eating.

Shrimp Floss

Makes about 2 oz / 3/4 cup

50 g / 1/2 cup medium-size dried shrimp

Fill a medium bowl with water, add the dried shrimp, and stir. Let the shrimp soak for 30 seconds or so, then drain well. Transfer the shrimp in a single layer to clean kitchen or paper towels and let them dry for 15 minutes.

Transfer the shrimp to a blender and blend, shaking the blender if necessary to help the shrimp catch in the blades and stopping to stir occasionally, until the shrimp are fully broken down into fluffy shreds, 2 to 3 minutes.

The floss will keep in an airtight container in the fridge for up to 1 week.

Khanom Jiin Naam Phrik

RICE VERMICELLI WITH SHRIMP, COCONUT MILK, AND TOASTED MUNG BEANS

ขนมจีนน้ำพริก

My initial dalliance with this preparation came in the city of Trang, in the south, at a night market famous for *khanom jiin* vendors. I chose a vendor working three pots, each with a different curry to be spooned over the coils of noodles, and ordered the one I didn't recognize.

I got my bowl and raided a nearby table of self-serve garnishes, loading up on dried chiles, pickled mustard greens, bean sprouts, and, especially, shredded green mango, which the vendor recommended. When I got stuck in, I found a compelling curry, rich from coconut as well as sweet and sour, with a slightly nutty flavor that I couldn't put my finger on. It was uncharacteristically fiery, too—attuned to the local palate.

Since then, I've learned that *khanom jiin naam phrik* belongs to the Central Thai canon and includes a Burmese element, as evidenced by toasted dried mung beans, the ingredient contributing that mysterious nuttiness as well as body to the sauce. (In the United States, you'll find the correct dried mung beans for this recipe—not whole and green, but split and yellow—in health food, Asian, and Indian stores, where they're often sold as "moong dal.") Also of note are the shrimp blended into the sauce, adding more texture and flavor, and the pairing of coconut and lime juice, a rarity in curries. I've carved out the aromatic, garlicky chile paste, so you can add as much or as little as you'd like.

Makes 8 bowls (8 servings)

»

THE PASTE

28 g chopped (1 inch) small Asian shallots, peeled

28 g garlic cloves, peeled

10 g thinly sliced (1/4 inch) peeled fresh or thawed frozen galangal

1 g dried Thai chiles, soaked in hot water until soft, then drained

THE CURRY

3 3/4 oz / 1/2 cup dried split yellow mung beans

2 cups water

3 g / 1 tsp kosher salt

1 tbsp neutral oil, such as canola, soybean, or rice bran, plus more as needed

5 cups unsweetened coconut milk (preferably boxed)

4 oz palm sugar (preferably Thai), roughly pounded

1/4 cup plus 2 tbsp Thai fish sauce, plus more as needed

1/4 cup fresh lime juice (preferably from Key limes or from regular [Persian] limes with a squeeze of Meyer lemon juice)

14 oz fresh or thawed frozen peeled and deveined medium-size shrimp

48 oz / 24 coils cooked khanom jiin (see page 44)

ACCOMPANIMENTS

Chile-Garlic Oil (facing page)

Khai Tom (Boiled Eggs; page 230; cooked 8 minutes), peeled

Very thinly sliced green cabbage

Julienned carrot

Sliced (1/4 inch) long beans

Small Thai basil sprigs

Phrik Haeng Khua (Pan-Toasted Dried Thai Chiles; page 243)

Halved Key limes or regular (Persian) lime wedges

Suggested khruang phrung

Make the Paste

Prepare a grill, preferably charcoal, to cook with medium-low heat (or set a heavy pan over medium heat). Combine the shallots, garlic, and galangal on a double sheet of aluminum foil in more or less one layer and fold to make a fairly tight packet. Set the packet on the grill (or in the pan) and grill, flipping the packet occasionally, until the shallots and garlic have spots of brown and are fully soft but still hold their shape (carefully open the packet to check), 15 to 20 minutes. Transfer to a small food processor, add the chiles, and process, occasionally stopping to scrape the sides and gradually adding a tbsp or two of water if the blades are struggling to catch the mixture, to a fairly smooth paste, 2 to 3 minutes.

Make the Curry

Meanwhile, set a dry small skillet or flat-bottomed wok over medium heat. Add the mung beans and cook, stirring and tossing constantly, until the beans are several shades darker with spots of brown, 4 to 5 minutes. Transfer to a medium pot, then pour in enough of the water to cover by about 2 inches and add the salt. Bring to a boil over high heat and cook, partially covered and adding more hot water if necessary to keep the mung beans submerged, until fully soft, 20 to 25 minutes. Drain well and set aside.

In a heavy medium pot over medium heat, warm the oil (add a little extra if necessary to thinly coat the surface) until it shimmers. Add the paste and cook, stirring constantly, until very aromatic, about 2 minutes. Add the coconut milk, palm sugar, fish sauce, and lime juice and bring to a simmer. Cook at a steady simmer for 10 minutes, then add the drained mung beans and 10 1/2 oz of the shrimp. Let the liquid return to a simmer and turn off the heat. Transfer to a blender in batches and blend (use caution when blending hot liquids) until smooth, 1 to 2 minutes per batch.

Return the mixture to the pot and simmer over medium heat, stirring occasionally, until slightly thickened, 8 to 10 minutes. Add the remaining 3 1/2 oz shrimp and cook, stirring occasionally, just until they're cooked through, about 1 minute, then turn off the heat. Let cool to warm or, even better, just above room temperature. Taste and consider adding more fish sauce, keeping in mind that the curry should be highly seasoned, since it'll be served with relatively bland noodles. (Fully cooled, the curry will keep in an airtight container in the fridge for up to 1 week.)

Divide the noodles among eight shallow bowls, then divide the curry and shrimp among them. Serve with the accompaniments and khruang phrung alongside. Tell guests to add these ingredients to their bowls to taste and to stir well before eating.

Chile-Garlic Oil

Makes about ¾ cup

½ cup neutral oil, such canola, soybean, or rice bran

42 g / 14 garlic cloves, peeled and finely chopped

50 g / ½ cup Phrik Pon Khua (Toasted-Chile Powder; page 240)

In a small saucepan, combine the oil and garlic, set over medium-high heat, and let it sizzle. Cook, stirring occasionally, until the garlic is just golden, 3 to 5 minutes. Pour into a small heatproof bowl and immediately stir in the toasted-chile powder. Let cool.

The chile-garlic oil will keep in an airtight container in the fridge for up to 3 months.

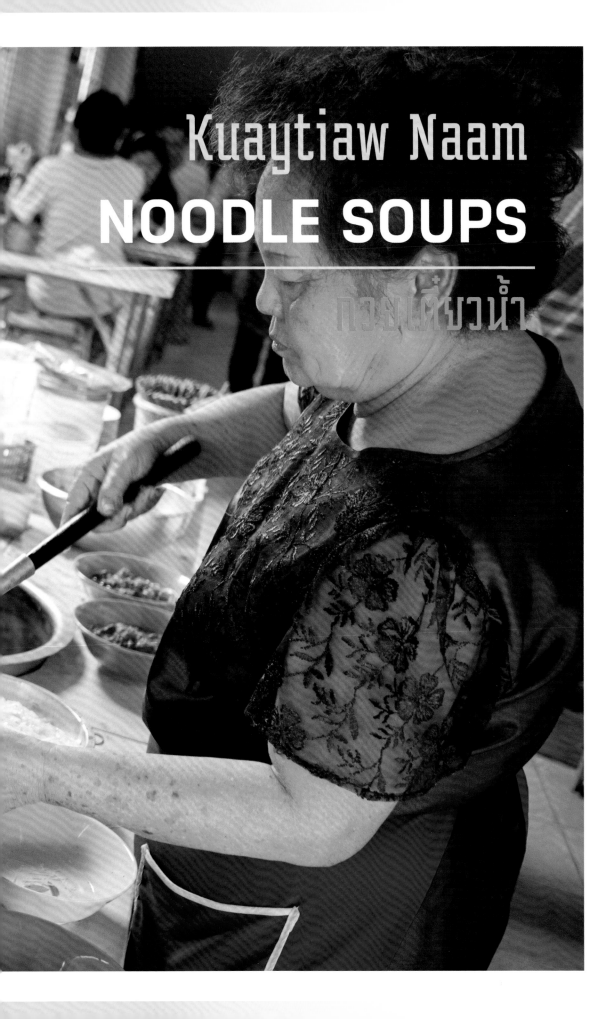

Kuaytiaw Naam

NOODLE SOUPS

ก๋วยเตี๋ยวน้ำ

Kuaytiaw Naam Kai

NOODLE SOUP WITH CHICKEN

ก๋วยเตี๋ยวน้ำไก่

The name of this dish has long struck me as a good demonstration of the grammatical simplicity of the Thai language. I'm no linguist—a better description would be "remedial student"—but I do enjoy the fact that stringing together the words *noodle*, *water*, and *chicken* is enough to get you lunch, not to mention one of this caliber.

Kuaytiaw naam kai might be the simplest of all Thai noodle dishes. I reckon it's one of the most craveable, too. This is still true for me a good quarter century after my first encounter with the dish, as a backpacker in Bangkok roaming Sukhumvit Road for sustenance. The dish is what it sounds like: noodles in chicken broth made in the Thai style—that is, made with aromatics such as lemongrass and cilantro root and then dosed with fish sauce, herbs, and fried garlic before serving. That's the ballgame, really, other than some shredded chicken, a handful of bean sprouts, the ubiquitous *khruang phrung*, and, of course, the noodle of your choice.

When I was new to Thai food, the noodle soup was a great initiation, providing comfort and adventure in equal measure. Now it gives me just comfort, and perhaps gratitude that I was initiated.

Makes 1 bowl (1 serving); to make more, double or quadruple the ingredients, but make each bowl separately

»

FLAVOR PROFILE

Mild, umami-rich

SUGGESTED KHRUANG PHRUNG

Phrik Naam Plaa
(Fish Sauce–
Soaked Chiles)
PAGE 236

Phrik Naam Som
(Vinegar-Soaked
Chiles)
PAGE 235

Phrik Pon Khua
(Toasted-Chile Powder)
PAGE 240

Sugar (preferably
raw cane sugar)

SUGGESTED UTENSILS

THE BOWL

1 tbsp Thai fish sauce

3 g / 1 tsp granulated sugar

1 tsp Naam Man Krathiam Jiaw (Fried Garlic in Garlic Oil; page 237), about half solids and half oil

Generous pinch of finely ground Asian white pepper

THE DISH

2½ oz / 1 cup tightly packed semidried sen lek (thin, flat rice noodles), snipped into approximately 8-inch lengths

28 g / ½ cup bean sprouts

3 oz / ⅓ cup Neua Kai Chiik (Shredded Poached Chicken; page 229), at room temperature

1½ cups Naam Sup Kai (Chicken Stock; page 112), hot

2 g / 1 tbsp very roughly chopped Chinese celery (thin stems and leaves)

2 g / 1 tbsp very roughly chopped cilantro (thin stems and leaves)

4 g / 1 tbsp sliced (¼ inch) green onion

Suggested khruang phrung

Prep the Bowl

In a wide soup bowl, combine the fish sauce, sugar, fried garlic in garlic oil, and pepper.

Make the Dish

Fill a large, tall pot with enough water to submerge a long-handled noodle basket and bring to a boil over high heat. Put the noodles and bean sprouts in the basket and submerge the contents in the boiling water. Cook, stirring occasionally, with chopsticks, until the noodles are tender, about 1 minute.

Firmly shake the basket to drain well and dump the contents into the prepared bowl. Add the shredded poached chicken, then pour on the hot chicken stock and stir briefly but well. Sprinkle on the Chinese celery, cilantro, and green onion. Serve with the khruang phrung alongside.

Kuaytiaw Muu Naam Sai

From my thoroughly scientific study, I can tell you that pork-based noodle soups are all the rage in Thailand. My data? Nine out of ten times when I approach an unfamiliar noodle shop, whether it's a scattering of outdoor stools near a couple of pots or a full-blown operation with a roof, what's on offer is porcine. There's the meat—stewed, poached, made into balls. There's stock boiled from bones. And there are innards simmered until chewable. There are also countless varieties, from spicy, sweet, tart *tom yam* (see page 79) to rich *naam tok* (spiked with blood, sugar, and chiles) to the comparatively spare *muu naam sai*, the clear broth seasoned with a little fish sauce, sugar, and garlic oil that you see here. This is pork noodle soup at its most simple and, in some ways, at its most compelling, since simplicity hides none of the care taken in making it.

Feel free to swap the pork loin for more pork balls, the pork balls for more pork loin, or the ground pork for cooked offal (see page 227). In other words, these details are up to you.

Makes 1 bowl (1 serving); to make more, double or quadruple the ingredients, but make each bowl separately

»

FLAVOR PROFILE

Mild, umami-rich

SUGGESTED KHRUANG PHRUNG

Phrik Naam Plaa
(Fish Sauce–
Soaked Chiles)
PAGE 236

Phrik Naam Som
(Vinegar-Soaked
Chiles)
PAGE 235

Phrik Pon Khua
(Toasted-Chile Powder)
PAGE 240

Sugar (preferably
raw cane sugar)

SUGGESTED UTENSILS

THE BOWL

1 tbsp Thai fish sauce

3 g / 1 tsp
granulated sugar

1 tsp Naam Man
Krathiam Jiaw (Fried
Garlic in Garlic Oil;
page 237), about half
solids and half oil

Generous pinch of
finely ground Asian
white pepper

THE DISH

42 g pork loin, cut
against the grain into
2 by 1 by ⅛-inch slices

Splash of Thai
fish sauce

Generous pinch of
finely ground Asian
white pepper

2½ oz / 1 cup tightly
packed semidried
sen lek (thin, flat rice
noodles), snipped into
approximately 8-inch
lengths

28 g / ¼ cup Muu Sap
Luak (Poached Ground
Pork; page 228)

4 fresh or thawed
frozen Luuk Chin Muu
(Pork Balls; page 214,
or use store-bought),
at room temperature

28 g / ½ cup
bean sprouts

1½ cups Naam Sup
Muu (Pork Stock;
page 111), hot

3 g / 1 tbsp crumbled
Khaep Muu (Pork
Cracklings; page 225,
or use store-bought)

2 g / 1 tbsp very roughly
chopped cilantro (thin
stems and leaves)

5 g / 1 tbsp sliced
(¼ inch) green onion

Suggested khruang
phrung

Prep the Bowl

In a wide soup bowl, combine the fish sauce,
sugar, fried garlic in garlic oil, and pepper.

Make the Dish

Put the pork loin in a small bowl and add the fish
sauce and pepper. Mix with your hands, then let
marinate while you continue.

Fill a large, tall pot with enough water to submerge
a long-handled noodle basket and bring to a boil
over high heat. Put the noodles, marinated pork
loin, poached ground pork, pork balls, and bean
sprouts in the basket and submerge the contents
in the boiling water. Cook, stirring occasionally with
chopsticks, until the noodles are tender and the
pork loin is cooked, about 1 minute.

Firmly shake the basket to drain well and dump the
contents into the prepared bowl. Pour on the hot
pork stock and stir briefly but well. Sprinkle on
the pork cracklings, cilantro, and green onion.
Serve with the khruang phrung alongside.

Kuaytiaw Tom Yam Plaa Naam Khon

SPICY, SWEET, TART NOODLE SOUP WITH COCONUT MILK AND FISH

ก๋วยเตี๋ยวต้มยำปลาน้ำข้น

This variation on *kuaytiaw tom yam* has a few delicious differences from its pork cousin, Kuaytiaw Tom Yam Muu Naam (Spicy, Sweet, Tart Noodle Soup with Pork, page 79). Most obvious among them is the protein: in this case fish, fish balls, and a few shrimp thrown in for good measure. Then there's the addition of coconut milk or evaporated milk, which makes a cloudy soup (*naam khon*), and the aromatics in each bowl, which perfume the dish once they're drowned in hot broth.

There are also the specific seasonings used to achieve the sweet, tart, spicy flavor. Instead of the chile vinegar and toasted-chile powder in the pork version, lime juice and *naam phrik phao* (chile jam) do the work; the latter is an oily, complex paste that's sweet from palm sugar, tangy from tamarind, aromatic from fried shallots and garlic, and spicy from dried chiles. Ideally, you would make it yourself, though you may successfully lean on the Pantainorasingh or Maepranom brands. Look for "chile paste" on the label and items such as dried shrimp and shallots in the ingredient list.

Makes 1 bowl (1 serving); to make more, double or quadruple the ingredients, but make each bowl separately

»

Note

The *naam sai* (clear soup) variation on *kuaytiaw tom yam plaa* has no coconut milk or evaporated milk. To make it, skip those ingredients and increase the hot stock added to the bowl to 1½ cups.

FLAVOR PROFILE

Tart, sweet, spicy

SUGGESTED KHRUANG PHRUNG

Phrik Naam Plaa (Fish Sauce–Soaked Chiles) PAGE 236

Phrik Naam Som (Vinegar-Soaked Chiles) PAGE 235

Phrik Pon Khua (Toasted-Chile Powder) PAGE 240

Sugar (preferably raw cane sugar)

SUGGESTED UTENSILS

THE BOWL

3 tbsp unsweetened coconut milk (preferably boxed) or evaporated milk

2 tbsp Thai fish sauce

2 tbsp fresh lime juice (preferably from Key limes or from regular [Persian] limes with a squeeze of Meyer lemon juice)

6 g / 2 tsp granulated sugar

10 g / 2 tsp Naam Phrik Phao (Chile Jam; page 232, or use store-bought)

6 g / 8 very thin slices (1/8 inch) unpeeled fresh or thawed frozen galangal

5 g / 4 diagonal slices (1/4 inch wide, 1 inch long) trimmed (outer layer, bottom 1 inch, and top 9 inches removed) lemongrass, bruised

1 g / 2 fresh or frozen large makrut lime leaves, torn

5 g / 4 fresh or frozen green Thai chiles, stemmed, smashed to split slightly

THE DISH

2 1/2 oz / 1 cup packed semidried sen lek (thin, flat rice noodles), snipped into approximately 8-inch lengths

2 oz firm white-fleshed fish fillet, such as basa, tilapia, porgy, or striped bass, cut into 1 1/2-inch pieces

28 g / 2 medium-size shrimp, peeled and deveined

2 fresh or thawed frozen Luuk Chin Plaa (Fish Balls; page 216, or use store-bought), at room temperature

1 cup Naam Sup Muu (Pork Stock; page 111), hot

2 g / 1 tbsp very roughly chopped cilantro (thin stems and leaves)

4 g / 1 tbsp sliced (1/4 inch) green onion

2 g / 1 tbsp thinly sliced (1/8 inch) sawtooth herb

2 g / 3 Phrik Haeng Thawt (Dried Thai Chiles Fried in Oil; page 242)

Suggested khruang phrung

Prep the Bowl

In a wide soup bowl, combine the coconut milk, fish sauce, lime juice, sugar, chile jam, galangal, lemongrass, lime leaves, and chiles.

Make the Dish

Fill a large, tall pot with enough water to submerge a long-handled noodle basket and bring to a boil over high heat. Put the noodles, fish, fish balls, and shrimp in the basket and submerge the contents in the boiling water. Cook, stirring occasionally with chopsticks, until the fish and shrimp are just cooked and the noodles are tender, about 1 minute. Meanwhile, pour the hot pork stock into the bowl and stir well.

When the noodles are ready, firmly shake the basket to drain well and dump the contents into the prepared bowl. Stir briefly but well. Sprinkle on the cilantro, green onion, and sawtooth herb and add the dried Thai chiles fried in oil. Serve with the khruang phrung alongside.

Kuaytiaw Luuk Chin Plaa

Like so many Thai dishes, *kuaytiaw luuk chin plaa* rewards cooks who make the extra effort. Each bowl, after all, contains little more than seasoned stock, fish balls, and noodles, so the success of the whole endeavor depends primarily on the quality of these three components. Make the first two and you've gone from night to day, from spaghetti with jarred sauce to fresh pappardelle with slow-simmered ragù. The stock you make yourself with fish, lemongrass, and green onions will be far better than anything you could hope to purchase. Same goes for the fish balls, whose superior texture and flavor will banish the bland, starchy packaged orbs from your memory. The noodles, however, require a different sort of exertion—locating a source of freshly made rice noodles. Even in Thailand you're better off buying them, since the people who make them daily do a better job than dabblers like you or I ever could.

Makes 1 bowl (1 serving); to make more, double or quadruple the ingredients, but make each bowl separately

»

FLAVOR PROFILE

Mild, umami-rich

SUGGESTED KHRUANG PHRUNG

Phrik Naam Plaa
(Fish Sauce–
Soaked Chiles)
PAGE 236

Phrik Naam Som
(Vinegar-Soaked
Chiles)
PAGE 235

Phrik Pon Khua
(Toasted-Chile Powder)
PAGE 240

Sugar (preferably
raw cane sugar)

SUGGESTED UTENSILS

THE BOWL

1 tbsp Thai fish sauce

2 g / ½ tsp granulated sugar

Generous pinch of finely ground Asian white pepper

14 g / 4 torn (3-inch pieces) green-leaf or iceberg lettuce

THE DISH

4½ oz / 1 cup sen yai (fresh wide rice noodles; ¾ inch wide)

6 fresh or thawed frozen Luuk Chin Plaa (Fish Balls; page 216, or use store-bought), at room temperature

28 g firm white-fleshed fish fillet, such as basa, tilapia, porgy, or striped bass, cut into 1½-inch pieces

1½ cups Naam Sup Plaa (Fish Stock; page 113), hot

2 g / 1 tbsp very roughly chopped cilantro (thin stems and leaves)

4 g / 1 tbsp sliced (¼ inch) green onion

Generous pinch of finely ground Asian white pepper

Suggested khruang phrung

Prep the Bowl

In a wide soup bowl, combine the fish sauce, sugar, and pepper. Add the lettuce to the bowl.

Make the Dish

Fill a large, tall pot with enough water to submerge a long-handled noodle basket and bring to a boil over high heat. Put the noodles, fish balls, and fish in the basket and submerge the contents in the boiling water. Cook, gently swirling occasionally, until the fish balls and noodles are hot and the fish is cooked, about 30 seconds.

Firmly shake the basket to drain well and dump the contents into the prepared bowl. Pour on the hot fish stock and stir briefly but well. Sprinkle on the cilantro, green onion, and pepper. Serve with the khruang phrung alongside.

Kuaytiaw Tom Yam Muu Naam

SPICY, SWEET, TART NOODLE SOUP WITH PORK

ก๋วยเตี๋ยวต้มยำหมูน้ำ

You might recognize the words *tom yam* as the name of the sweet, tart, and spicy soup ubiquitous at Thai restaurants in America. This is a different dish that has some of that soup's appeal. They share a general flavor profile, which is what earns it the designation *tom*, meaning "boiled" and suggesting "soup," and *yam*, the Thai word for the genre of sweet, tart, and spicy salads.

Among Thais and, in particular, young people in Thailand, the popularity of this noodle soup seems to outstrip that of all others. Not being Thai nor young, I can only speculate about the reason. Perhaps it's the abattoir's worth of pork that graces the typical bowl, or the overall sweetness of the broth. My favorite versions, however, tread lightly on both of these qualities, scaling back a bit on the pig products and matching sweetness with plenty of acidity in the form of chile-spiked vinegar and additional heat from toasted-chile powder.

Makes 1 bowl (1 serving); to make more, double or quadruple the ingredients, but make each bowl separately

»

FLAVOR PROFILE

Tart, sweet, spicy

SUGGESTED KHRUANG PHRUNG

Phrik Naam Plaa (Fish Sauce–Soaked Chiles)
PAGE 236

Phrik Naam Som (Vinegar-Soaked Chiles)
PAGE 235

Phrik Pon Khua (Toasted-Chile Powder)
PAGE 240

Sugar (preferably raw cane sugar)

SUGGESTED UTENSILS

THE BOWL

28 g / ¼ cup Phat Muu Sap (Stir-Fried Ground Pork; page 228)

20 g / 2 tbsp coarsely pounded (⅛- to ¼-inch pieces) unsalted roasted peanuts

14 g / 1 tbsp shredded Thai salted radish (soaked in cold water for 10 minutes, rinsed, and drained well)

1 tbsp Thai fish sauce

6 g / 2 tsp granulated sugar

1 tsp Phrik Phao Naam Som (Grilled-Chile Vinegar; page 235)

2 g / 1 tsp Phrik Pon Khua (Toasted-Chile Powder; page 240)

1 tsp Naam Man Krathiam Jiaw (Fried Garlic in Garlic Oil; page 237), about half solids and half oil

THE DISH

28 g pork loin, cut against the grain into 2 by 1 by ⅛-inch strips

Splash of Thai fish sauce

Generous pinch of finely ground Asian white pepper

2½ oz / 1 cup tightly packed semidried sen lek (thin, flat rice noodles), snipped into approximately 8-inch lengths

3 fresh or thawed frozen Luuk Chin Muu (Pork Balls; page 215, or use store-bought)

28 g / ½ cup bean sprouts

28 g / ¼ cup diagonally sliced (¼ inch thick, ¾ inch long) long beans

1 cup Naam Sup Muu (Pork Stock; page 111), hot

3 g / 1 tbsp crumbled Khaep Muu (Pork Cracklings; page 225, or use store-bought)

2 g / 1 tbsp very roughly chopped cilantro (thin stems and leaves)

4 g / 1 tbsp sliced (¼ inch) green onion

2 g / 1 tbsp thinly sliced (⅛ inch) sawtooth herb

ACCOMPANIMENTS

Halved Key limes or regular (Persian) lime wedges

Coarsely pounded unsalted roasted peanuts

Suggested khruang phrung

Prep the Bowl

In a wide soup bowl, combine the stir-fried ground pork, peanuts, salted radish, fish sauce, sugar, grilled-chile vinegar, toasted-chile powder, and fried garlic in garlic oil.

Make the Dish

Put the pork loin in a small bowl and add the fish sauce and pepper. Mix with your hands, then let marinate while you continue.

Fill a large, tall pot with enough water to submerge a long-handled noodle basket and bring to a boil over high heat. Put the noodles, marinated pork loin, pork balls, bean sprouts, and long beans in the basket and submerge the contents in the boiling water. Cook, stirring occasionally with chopsticks, until the pork loin is just cooked and the noodles are tender, about 1 minute.

Firmly shake the basket to drain well and dump the contents into the prepared bowl. Pour on the hot pork stock and stir briefly but well. Sprinkle on the pork cracklings, cilantro, green onion, and sawtooth herb. Serve with the accompaniments and khruang phrung alongside.

Kuaytiaw Reua Neua

Boat noodles hail from Ayutthaya, a Central Thai city that, beginning in the mid-fourteenth century, was home base to the Kingdom of Thailand for about four hundred years. In those days, the noodles were sold from canoe-like watercraft called *reua phai* that paddled along the Chao Phraya River and the network of *khlong* (canals) that ultimately connected the city to Bangkok, a good fifty miles to the south. These waterways were hubs of commerce, and the floating vendors took advantage, selling bowls of this rich, tart, spicy noodle soup to customers on the banks.

Today, most of the canals are gone and the vendors have moved their operations to dry land, though a boat in some form or another—a drawing on the sign, an actual boat parked inside the establishment— often signifies the presence of *kuaytiaw reua*. The dish's broth, at least in the popular beef version, closely resembles *neua tuun* ("Dry" Stewed Beef Noodles)—flavored with meat stewed with soy sauce; aromatics such as lemongrass, galangal, and pandan leaf; and spices like star anise—which inspires noodle dishes of its own. One major distinction is the seasonings in each bowl. These typically include, among other things, vinegar mixed with grilled Thai chiles, toasted-chile powder, and, occasionally, blood.

As always, the customer has the final say on matters of bovinity (this recipe's array of stewed shank, poached chuck flap, springy meatballs, and gelatinous tendon is just one option) and noodles (the thin, flat noodles called *sen lek* are the standard but by no means the only choice). So do you. People often ask for additional blanched water spinach on the side. It's a nice way to add a crunchy, fresh element to the meaty dish, so consider prepping extra.

Makes 10 bowls (10 servings)

»

FLAVOR PROFILE

Rich, salty, slightly smoky, a bit sour and sweet

SUGGESTED KHRUANG PHRUNG

Phrik Naam Plaa (Fish Sauce– Soaked Chiles)
PAGE 236

Phrik Naam Som (Vinegar-Soaked Chiles)
PAGE 235

Phrik Pon Khua (Toasted-Chile Powder)
PAGE 240

Sugar (preferably raw cane sugar)

SUGGESTED UTENSILS

THE BOWLS

½ cup plus 2 tbsp Thai fish sauce

3 tbsp plus 1 tsp Phrik Phao Naam Som (Grilled-Chile Vinegar; page 235)

50 g / 3 tbsp plus 1 tsp granulated sugar

10 tbsp Naam Man Krathiam Jiaw (Fried Garlic in Garlic Oil; page 237), about half solids and half oil

20 g / 3 tbsp plus 1 tsp Phrik Pon Khua (Toasted-Chile Powder; page 240)

3 tbsp plus 1 tsp fresh or thawed frozen raw cow's or pig's blood (optional)

THE DISH

1¼ lb beef chuck flap or flank steak, cut against the grain into 2 by 1 by ⅛ inch strips

30 fresh or thawed frozen Luuk Chin Neua (Beef Balls; page 215, or use store-bought), at room temperature

4¼ oz / ¾ cup sliced cooked beef tendon (recipe follows)

1 lb 8 oz / 10 cups tightly packed semidried sen lek (thin, flat rice noodles), snipped into approximately 8-inch lengths

5 oz / 5 cups roughly chopped water spinach (bottoms trimmed by 2 inches), stems and leaves in 2-inch pieces

10 oz / 5 cups bean sprouts

1 recipe broth from Kuaytiaw Haeng Neua Tuun ("Dry" Stewed Beef Noodles; page 185), hot

20 g / 10 tbsp very roughly chopped Chinese celery (thin stems and leaves)

20 g / 10 tbsp very roughly chopped cilantro (thin stems and leaves)

20 g / 10 tbsp thinly sliced (⅛ inch) sawtooth herb

Suggested khruang phrung

Prep the Bowls

In each wide soup bowl, combine 1 tbsp fish sauce, 1 tsp grilled-chile vinegar, 3 g / 1 tsp sugar, 1½ tsp fried garlic in garlic oil, 1 tsp toasted-chile powder, and 1 tsp blood, if desired.

Make the Dish

Fill a large, tall pot with enough water to submerge a long-handled noodle basket and bring to a boil over high heat.

Set up an assembly line. In each of ten containers, combine 2 oz raw beef, 3 beef balls, 18 g / heaping 1 tbsp cooked tendon, 2½ oz / 1 cup noodles, ½ oz / ½ cup water spinach, and 1 oz / ½ cup bean sprouts. Measure the ingredients at first, then eyeball once you get the hang of it.

Make one bowl at a time (or two if you have two noodle baskets). Add one prepared portion of the noodle mixture to the noodle basket and submerge the contents in the boiling water. Cook, stirring occasionally with chopsticks, just until the raw beef is cooked through and the noodles are tender, about 1 minute.

Firmly shake the basket to drain the ingredients well and dump the contents back into the bowl. Add about ¼ cup stewed-beef broth to the bowl. Stir gently but well. Add 6 g / 1 tbsp Chinese celery, 2 g / 1 tbsp cilantro, and 2 g / 1 tbsp sawtooth herb to each bowl. Serve with the khruang phrung alongside and get to work on the next bowl.

Beef Tendon

Beef tendon, long cooked until it's soft and gelatinous, is a common addition to boat noodles. It's optional but recommended.

Makes about ¾ lb / 2 cups sliced

1 lb / 3 beef tendons	Kosher salt

In a medium pot, combine the tendons and enough water to cover by 2 inches. Stir in plenty of salt, as if you were cooking pasta. Set over high heat, bring the water to a simmer, cover the pot, and lower the heat to maintain a simmer. Cook, stirring occasionally and adding more hot water if necessary to cover the tendons, until the tendons are fairly tender (soft enough to slice but still with some chew to them), 3 to 3½ hours. Drain the tendons.

When the tendons are cool enough to handle, cut them crosswise into ⅛- to ¼-inch-thick slices. Store in an airtight container in the fridge for up to 1 week or in the freezer for up to 6 months.

Kuaytiaw Kai Tuun

STEWED-CHICKEN NOODLE SOUP

ก๋วยเตี๋ยวไก่ตุ๋น

If this is medicine, I'll take another bowl. Heavy on roots, herbs, and spices, the broth has an unmistakable curative character even before you hear it's commonly made with black chicken—that is, the dusky-skinned Silkie breed that some believe has restorative properties—and occasionally *gancha* (ganja), not high-test stuff dried to activate its psychoactive effects but the fresh plant grabbed from the ground, that is, *weed* in the literal sense. (Depending on your access to the black chicken and whether you have marijuana legally flourishing in your yard, you can do either or neither.)

But to the unaware, the broth strikes you only as delicious, homeopathy be damned. It's slightly sweet and salty, complex and rich in flavor but light going down thanks to the relatively lean meat used to make it. It takes particularly well to fresh, wide rice noodles and benefits from *khruang phrung*, as do most noodle soups, but especially from a dose of chile vinegar. For a treat, drop in a few boiled eggs (see page 230) as soon as you turn off the heat and let them soak up some of the flavor of the broth for an hour or two or until you're ready to eat.

Makes 6 bowls (6 servings)

»

Note

Look for clear plastic packages of dried ingredients, often labeled "herbal soup," at Chinese markets. Their contents vary, but if you purchase those that contain goji berries (aka wolfberries or lycium berries) and a few strips of various dried roots (such as angelica) and rhizomes (such as Solomon's seal), you're good.

FLAVOR PROFILE

Rich, salty, a little sweet

SUGGESTED KHRUANG PHRUNG

Phrik Naam Plaa (Fish Sauce-Soaked Chiles)
PAGE 236

Phrik Naam Som (Vinegar-Soaked Chiles)
PAGE 235

Phrik Pon Khua (Toasted-Chile Powder)
PAGE 240

Sugar (preferably raw cane sugar)

SUGGESTED UTENSILS

THE BROTH

50 g / 1½ cups very roughly chopped (3 inch) Chinese celery (stems and leaves)

20 g / 2 tbsp thinly sliced (⅛ inch; against the grain) unpeeled fresh or thawed frozen galangal

14 g / 14 cilantro roots, bruised

2½ oz / 2 large stalks lemongrass (outer layer, bottom 1 inch, and top 9 inches removed), bruised

1 (20 g) packet Chinese herbal soup seasoning (see Note, page 85)

9 g / 1 tbsp black peppercorns

1 g / 4 dried bay leaves

2 g / 1-inch cinnamon (cassia) stick

2 g / 2 whole star anise

6 chicken legs (thigh and drumstick), ¾ to 1 lb each, rinsed well

8 cups water

1 cup Thai thin soy sauce

½ cup Thai black soy sauce

2 oz / 12 dried shiitake mushrooms

42 g / 3 tbsp Chinese rock sugar

4¼ oz / 1 bunch fresh or thawed frozen pandan leaves, folded to fit in pot and tied into a bundle

THE BOWLS

36 oz / 7½ cups sen yai (fresh wide rice noodles; ¾ to 1 inch wide)

6 tbsp Naam Man Krathiam Jiaw (Fried Garlic in Garlic Oil; page 237), about half solids and half oil

12 g / 6 tbsp very roughly chopped Chinese celery (thin stems and leaves)

12 g / 6 tbsp very roughly chopped cilantro (thin stems and leaves)

Suggested khruang phrung

Make the Broth

On a large square of cheesecloth, combine the Chinese celery, galangal, cilantro roots, lemongrass, soup seasoning packet, peppercorns, bay leaves, cinnamon, and star anise. Gather the edges around the ingredients, then twist and knot the cheesecloth to secure the bundle.

In a large pot, combine the cheesecloth bundle, chicken legs, water, thin soy sauce, black soy sauce, mushrooms, rock sugar, and pandan leaves and bring to a simmer over high heat. Cover the pot, lower the heat to maintain a steady simmer, and cook, adjusting the heat as needed to maintain a steady simmer, until the chicken is tender, about 30 minutes. Uncover the pot and cook at a steady simmer until the meat is very tender but not falling off the bone and the flavor of the broth has concentrated slightly, 20 to 25 minutes more. Remove and discard the cheesecloth and pandan leaf bundles, but reserve the chicken and mushrooms. (Fully cooled, the chicken, mushrooms, and broth will keep in an airtight container in the fridge for up to 1 week.)

Assemble the Bowls

Before you're ready to serve, bring the stewed chicken to a bare simmer over medium-low heat.

Fill a large, tall pot with enough water to submerge a long-handled noodle basket and bring to a boil over high heat.

Make one bowl at a time (or two if you have two noodle baskets). Put 6 oz / 1¼ cups noodles in the basket and submerge the noodles in the boiling water. Cook, gently swirling the basket occasionally, until the noodles are hot, about 30 seconds. Firmly shake the basket to drain well and dump the noodles into a wide soup bowl.

Spoon on 1 tbsp of the fried garlic in garlic oil, then pull a chicken leg and a few mushrooms out of the broth and add them to the bowl. Spoon on a generous 1 cup of the hot broth and add 2 g / 1 tbsp Chinese celery and 2 g / 1 tbsp cilantro. Serve with the khruang phrung alongside and get to work on the next bowl.

MAMA Naam

SPICY INSTANT RAMEN NOODLE SOUP

มาม่าน้ำ

At Mama Fah Thani, Pa Riang goes all in on instant noodles. Known as MAMA, after a brand that has come to refer to a product, instant noodles are an option at most shops selling noodle soup, and one of no less esteem than fresh wheat or rice noodles. At her restaurant, they're all that's on offer.

Hers isn't the only shop that specializes in MAMA, but it's the best I've been to; good enough to inspire copycats around town. She started almost twenty years ago with a cart on Nimmanhemin Road near Chiang Mai University. After business boomed, she moved the operation to a storefront in the neighborhood of Santitham, once a red-light district that's now a hub for students who attend nearby Rajabhat University. The stools are populated mostly by undergrads, who have a particular affinity for instant noodles, and former students who got hooked on Pa Riang's fiery MAMA *naam* during their studies and can't kick the habit. Her old cart sits inside the restaurant, a testament to how far she's come as well as a place to warehouse clutter.

Each bowl is an unsightly marvel: a ruddy broth that includes pork stock, tamarind, and the *tom yam*-flavored powder found in packages of MAMA; rings of reconstituted dried cephalopod; *yu choy*; two types of pork balls—store-bought and craggy homemade; an egg, cracked right into the boiling broth and cooked hard; and, of course, the noodles, which retain some of the undulating shape they had in their past dried-block form. It won't win any beauty contests, but it tastes damn good.

On each table, you'll find repurposed beer bottles filled with her famous *naam phrik*, an enigmatic concoction that I suspect involves chiles fermented with tamarind. In any case, it's *khot phet*—"fucking hot"—so much so that it necessitates the posting of paper signs throughout the restaurant: an illustration of a crying man and a warning in Thai, "Please taste first, the chiles are spicy."

My recipe is an homage to her signature noodle soup. I took some guesses and I made some adjustments, like trading the dried squid (high-quality stuff is tough to find) for shrimp and poaching, rather than hammering, the eggs. But I try to stay true to its spirit. I don't, for instance, ditch the envelopes of powdered flavoring. I add them to the broth just like she does. I certainly don't upgrade to fresh rice noodles. MAMA might be a cheap, industrial product, but it's welcome in my bowl anytime.

Makes 1 bowl (1 serving); to make more, double or quadruple the ingredients, but make each bowl separately

FLAVOR PROFILE

Hot, sour, a bit salty

SUGGESTED KHRUANG PHRUNG

Naam Phrik Makham (Tamarind-Chile Sauce)
PAGE 88

SUGGESTED UTENSILS

»

THE BOWL

2 tbsp Naam Makham Piak (Tamarind Water; page 238)

1 tbsp Thai fish sauce

2 g / 1 tsp Phrik Pon Khua (Toasted-Chile Powder; page 240)

5 g / 1 tsp granulated sugar

1 (60 g) package tom yam–flavored Thai instant ramen (such as MAMA brand), noodles, seasoning powder, and seasoning paste reserved

THE DISH

1½ cups Naam Sup Muu (Pork Stock; page 111)

1 egg, at room temperature

28 g / 2 medium-size shrimp, peeled and deveined

4 Muu Sap Sawng Khreuang (Minced-Pork Balls; page 224)

42 g / ½ cup roughly chopped (2 inches) yu choy (tender stems and leaves)

2 g / 1 tbsp very roughly chopped cilantro (thin stems and leaves)

ACCOMPANIMENTS

Roughly chopped (2 inches) yu choy (tender stems and leaves)

Suggested khruang phrung

Prep the Bowl

In a wide soup bowl, combine the tamarind water, fish sauce, toasted-chile powder, and sugar. In a small bowl, combine the seasoning powder and seasoning paste from the instant ramen package, stir well, then add 3 g / 1 tsp of the mixture to the wide bowl, reserving the rest for other bowls of soup.

Make the Dish

Fill a large, tall pot with enough water to submerge a long-handled noodle basket and bring to a boil over high heat.

Meanwhile, pour the pork stock into a small pot and bring to a boil over high heat. Crack in the egg, lower the heat to maintain a gentle simmer, and poach the egg for 2 to 3 minutes, until cooked to your liking. Use a slotted spoon or spider to transfer the egg to a plate and set it aside. Keep the stock warm.

Put the block of instant ramen noodles in the noodle basket (breaking the noodles slightly to fit if need be), then add the shrimp, minced-pork balls, and yu choy. Submerge the contents in the boiling water and cook, stirring occasionally with chopsticks to separate the noodles, until the shrimp are cooked and the noodles are tender, about 2 minutes. Firmly shake the basket to drain well and dump the contents into the prepared bowl.

Pour on the hot stock and stir briefly but well. Add the poached egg and sprinkle on the cilantro. Serve with the accompaniments and khruang phrung alongside.

Naam Phrik Makham

TAMARIND-CHILE SAUCE

This is not Pa Riang's recipe for her inscrutable, delicious *naam phrik*. But it's similarly sour and hot and great for stirring into MAMA Naam.

Makes about 1 cup

40 g / 2 tbsp packed Vietnamese or Thai seedless tamarind pulp (also called tamarind paste)

½ cup hot water

3 tbsp Phrik Pon Khua (Toasted-Chile Powder; page 240)

1 tbsp Thai fish sauce

13 g / 1 tbsp granulated sugar

In a small mixing bowl, combine the tamarind pulp and hot water. Let the mixture sit until cool enough to handle, then use your hands to break up the softened tamarind pulp. Pour the mixture through a medium-mesh strainer into a bowl, stirring and pressing the solids to extract as much liquid as you can. Stir in the toasted-chile powder, fish sauce, and sugar until well combined.

The sauce will keep in an airtight container in the fridge for up to 1 week.

Kuaytiaw Kai Mara

NOODLE SOUP WITH STEWED CHICKEN AND BITTER MELON

ก๋วยเตี๋ยวไก่มะระ

I can't tell you how often it's happened. I'll be driving in Thailand—en route to shop at Talaat Chedi Mae Khrua, to grab lunchtime *laap*, or to score bags of one of my favorite snacks, *khao taen* (watermelon juice–soaked sticky rice that's sun-dried and then deep-fried)—when some shrewd passenger in my pickup, one who both reads Thai and knows where my interests lie, spots a new sign that derails our mission.

One day a couple of years ago, that sign read "Kuaytiaw Kai Mara" and inspired a hasty jerk of the steering wheel. It pointed me and Kung, now my wife, toward an unnamed restaurant that served the dish and nothing but the dish. We approached a small kiosk, ordered, and took our bowls to an open-faced shed that offered seating and respite from the sun. In those bowls was the finest version of the dish I've ever had, a delicately sweet, spiced broth similar to that of Kuaytiaw Kai Tuun (page 85), but a bit lighter, the result of simmering cartilaginous chicken feet instead of the whole chicken, with the same combination of Chinese and Thai ingredients. Among the noodles and poultry were stewed chunks of *mara* (bitter melon), an ingredient beloved in Thailand for its medicinal qualities and its fierce astringent flavor, which here had been mercifully tamed by long cooking. Alongside the bowls came thin half-moon slices of the raw vegetable, which was not tamed in the slightest.

Makes 6 bowls (6 servings)

»

Note

For those new to the project, be aware that the edible portion of a chicken foot is made up of skin, cartilage, and tendon, which become soft and gelatinous after long, slow cooking. As anyone familiar with their own extremities might guess, chicken feet contain bones, which are to be discarded once they're sucked clean.

FLAVOR PROFILE

Salty, slightly sweet, a little bitter

SUGGESTED KHRUANG PHRUNG

Phrik Naam Plaa
(Fish Sauce–
Soaked Chiles)
PAGE 236

Phrik Naam Som
(Vinegar-Soaked
Chiles)
PAGE 235

Phrik Pon Khua
(Toasted-Chile Powder)
PAGE 240

Sugar (preferably
raw cane sugar)

SUGGESTED UTENSILS

THE BROTH

32 g / 1 cup lightly packed, very roughly chopped (3 inches) Chinese celery (stems and leaves)

20 g / 1 medium stalk lemongrass (outer layer, bottom 1 inch, and top 9 inches removed), bruised and sliced ½ inch thick

10 g / 1 tbsp thinly sliced (⅛ inch; against the grain) unpeeled fresh or thawed frozen galangal

7 g / scant 1 tbsp thinly sliced (⅛ inch; against the grain) ginger

6 g / 6 cilantro roots, bruised

2 g / 1-inch cinnamon (cassia) stick

2 g / 2 whole star anise

1 dried bay leaf

4 g / 1½ tsp black peppercorns

2 lb chicken feet, rinsed well, toenails clipped off if necessary

10 cups water

½ cup Thai thin soy sauce

¼ cup Thai black soy sauce

1 tbsp Thai fish sauce

14 g / 2 fresh or thawed frozen pandan leaves, folded to fit in pot and tied in a bundle

16 g / 1 tbsp Chinese rock sugar

THE BITTER MELON

Kosher salt

6 oz / 1 medium bitter melon, halved lengthwise, spongy white center and seeds scraped out, then cut into 3-inch lengths

1 tsp Thai black soy sauce

THE BOWLS

10½ oz / 1½ cups Neua Kai Chiik (Shredded Poached Chicken; page 229), at room temperature

6 tbsp Thai fish sauce

30 g / 6 tsp granulated sugar

6 pinches of finely ground Asian white pepper

15 oz / 6 cups tightly packed semidried sen lek (thin, flat rice noodles), snipped into approximately 8-inch lengths

12 g / 6 tbsp very roughly chopped cilantro (thin stems and leaves)

ACCOMPANIMENTS

Bitter melon, halved lengthwise, spongy white center and seeds scraped out, then thinly sliced into half-moons

Whole Thai basil sprigs

Bean sprouts

Suggested khruang phrung

Make the Broth

On a large square of cheesecloth, combine the Chinese celery, lemongrass, galangal, ginger, cilantro roots, cinnamon, star anise, bay leaf, and peppercorns. Twist and knot to secure the bundle.

In a large pot, combine the cheesecloth bundle, chicken feet, water, thin soy sauce, black soy sauce, fish sauce, pandan leaves, and rock sugar and bring to a simmer over high heat. Cover, lower the heat to maintain a gentle simmer, and cook, stirring occasionally, until the chicken feet are very tender but not falling apart, about 1 hour. Remove and discard the cheesecloth and pandan leaf bundles. Turn off the heat and leave the pot covered to keep the broth warm.

Cook the Bitter Melon

While the broth is cooking, in a medium pot, bring 2 inches or so of water to a boil over high heat and salt the water as if you are cooking pasta. Add the bitter melon to the boiling water, cover, and lower the heat to maintain a simmer. Cook until the melon is fork-tender, about 8 minutes. Drain well and transfer to a small pot.

When the broth is ready, spoon just enough of it into the small pot to submerge the melon and add the black soy sauce. Bring to a simmer over high heat, cover, and lower the heat to cook at a simmer until the melon is very tender but not falling apart, about 25 minutes. Transfer the melon to a plate, discarding the liquid, and set aside.

Assemble the Bowls

Before you're ready to serve, bring the remaining broth to a simmer.

In each of six wide soup bowls, combine 2 chicken feet, 50 g / ¼ cup shredded chicken, 1 tbsp fish sauce, 5 g / 1 tsp sugar, and a pinch of pepper.

Fill a large, tall pot with enough water to submerge a long-handled noodle basket and bring to a boil over high heat. Finish one bowl at a time. Put 2½ oz / 1 cup of the noodles in the basket and submerge them in the boiling water. Cook, stirring occasionally with chopsticks, until the noodles are tender, about 1 minute. Meanwhile, ladle 1½ cups of the hot broth into one of the prepared bowls.

When the noodles are ready, firmly shake the basket to drain well and dump them into the prepared bowl. Stir briefly but well. Top the bowl with a piece of cooked bitter melon and sprinkle on 2 g / 1 tbsp cilantro. Serve with the accompaniments and khruang phrung alongside and get to work on the next bowl.

Yen Ta Fo

SOUR-SWEET NOODLE SOUP WITH SEAFOOD AND FERMENTED TOFU

เย็นตาโฟ

If you've spent a few weeks in Thailand, you've likely spotted bowls of *yen ta fo*, even if you haven't ordered one yourself. The modern version of this noodle soup tends to turn the heads of those not used to the color of its broth—a vivid pink. Crowded with fish balls, shrimp, and crunchy pickled cuttlefish, the dish is as popular in Thailand as it is uncommon in the States. It's one of dozens of Thai foods relegated to obscurity in the West, and for no good reason, if you ask me.

Like most dishes, *yen ta fo* has murky origins, though it almost certainly has a Chinese pedigree, as most noodle dishes do and especially those with a distinctly Chinese ingredient at their heart. In this case, it's a type of tofu fermented with so-called red-yeast rice (called *taohu yii* in Thai), which provides the old-school broth's pale pink color. In the version that prevails nowadays, the tofu is nowhere to be found. Instead, a sugary, electric-pink gloop both flavors and colors the broth. Yet in the best versions, those made in the traditional manner, *taohu yii* joins forces with tomatoes and pickled garlic to give a tangy, sweet, and slightly funky flavor to pork stock.

It is to this outcome that this recipe is meant to guide you. Between making the elements of the broth and fashioning your own fish balls, the dish asks a lot of the home cook. Each bowl gives plenty back.

Makes 8 bowls (8 servings)

Note

White fungus is sold dried at Chinese or Southeast Asian markets and labeled variously as "silver fungus" or "snow fungus." To rehydrate the fungus for this dish, soak it in enough lukewarm (about 100°F) water to cover, weighting it down if necessary to keep it submerged, until softened but still very crunchy, at least 1 hour or up to overnight. Trim off and discard the woody base before proceeding with the recipe.

FLAVOR PROFILE

Sour, sweet, a bit funky

SUGGESTED KHRUANG PHRUNG

Phrik Naam Plaa (Fish Sauce–Soaked Chiles)
PAGE 236

Phrik Naam Som (Vinegar-Soaked Chiles)
PAGE 235

Phrik Pon Khua (Toasted-Chile Powder)
PAGE 240

Sugar (preferably raw cane sugar)

SUGGESTED UTENSILS

THE YEN TA FO SAUCE

10 oz / 1¾ cups halved cherry tomatoes or cored and chopped (1 inch) regular red tomatoes

42 g / 15 garlic cloves, peeled

42 g / 2½ tbsp packed red fermented bean curd

½ cup distilled white vinegar

2 tbsp pickled garlic liquid

3½ oz / ½ cup granulated sugar

10 g / 1 tbsp kosher salt

THE STOCK

10 cups Naam Sup Muu (Pork Stock; page 111)

50 g / 2 pickled garlic heads, drained

3 tbsp Thai thin soy sauce

15 g / 1 tbsp Chinese rock sugar

15 g / 5 garlic cloves, crushed into small pieces in a mortar

2 g / ¾ tsp black peppercorns, very coarsely cracked

THE BOWLS

8 tbsp Thai fish sauce

8 tsp Naam Man Krathiam Jiaw (Fried Garlic in Garlic Oil; page 237), about half solids and half oil

36 oz / 8 cups sen yai (fresh wide rice noodles; ¾ inch wide)

4 oz / 2 cups bean sprouts

4 oz / 4 cups chopped water spinach (bottoms trimmed by 2 inches), stems and leaves in 1-inch pieces

32 sen plaa (fish noodles; see page 216)

4½ oz / 32 (½ by 2-inch) pieces cleaned cuttlefish, or 16 g / 4 cleaned squid bodies, cut into ½-inch-wide rings

16 fresh or thawed frozen Luuk Chin Plaa (Fish Balls; page 216, or use store-bought), at room temperature

8 oz / 16 medium-size shrimp, peeled and deveined

10 oz / 16 store-bought tofu puffs

4 oz / 16 (1½-inch) pieces, roughly chopped, trimmed, rehydrated white fungus (see Note, page 93)

8 pinches of very roughly chopped Chinese celery (thin stems and leaves)

16 triangles Kiaw Thawt (Fried Wonton Skins; page 243; optional)

Suggested khruang phrung

Make the Sauce

In a medium pot, combine the tomatoes, garlic, bean curd, vinegar, pickled garlic liquid, sugar, and salt and bring to a boil over high heat. Lower the heat to maintain a gentle but steady simmer and cook, stirring once or twice, until the tomatoes have broken down, the garlic is tender but not falling apart, and the liquid has thickened slightly, about 30 minutes.

Let cool slightly, then transfer to a blender and blend until smooth. The sauce will keep in an airtight container in the fridge for up to 1 week.

Make the Stock

In a medium pot, combine the pork stock, pickled garlic heads, thin soy sauce, rock sugar, garlic cloves, and peppercorns. Bring to a gentle but steady simmer over high heat, lower the heat to maintain the simmer, and cook, occasionally skimming off any scum, for 15 to 20 minutes to combine the flavors. Strain the stock, discarding the solids. If you're using it right away, keep it warm.(Fully cooled, it will keep in airtight containers in the fridge for up to 1 week or in the freezer for up to 6 months.)

Assemble the Bowls

Just before you're ready to serve, bring the stock to a simmer.

In each of eight wide soup bowls, combine 3 tbsp of the yen ta fo sauce, 1 tbsp fish sauce, and 1 tsp fried garlic in garlic oil.

Fill a large, tall pot with enough water to submerge a long-handled noodle basket and bring to a boil over high heat. Finish one bowl at a time (or two if you have two noodle baskets). Put 4½ oz / 1 cup noodles, 14 g / ¼ cup bean sprouts, 14 g / ½ cup water spinach, 4 fish noodles, 16 g / 4 pieces cuttlefish, 2 fish balls, 28 g / 2 shrimp, 35 g / 2 tofu puffs, and 14 g / 2 pieces white fungus in the basket and submerge the contents in the boiling water. Cook, swirling the basket occasionally, just until the cuttlefish and shrimp are cooked through, about 1 minute. Meanwhile, pour 1½ cups of the hot stock into one of the bowls. Stir briefly but well.

When the noodles are ready, firmly shake the basket to drain well and dump the contents into the prepared bowl. Stir briefly but well. Sprinkle with a pinch of Chinese celery and garnish with 2 fried wonton skins. Serve with the khruang phrung alongside and get to work on the next bowl.

Kuay Chap Naam Sai

PEPPERY PORK AND OFFAL SOUP WITH ROLLED NOODLES

ก๋วยจั๊บน้ำใส

Beneath the towering signs and giant TV screens of Yaowarat, Bangkok's frenetic Chinatown, you'll find diners crowded at metal tables, ending their nights with *kuay chap*, bowls of short tubular noodles, a ferociously peppery broth, and enough pork guts to scare off most Western sight-seers. Years ago, you could nab a seat and enjoy your bowl a few feet from the traffic buzzing by—street food with emphasis on the street. Nowadays, barricades surround the best-known *kuay chap* vendors, corralling the tourists and creating the sort of melee that men of a certain age can no longer abide.

Lucky for me, then, there's Kuay Chap Chang Moi. Fifty-odd years ago, the family ran a restaurant in Bangkok before migrating it to this old shophouse near Talaat Warorot (or Kat Luang, in the local parlance), the market in Chiang Mai's Chinatown. Their *kuay chap* goes lighter on the white pepper, though each table has a shaker for those who miss the sting, and contains as much meat as it does offal, not to mention an unusual uncured sausage that's little more than pork, salt, pepper, garlic, and rice. It's all damn delicious.

When making the noodle soup at home, I recommend using plenty of innards—without them, the dish is fundamentally different, like spaghetti carbonara made vegan—as well as meat, whether it's ground pork, pork loin, pork balls, or cooked ribs left over from *bak kut teh* (see page 107). I have spared you instructions for the sausage, which I have yet to master. Because the primary seasoning, along with soy sauce, is white pepper added by the boatload, it's worth stressing that you should seek out the more mellow white pepper from Southeast Asia, rather than the more hectic stuff from Europe, which, when used unstintingly, tends to add a flavor and scent reminiscent of cowshit.

Makes 1 bowl (1 serving); to make more, double or quadruple the ingredients, but make each bowl separately

»

FLAVOR PROFILE

Very peppery, salty, offal-y

SUGGESTED KHRUANG PHRUNG

Phrik Naam Plaa
(Fish Sauce-
Soaked Chiles)
PAGE 236

Phrik Naam Som
(Vinegar-Soaked
Chiles)
PAGE 235

Phrik Pon Khua
(Toasted-Chile Powder)
PAGE 240

Sugar (preferably
raw cane sugar)

SUGGESTED UTENSILS

2¼ oz / 3 cups sen kuay chap (dried bean sheet noodles)

1 tbsp Thai thin soy sauce

1 g / ½ tsp finely ground Asian white pepper

3 oz / ½ cup cooked Khruang Nai (Offal; page 227), such as heart, liver, and intestines

4 oz boneless pork loin, cut into 2 by ½ by ⅛-inch strips, or 2½ oz / ½ cup Muu Sap Luak (Poached Ground Pork; page 228)

1½ cups Naam Sup Muu (Pork Stock; page 111), hot

4 g / 1 tbsp sliced (¼ inch) green onion

4 g / 1 tbsp crumbled Khaep Muu (Pork Cracklings; page 225, or use store-bought)

Suggested khruang phrung

In a large bowl, combine the noodles and enough lukewarm (about 100°F) water to cover by an inch or so. Let soak for 5 minutes, occasionally using your hands to make sure the noodles don't stick together. The noodles will curl to form a tubular shape. Drain well.

Meanwhile, fill a large, tall pot with enough water to submerge a long-handled noodle basket and bring to a boil over high heat.

In a wide soup bowl, combine the thin soy sauce and pepper.

Put the soaked noodles, offal, and pork loin or poached ground pork in the basket and submerge the contents in the boiling water. Cook, stirring with chopsticks, until the noodles are fully cooked (they'll still be chewy), about 1 minute.

Firmly shake the basket to drain well and dump the contents into the prepared bowl. Pour on the hot pork stock and stir briefly but well. Sprinkle on the green onion and pork cracklings. Serve with the khruang phrung alongside.

I first encountered this dish while traveling in China's Yunnan Province, where I found migrant Muslims from Northern China hawking their wares streetside: grilled lamb skewers, flatbread, and hand-pulled noodles in smoky broth made from lamb cooked over a charcoal fire. As a noodle freak, I was immediately taken with the dish and proceeded to seek it out in every town I visited.

Besides the noodles—hand pulled, if you're adept at the simple, riveting technique, or purchased, if, like me, you're not—the dish is all about the broth. My recipe is an educated guess about its composition and gives you something quite good and not too far from what I had in Yunnan. To do it justice, I strongly recommend grilling the lamb bones and meat over charcoal. It's how I ape the smoky quality of the broths I loved in China, which came from, I assume based on practically every setup I saw, hunks of lamb hanging near open fire. Don't skip the fiery, oily paste of dried chiles meant to be served alongside.

Makes 8 bowls (8 servings, plus leftover stock and meat)

FLAVOR PROFILE

Mild, meaty, a bit salty

SUGGESTED KHRUANG PHRUNG

Thai thin soy sauce

SUGGESTED UTENSILS

»

THE STOCK AND LAMB

5 lb meaty lamb bones (such as neck or ribs), rinsed and patted dry

1 tbsp neutral oil, such as canola, soybean, or rice bran

2 lb boneless lamb leg or shoulder, in a single piece, fat scored in a crisscross pattern

7 g / 2 tsp kosher salt

Ground black pepper

35 g / 1 small whole unpeeled head garlic

28 g / 1½ by 1-inch knob unpeeled ginger

10 g / 3 cilantro roots (with several inches of stem attached), or 10 g / 3 whole cilantro sprigs

20 g / 1 medium stalk lemongrass (outer layer, bottom 1 inch, and top 9 inches removed), halved crosswise

6 oz / 1 small unpeeled daikon radish, halved lengthwise, then cut crosswise into about ¼-inch-thick slices

6 oz / ½ small unpeeled yellow onion, very roughly chopped

2¼ oz / 3 green onions, torn in half

35 g / 3 leafy Chinese celery stalks, torn in half

2 g / ¾ tsp black peppercorns

THE BOWLS

½ cup Thai thin soy sauce

16 g / 4 tsp granulated sugar

8 generous pinches of finely ground Asian white pepper

THE DISH

1½ lb / 6 cups fresh wheat noodles, preferably ⅛ inch thick and white

8 oz / 2 cups thinly sliced (1/16 inch; with the grain) yellow onion

16 g / 1 cup very roughly chopped mint leaves

16 g / ½ cup very roughly chopped cilantro (thin stems and leaves)

32 g / ½ cup sliced (¼ inch) green onion

10 g / 1 tbsp untoasted sesame seeds

½ cup Naam Phrik Phao (Roasted-Chile Paste; page 233)

Suggested khruang phrung

Cook the Stock and Lamb

Prepare a grill, preferably charcoal, to cook with medium-high heat. Alternatively, preheat the oven to 375°F. Grill the lamb bones, or roast them in a single layer on a sheet pan in the oven, turning them over occasionally, until golden brown, 45 minutes to 1 hour. Keep the grill or oven going.

Transfer the bones to a large, tall pot and add enough water to cover by an inch or so. Bring the water to a bare simmer over high heat, then lower the heat to maintain the bare simmer. Cook, occasionally skimming off any surface scum, until all the flavor has been cooked out of the meat remaining on the lamb bones, about 2 hours.

While the stock is cooking, rub the oil all over the lamb leg, then season all over with the salt and with ground black pepper. Grill the lamb with the grill covered, or roast uncovered on a sheet pan in the oven, until well browned and cooked to medium doneness (about 135°F), 45 minutes to 1 hour. Let the lamb rest on a cutting board for 15 minutes or so. Cut it against the grain into ⅛- to ¼-inch-thick bite-size pieces. Reserve 1¼ lb / 4 cups for this dish. Let the remainder cool, then refrigerate in an airtight container for up to 1 week.

When the stock has simmered for 2 hours, working with one ingredient at a time, use a pestle or heavy pan to lightly whack the garlic, ginger, cilantro roots, and lemongrass to bruise them. Very roughly slice the ginger and lemongrass. Add the bruised aromatics to the pot along with the daikon, yellow onion, green onions, Chinese celery, and peppercorns. Simmer gently for 30 minutes more. Strain the stock into a very large container or pot (don't press the solids) and discard the solids. Return 12 cups of the stock to the pot and keep hot. (Fully cooled, the remaining stock will keep in airtight containers in the fridge for up to 1 week or in the freezer for up to 6 months.)

Prep Each Bowl

In each of eight wide soup bowls, combine 1 tbsp of the thin soy sauce, ½ tsp of the sugar, and a generous pinch of white pepper.

Make the Dish

Fill a large, tall pot with enough water to submerge a long-handled noodle basket and bring to a boil over high heat. Make one bowl at a time. Put 3 oz / ¾ cup noodles in the basket and submerge them in the boiling water. Cook, stirring occasionally with chopsticks, until the noodles are tender, 3 to 4 minutes. Firmly shake the basket to drain well and dump the noodles into one of the prepared bowls.

Add 2½ oz / ½ cup of the lamb, pour on 1½ cups of the hot stock, and stir briefly but well. Sprinkle on 25 g / ¼ cup yellow onion, 4 g / 2 tbsp mint, 2 g / 1 tbsp cilantro, 4 g / 1 tbsp green onion, and a generous pinch of sesame seeds. Serve the first bowl with the roasted-chile paste and khruang phrung alongside and get to work on the next bowl.

Laksa Nyonya

ละก์ซาย่าหยา

Inspiration for this recipe struck when I employed a well-worn traveler's trick during a trip to Singapore: asking my taxi driver for recommendations. I was venturing out for lunch on what would become a multiday slog around the city with the goal of tasting as many of the best versions of *laksa nyonya* as I could physically tolerate. I told my driver about my mission, and without hesitation, he said something to the effect of "hold my beer." With me cheering him on, we sped off into the tropical heat.

Anyone who's tried the dish will sympathize with my zeal. While *laksa nyonya* is but one twig sprouted from the vast *laksa* family tree, it is deservedly fawned over. Created by Peranakan Chinese, immigrants to Singapore and to the Malaysian port cities of Melaka and Penang, the noodle soup features the deft melding of culinary influences that developed over the intervening centuries and has come to define their cuisine. The food is colloquially called *nyonya*, a term of endearment for women, who were, by all accounts, historically the ones doing the cooking.

When my driver pulled up in front of an office building, I began to fear my enthusiasm had been misplaced. At his insistence, I entered a cafeteria-style restaurant on the first floor that looked as unexceptional as the facade of the building itself. I took my place in line, ordered, and received a stainless-steel bowl of noodles drowned in a gravy-like sauce fragrant from coconut, lemongrass, and the fermented shrimp paste called *belacan*. On top were shrimp, fish cakes, tiny clams, tofu puffs, shredded chicken, and still more accessories. Alongside came fiery sambal, a paste of chiles and aromatics meant for adjusting flavor. It was the best bowl I had all trip. Alas, these were the days before check-in apps and pin drops. I neglected to write down the location, so I have no clue how to find it again.

My goal was to re-create its intense, complex flavor, complete with the thickening effects of candlenut and the herb *daun kesum* (called *phak phai* in Thai, *rau ram* in Vietnamese, and Vietnamese mint in English), which is considered so vital to the dish that it also goes by *duan laksa* (*laksa* leaf). Both, by the way, are easy enough to get in the States. I make one major concession to my palate. I substitute some of the coconut cream most bowls rely on with evaporated milk, an ingredient you sometimes find in bowls around Singapore and a holdover from days past when the only available dairy came in cans.

Makes 10 bowls (10 servings)

»

FLAVOR PROFILE

Rich, umami, a bit salty

SUGGESTED KHRUANG PHRUNG

Sambal Belacan (Spicy Shrimp Paste)
PAGE 229

SUGGESTED UTENSILS

THE PASTE

42 g Malaysian fermented shrimp paste

283 g small Asian shallots, peeled and roughly chopped

56 g peeled fresh or thawed frozen galangal, roughly sliced against the grain

64 g roughly sliced lemongrass, tender parts only (from about 9 large stalks)

18 g peeled fresh or thawed frozen yellow turmeric root, thinly sliced against the grain

15 g medium-size dried shrimp, soaked in cold water for 10 minutes and then drained

50 g stemmed dried puya chiles, split open, seeded, and soaked in hot tap water until fully soft, about 20 minutes

35 g raw candlenuts or macadamia nuts

4 g coriander seeds (preferably Asian)

1/2 cup water, plus more as needed

THE BROTH

3 1/2 lb / 40 Manila or littleneck clams, rinsed

Up to 5 cups shrimp stock (recipe follows) or Naam Sup Muu (Pork Stock; page 111)

1/4 cup neutral oil, such as canola, soybean, or rice bran

6 1/2 oz / 1 1/2 cups chopped (1/2 inch) yellow onions

50 g / 1/4 cup granulated sugar

4 cups unsweetened coconut cream (preferably boxed)

1 cup evaporated milk

2 tbsp Thai fish sauce

10 g / 1 tbsp kosher salt

2 g / 1 tsp finely ground Asian white pepper

THE DISH

14 1/2 oz bun (dried spaghetti-shaped rice noodles)

1 tbsp neutral oil, such as canola, soybean, or rice bran

1 1/4 lb / 40 medium-size shrimp, peeled and deveined, shells (and heads, if you have them) reserved for the stock

10 oz / 5 cups bean sprouts

30 thinly sliced (1 1/2 by 1/8 inches) Luuk Chin Plaa (Fish Balls; page 216, or use store-bought)

13 oz / 20 store-bought tofu puffs

10 oz / 1 1/4 cups Neua Kai Chiik (Shredded Poached Chicken; page 229), at room temperature

1/2 cup plus 2 tbsp Thai fish sauce

10 Khai Tom (Boiled Eggs; page 230; cooked 7 minutes), peeled and quartered

10 oz / 2 1/2 cups julienned (2 by 1/8 inch) seeded cucumber (peeled, if thick skinned)

20 g / 1/2 cup plus 2 tbsp very thinly sliced Vietnamese mint

Suggested khruang phrung

Make the Paste

Make a double layer of aluminum foil (or banana leaves, if you've got them), put the shrimp paste on the center, and fold in the sides to make a packet (securing it with wet toothpicks if using banana leaves). Set a heavy pan over medium heat and add the packet (or better yet, grill it over a low charcoal fire). Cook, flipping the packet occasionally, until the shrimp paste is very fragrant, about 12 minutes.

Meanwhile, combine the shallots, galangal, lemongrass, turmeric, and dried shrimp in a food processor. When the shrimp paste is ready, open the package and dump the paste into the processor. Drain the chiles well. Wrap them in paper towels, gently wring out the water, and add them to the processor.

Put the candlenuts in a small pan, set it over medium-low heat, and cook, stirring and tossing often, until the nuts are golden brown outside and hot all the way through, 6 to 8 minutes. Transfer to a mortar, pound to a fairly fine powder, and scoop into the food processor. Add the coriander seeds to the pan and toast over medium-low heat until fragrant, 1 to 2 minutes. Transfer to the mortar, pound to a fairly fine powder, and scoop into the food processor.

Add the water to the food processor and process, occasionally stopping to scrape the sides and gradually adding more water if the blades are struggling to catch the mixture, to a fairly smooth paste, 2 to 3 minutes.

You'll have about 25 1/2 oz / 2 3/4 cups paste. Reserve 12 3/4 oz / 1 1/3 cups for this recipe. The remaining paste will keep in an airtight container in the fridge for up to 1 week or in the freezer for up to 6 months.

Make the Broth

Put the clams in a wide saucepan and pour in 1/2 inch of water. Cover the pan, set over high heat, and bring the water to a boil. Cook, shaking the pan occasionally, just until the clams have popped open, about 5 minutes.

Remove the clams, reserving the liquid in the pan. When the clams are cool enough to handle, pull the meat from each one and reserve in a bowl. Discard the shells and any clams that didn't open.

Strain the liquid from the pan through a fine-mesh strainer into a heatproof measuring cup. Add enough shrimp stock to make 6 cups liquid total.

In a medium pot over medium heat, warm the oil until it shimmers. Add the onions and cook, stirring, until slightly softened, about 2 minutes. Stir in the paste and cook, stirring frequently, until the paste is very fragrant and loses the smell of raw shallots, 5 to 7 minutes.

Stir in the mixed clam broth and shrimp stock and the sugar and bring to a boil over high heat. Add the coconut cream, evaporated milk, fish sauce, salt, and pepper and bring to a simmer (don't let it boil). Lower the heat to maintain a gentle simmer and cook, stirring occasionally, until the flavors have had a chance to come together, about 30 minutes. Keep the broth warm.

Make the Dish

Fill a large, tall pot with enough water to submerge a long-handled noodle basket and bring to a boil over high heat. Add the noodles and cook, stirring occasionally, until fully tender but not mushy, 10 to 15 minutes. Drain them well. Reserve the pot of water. To prevent clumping, toss the noodles with the oil to coat well.

Set up an assembly line. In each of ten containers, combine 5 oz / ¾ cup noodles, 4 shrimp, 28 g / ½ cup bean sprouts, 3 slices fish ball, and 36 g / 2 tofu puffs. Measure at first, then eyeball once you get the hang of it.

Make one bowl at a time (or two if you have two noodle baskets). Add one portion of the noodle mixture to the noodle basket and submerge the contents in the water. Cook, occasionally stirring the contents with chopsticks, just until the shrimp are cooked through, about 1 minute. Firmly shake the basket to drain the ingredients well and dump the contents into a wide soup bowl. Add 28 g / 2 tbsp shredded poached chicken, 10 g / 4 clams, and 1 tbsp fish sauce.

Ladle in 1 cup of the hot broth. Stir gently but well. Add 4 egg quarters, 28 g / ¼ cup cucumber, and 2 g / 1 tbsp Vietnamese mint leaves. Serve with the khruang phrung alongside and get to work on the next bowl.

Shrimp Stock

You'll get the best results if you make *laksa* with shrimp stock. It requires plenty of shells, which you can collect from other shrimp-cooking endeavors and freeze until you're ready to use them.

Makes about 9 cups

1½ tsp neutral oil, such as canola, soybean, or rice bran	15 g / 3 leafy Chinese celery stalks
Shrimp shells (and heads, if you have them) from about 1¼ lb shrimp, rinsed	15 g / 1 small stalk lemongrass (outer layer, bottom 1 inch, and top 9 inches removed), bruised and roughly chopped
12 cups water	28 g / 1½ by 1-inch knob unpeeled ginger, smashed
28 g / 1 small unpeeled head garlic, smashed	3 g / 1 tsp black peppercorns or Asian white peppercorns
20 g / 2 green onions	1 small dried bay leaf
15 g / 10 whole cilantro sprigs	

In a medium pot over medium heat, warm the oil until it shimmers. Add the shrimp shells and heads and cook, stirring occasionally, until they turn pink and are golden brown at the edges, about 5 minutes. Pour in the water, turn the heat to high, and bring the water to a simmer. Add the garlic, green onions, cilantro, Chinese celery, lemongrass, ginger, peppercorns, and bay leaf; lower the heat to maintain a gentle simmer and cook for 1 hour.

Strain the stock into a large bowl or pot (don't press the solids) and discard the solids. Use the stock now, or let it cool fully and store it in an airtight container in the fridge for up to 5 days or in the freezer for up to 6 months.

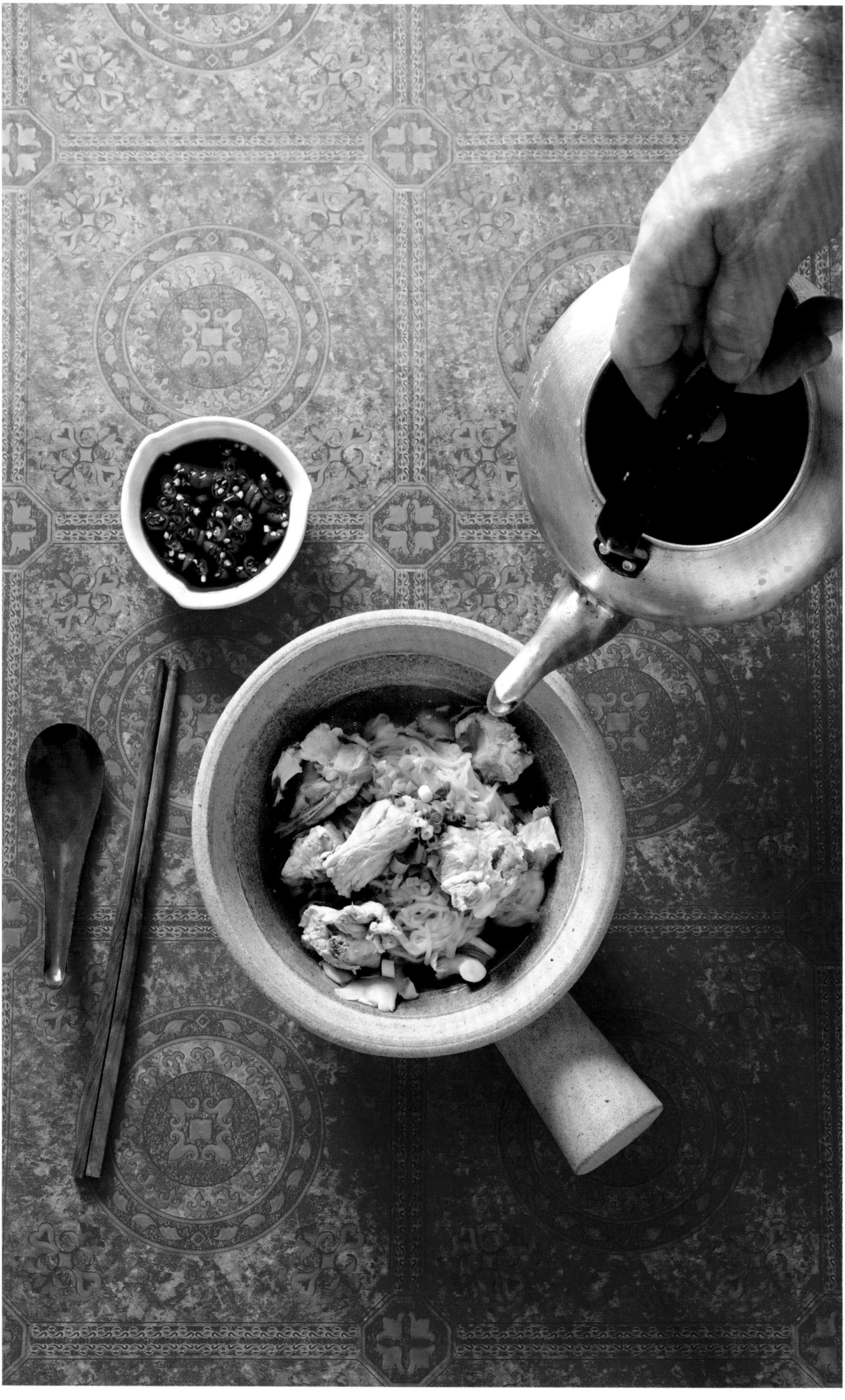

Ba Mii Bak Kut Teh

NOODLES WITH PORK BONE TEA

บะหมี่บะกุดเต๋

FLAVOR PROFILE

Peppery, umami-rich, salty

SUGGESTED UTENSILS

I had my first bowl of *bak kut teh* in Singapore. Early one morning, I wandered into a shop where every customer had a bowl of stubby pork ribs wading in broth. There was nothing to do but join them. The broth was subtly seasoned, judiciously salted, and only slightly sweet, but rich with flavor, complex from medicinal spices such as star anise and clove, and sharp from white pepper. Like my neighbors, I sipped the broth from the bowl and nabbed the ribs with chopsticks, dipping them in a mixture of molasses-like black soy sauce and sliced fresh chile. An older woman made the rounds with a kettle—befitting a dish whose name translates as "meat bone tea"—remedying broth levels that got too low.

Food this satisfying encourages further exploration. So I sought out this staple when I visited *bak kut teh* hubs; like Singapore and Malaysia, two contenders for the elusive title of Where The Dish Came From. The dish was likely cooked up by migrants from southern China, perhaps the Teochew or Hokkien people, who came to these countries to toil in mines, at ports, and on plantations. Whatever the specifics, the dish is now one of the many that have transcended their origins and morphed with the tastes of cooks throughout Southeast Asia.

On my travels, I encountered broths dark and light, sweet and not, heavily and sparely spiced. I ate those containing just pork ribs and others with tofu skins, tofu puffs, mushrooms, and organs. On the side, I found some combination of fried crullers called *youtiao*, boiled peanuts, salted vegetables, and rice. I started seeing the dish in Thailand, too, from shops in Chiang Mai and Bangkok to a very famous joint in Hat Yai, a Southern Thai city close to the Malaysian border. And it was sometimes served with noodles, something I hadn't seen before. Its presence in Thailand is yet another testament to the country's welcoming culinary culture and to the simple logic behind its innovation—Thais just love noodles.

Makes 4 bowls (4 servings)

»

THE PORK BONE TEA

2½ lb pork spare ribs, cut crosswise through the bone into 2-inch-wide racks, then into individual riblets, rinsed

4 quarts water

½ cup Thai thin soy sauce

2 tbsp Thai black soy sauce

14 g / 1 tbsp Chinese rock sugar

20 g / 2 tbsp plus 1 tsp kosher salt

40 g / 1 whole small unpeeled head garlic, smashed to break apart and bruise

1 packet bak kut teh spices (see facing page)

THE BOWLS

64 g / 4 cups roughly chopped (2 inches) green-leaf lettuce

4 tbsp Thai fish sauce

4 generous pinches of finely ground Asian white pepper

12 oz / 3 cups packed round thin ba mii (fresh yellow Chinese wheat noodles)

4 oz / 1 cup trimmed and torn (2- to 3-inch pieces) oyster mushrooms

16 g / 4 tbsp sliced (¼ inch) green onion

ACCOMPANIMENTS

Naam Jim Si Ew Dam Phrik Sot (Black Soy-Chile Dipping Sauce; page 234)

Make the Pork Bone Tea

Put the ribs in a large pot, add enough water to cover the bones by an inch or so, and set the pot over high heat. Bring the water to a simmer, then turn off the heat. Skim any scum from the surface, then drain the ribs and rinse them well under cold running water. All this is to get any schmutz off the ribs, which will give you a cleaner-tasting, clearer product.

Clean the pot, return the ribs to the pot, and add the 4 quarts water. Bring to a bare simmer over high heat, then lower the heat to maintain the bare simmer. Add the thin soy sauce, black soy sauce, rock sugar, salt, and garlic. Put the spice packet ingredients on a double layer of cheesecloth, gather the edges around them, then twist the edges and knot the cheesecloth to secure the bundle. Add the bundle to the pot. Cook, occasionally skimming off any surface scum, until the meat on the ribs is tender but still has some chew to it, about 20 minutes. Turn off the heat and remove and discard the spice bundle. Cover the pot to keep warm. (Fully cooled, the bone tea and ribs will keep in an airtight container in the fridge for up to 5 days.)

Assemble the Bowls

In each of four wide soup bowls, combine 16 g / 1 cup lettuce, 1 tbsp fish sauce, and a generous pinch of pepper.

Fill a large, tall pot with enough water to submerge a long-handled noodle basket and bring to a boil over high heat. Finish one bowl at a time (or two if you have two noodle baskets). Put 3 oz / ¾ cup noodles and 28 g / ¼ cup mushrooms in the basket and submerge the contents in the boiling water. Cook, stirring occasionally with chopsticks, until the mushrooms are cooked and the noodles are tender, about 3 minutes. Firmly shake the basket to drain well and dump the contents into one of the prepared bowls.

Pour on 1½ cups of the hot bone tea, add 3 or 4 pork ribs, and stir briefly but well. Sprinkle on 4 g / 1 tbsp green onion. Serve with a small bowl of black soy–chile dipping sauce alongside for dipping the ribs and get to work on the next bowl.

Bak Kut Teh Spice Packets

Most Chinese and Southeast Asian markets and some Chinese herbalists sell small packets of the medicinal dried spices used to make *bak kut teh*. The contents vary by composer, though certain ingredients, such as cinnamon, star anise, angelica root, and wolfberries, seem more or less mandatory. Buying these premade packets is an easy way to gather the ingredients necessary, particularly those less familiar to the non-Chinese among us (angelica root and Solomon's seal rhizome, for example) that might take effort to track down. Feel free to use a packet meant for 1 kg of meat (the instructions on the package should guide you). Or use the packet for its Solomon's seal et al., and your own pantry and this formula for the rest.

Makes 1 packet (enough for 2¹/₂ lb of meat)

3 g / 8 inches dried Solomon's seal rhizome (in one or more pieces)

4 g / 5 inches Chinese dried orange peel (in one or more pieces)

5 g / 5 inches dried angelica root (in one or more pieces)

8 goji berries (aka wolfberries or lycium berries)

9 g / 1 tbsp Asian white peppercorns

2 g / 1¹/₂-inch cinnamon (cassia) stick

3 g / 1 tsp black peppercorns

1 g / 1 tsp coriander seeds (preferably Asian)

2 g / 1 tsp fennel seeds

3 whole cloves

1 whole star anise

Naam Sup / Stocks

Naam Sup Muu

PORK STOCK

น้ำซุปหมู

While pork stock is called for most frequently in this book, all three of the following stocks are required cooking for anyone who wants to delve into the ensuing recipes. The process is essentially the same. First, you extract the flavor of the protein through simmering. Next, you infuse the stock with aromatics. Finally, you strain the result, reserving it to fill bowls of noodle soups or to add a splash of richness and umami to stir-fries.

While I rarely part ways with Thai cooking techniques, I'll cop to cooking my stocks gently—at about 160°F, to be precise—compared to the full-on boil that I've noticed in vendors' pots. And though precision is key to practically every recipe in this book, these stocks will survive your omitting a few of the aromatics, slightly fudging their amounts, or both.

Makes about 14 cups

Put the bones in a large pot and add enough cold water to cover them by 1 inch or so. Cover the pot and bring the water to a simmer over high heat, then turn off the heat. Skim any scum from the surface, then drain the bones and rinse them well under cold running water. All this is to get any blood off the bones, which will give you a cleaner-tasting, clearer stock.

Clean the pot, return the bones to the pot, and add enough of the 5 quarts water to cover by an inch or so. Bring the water to a bare simmer over high heat, lower the heat to maintain a bare simmer, and cook, skimming off any surface scum occasionally, until all of the flavor has been cooked out of the meat on the bones, about 2½ hours.

Working with one ingredient at a time, use a pestle or heavy pan to lightly whack the garlic, ginger, cilantro roots, and lemongrass to bruise them. Very roughly slice the ginger and lemongrass. After the bones have simmered for 2½ hours, add the bruised aromatics to the pot along with the daikon, green onions, Chinese celery, and peppercorns. Simmer gently for 30 minutes more. Strain the stock into a large bowl or pot (don't press the solids) and discard the solids.

Use the stock now, or let it cool and then store in airtight containers in the fridge for up to 5 days or in the freezer for up to 6 months.

5 lb pork neck bones, cut by the butcher, if necessary, to fit in your pot

5 quarts water

35 g / 1 unpeeled whole head garlic

28 g / 1½ by 1-inch knob unpeeled ginger

20 g / 8 cilantro roots, with several inches of stem attached, or 20 g / 5 whole cilantro sprigs

1½ oz / 1 large stalk lemongrass (outer layer, bottom 1 inch, and top 9 inches removed), halved crosswise

6 oz / ½ small unpeeled daikon radish, halved lengthwise, then cut crosswise into about ¼-inch-thick slices

2½ oz / 3 green onions, halved crosswise

2 oz / 3 leafy Chinese celery stalks, halved crosswise

3 g / 1 tsp black peppercorns or Asian white peppercorns

Naam Sup Kai

CHICKEN STOCK

ก๋วยเตี๋ยวน้ำ

To find the small, lean fowl ideal for making this chicken stock, your best bet is a Chinese market, where they're sold fresh and frozen, often with the head and feet intact.

Makes about 13 cups

1 (2½- to 3-lb) fresh or thawed frozen whole lean stewing chicken, innards removed

5 quarts water

35 g / 1 unpeeled whole head garlic

28 g / 1½ by 1-inch knob unpeeled ginger

20 g / 8 cilantro roots, with several inches of stem attached, or 20 g / 5 whole cilantro sprigs

1½ oz / 1 large stalk lemongrass (outer layer, bottom 1 inch, and top 9 inches removed), halved crosswise

6 oz / ½ small unpeeled daikon radish, halved lengthwise and then cut crosswise into about ¼-inch-thick slices

2½ oz / 3 green onions, halved crosswise

2 oz / 3 leafy Chinese celery stalks, halved crosswise

3 g / 1 tsp black peppercorns or Asian white peppercorns

Rinse the chicken well, put it in a large pot, and add enough cold water to cover by an inch or so. Cover the pot and bring the water to a simmer over high heat, then turn off the heat. Skim any scum, then drain the chicken and rinse it well under cold running water. All this is to get any schmutz off, which will give you a cleaner-tasting, clearer stock.

Clean the pot, return the chicken to the pot, and add enough of the 5 quarts water to cover by an inch or so. Bring the water to a bare simmer over high heat, lower the heat to maintain a bare simmer, and cook, skimming off any surface scum occasionally, until all of the flavor has been cooked out of the chicken, about 2 hours.

Meanwhile, working with one ingredient at a time, use a pestle or heavy pan to lightly whack the garlic, ginger, cilantro roots, and lemongrass to bruise them. Very roughly slice the ginger and lemongrass. After the chicken has simmered for 2 hours, add the bruised aromatics to the pot along with the daikon, green onions, Chinese celery, and peppercorns. Simmer gently for 30 minutes more. Strain the stock into a large bowl or pot (don't press the solids) and discard the solids.

Use the stock now, or let it cool and then store in airtight containers in the fridge for up to 5 days or in the freezer for up to 6 months.

Naam Sup Plaa

FISH STOCK

น้ำชุปปลา

If you've got shrimp shells stored in the freezer, add a cup or two for even better flavor.

Makes about 14 cups

About 2 lb whole white-fleshed fish, such as tilapia, porgy, or striped bass, roughly sliced crosswise into 2-inch slabs, or 2 lb fish heads, rinsed well inside and outside

4 quarts water

35 g / 1 unpeeled whole head garlic

28 g / 1½ by 1-inch knob unpeeled ginger

20 g / 8 cilantro roots, with several inches of stem attached, or 20 g / 5 whole cilantro sprigs

1½ oz / 1 large stalk lemongrass (outer layer, bottom 1 inch, and top 9 inches removed), halved crosswise

6 oz / ½ small unpeeled daikon radish, halved lengthwise and then cut crosswise into about ¼-inch-thick slices

4 oz / 1 cup sliced (¼ inch) yellow onion

2½ oz / 3 green onions, halved crosswise

2 oz / 3 leafy Chinese celery stalks, halved crosswise

3 g / 1 tsp black peppercorns or Asian white peppercorns

In a large pot, combine the fish and water, set over high heat, and bring to a simmer.

Meanwhile, working with one ingredient at a time, use a pestle or heavy pan to lightly whack the garlic, ginger, cilantro roots, and lemongrass to bruise them. Very roughly slice the ginger and lemongrass. Once the water reaches a simmer, skim off any surface scum, then add the bruised aromatics to the pot along with the daikon, yellow onion, green onions, Chinese celery, and peppercorns. Lower the heat to maintain a bare simmer and cook for 45 minutes. Strain the stock into a large bowl or pot (don't press the solids) and discard the solids.

Use the stock now, or let it cool and then store in airtight containers in the fridge for up to 1 week or in the freezer for up to 6 months.

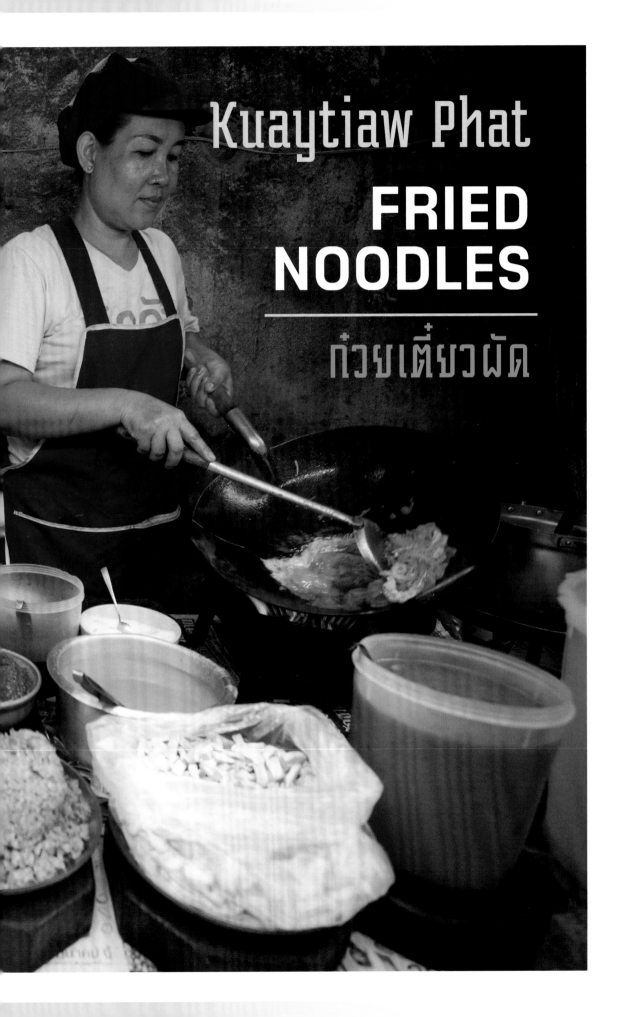

Kuaytiaw Phat

FRIED NOODLES

ก๋วยเตี๋ยวผัด

How Sen Kuaytiaw is Made

Sen kuaytiaw are fresh rice noodles made every morning in a hot, sweaty, laborious process.

1

First, raw long-grain rice is ground with some tapioca starch and water into a thin batter using a giant stone grinder.

2

The batter is pumped into a large hopper at the mouth of a long, complex steamer and then gravity-fed into a reservoir. There it is picked up by a heated steel roller that feeds the batter in a thin, continuous sheet onto an oiled conveyor belt and into a long steam tunnel.

3

The sheet cooks as it travels through the nine-foot-long steam tunnel fed by a giant wood-fueled boiler.

4 & 5

As the cooked sheet of noodles emerges from the tunnel, it is picked up by an elaborate array of vegetable oil–slicked steel rollers, then folded back and forth into piles with the help of more oil-slicked machinery.

6 & 7

The stacks are then cut by hand into whatever width the customer prefers (*sen yai* is usually ¾ to 1 inch wide) or just left in sheet form before being packaged in plastic bags or butcher paper for sale. In Thailand, these noodles never see the refrigerator and only require a minute or two in a wok or boiling water to be ready to eat.

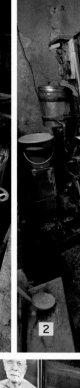

Kuaytiaw Khua Pet

STIR-FRIED WIDE NOODLES WITH CUTTLEFISH AND DUCK

ก๋วยเตี๋ยวผัด

I was in Bangkok's Chinatown with Austin Bush, my frequent dining companion and the photographer of this book, en route to my favorite vendor of *kuaytiaw khua kai*, the spare but spectacular dish of fresh wide rice noodles, egg, preserved cuttlefish, and chicken, when we stopped short. At the mouth of the alley that led to it, a different vendor presided over two small woks set atop glowing charcoal and made the same dish but with *pet* (duck) instead of chicken. The place was called Kuaytiaw Pak Soi, which means "mouth of the alley noodles." You don't need a catchy name when you make food this good.

Duck is a welcome, bolder stand-in for chicken, yet the general pleasures of the dish are unchanged. There's still no, say, tamarind to deliver tang or chile paste to provide fireworks. There's just the subtle alchemy that comes from combining compatible ingredients and cooking them well. In the case of this dish, part of the magic comes from the method. Unlike so many noodles cooked in a wok, this one isn't stir-fried over high heat. Rather, the components fry relatively slowly in rendered pork fat and without the customary frequent stirring, so they coalesce into a disk and the noodles develop patches of crispness and char.

Makes 1 bowl (1 serving)

»

FLAVOR PROFILE

Rich, fatty, umami-bomby

SUGGESTED KHRUANG PHRUNG

Phrik Naam Plaa (Fish Sauce–Soaked Chiles)
PAGE 236

Phrik Naam Som (Vinegar-Soaked Chiles)
PAGE 235

Phrik Pon Khua (Toasted-Chile Powder)
PAGE 240

Sugar (preferably raw cane sugar)

SUGGESTED UTENSILS

THE SAUCE

¾ cup Thai
oyster sauce

½ cup Naam Cheuam
(Simple Syrup;
page 239)

¼ cup Thai fish sauce

THE DISH

2 duck or chicken eggs,
at room temperature

2 oz skinless duck
breast meat, cut
against the grain into
2 by ½ by ¼-inch
strips

2 oz cleaned raw
cuttlefish or squid
bodies, cut into 2 by
½-inch pieces

16 g / ¼ cup sliced
(¼ inch) green onion,
plus 4 g / 1 tbsp

Generous pinch of
finely ground Asian
white pepper

16 g / 1 cup torn (2-inch
pieces) green-leaf or
iceberg lettuce

2 tbsp Naam Man Muu
(Rendered Pork Fat;
page 226, or use store-
bought) or neutral
oil, such as canola,
soybean, or rice bran

6 oz / 1½ cups
sen yai (fresh wide
rice noodles; about
1½ inches wide)

Suggested khruang
phrung

Make the Sauce

In an airtight container, combine the oyster sauce,
simple syrup, and fish sauce and stir well. You'll
have about 1½ cups. Reserve 2 tbsp for this dish.
The remaining sauce will keep, covered, in the
fridge for up to 6 months.

Make the Dish

In a medium bowl, beat one of the eggs with a
splash of water, then add the duck, cuttlefish,
16 g / ¼ cup green onion, white pepper, and
4 g / ¼ cup lettuce, and reserved 2 tbsp sauce.
Stir well. Put the lettuce in a serving bowl.

Set a flat-bottomed wok over medium-high heat
and heat until it begins to smoke lightly. Add the
pork fat and swirl the wok to coat the sides. Add
the noodles, spread them out slightly to cover
the bottom of the wok, and cook, without stirring,
until the edges begin to bubble and crisp, about
1½ minutes.

Pour the egg mixture onto the noodles and cook,
without stirring, until the bottom of the noodles is
crispy and lightly golden with spots of brown, about
2 minutes. Carefully but quickly use a wok spatula
to flip the raft of noodles and cook, without stirring,
until the egg is nearly set, about 30 seconds. Break
the noodles and egg into several pieces, crack in the
remaining egg, add a splash of water to the side of
the wok, and cover with a lid. Cook, without stirring,
until the egg white has set, 2 to 3 minutes.

Transfer to the serving bowl over the lettuce and
sprinkle with the remaining 4 g / 1 tbsp green
onion. Serve with the khruang phrung alongside.

Phat Wun Sen

STIR-FRIED GLASS NOODLES WITH PORK, PICKLED GARLIC, AND TOMATO

ผัดวุ้นเส้น

I first had this simple stir-fry at a restaurant specializing in *aahaan tham sang*, or "food made to order." Essentially, customers sidle up to these establishments and choose from a collection of dishes unlisted on any menu but understood as part of the general repertoire. Sophisticated outfits—those with multiple woks and vast expanses of raw vegetables and seafood and meat—might have unspoken options so extensive that one can ask for, more or less, whatever he or she wants, from crab stir-fried with eggs and curry powder to *phat si ew* to green curry. More modest establishments, due to the limitations of their setups, might offer just a handful of dishes. Whatever the case, the details of the food are flexible. You can request, for example, that the fried rice be made with shrimp or pork or sour sausage, so long as you see the item you want displayed.

I did no such thing when this version of *phat wun sen* wound up on my plate. At a restaurant known for offerings with a Chinese bent, I asked for *phat wun sen* without further specification and received a composition I'd never had before. In the past, I'd eaten stir-fried glass noodles with egg and pickled mustard greens, and with shrimp and cabbage. Now I was enjoying one with pork, tomatoes, and sweet-tart pickled garlic cloves, a combination of flavors that made for such good eating that it's worth re-creating in your kitchen.

Makes 1 plate (1 serving)

»

FLAVOR PROFILE

Salty, sweet

SUGGESTED KHRUANG PHRUNG

Phrik Naam Plaa
(Fish Sauce–
Soaked Chiles)
PAGE 236

Phrik Naam Som
(Vinegar-Soaked
Chiles)
PAGE 235

Phrik Pon Khua
(Toasted-Chile Powder)
PAGE 240

Sugar (preferably
raw cane sugar)

SUGGESTED UTENSILS

THE NOODLES AND PORK

2¼ oz wun sen (dried glass noodles)

2½ oz pork loin or lean shoulder, cut against the grain into 2 by ½ by ⅛-inch strips

15 g / 5 garlic cloves, peeled and crushed into small pieces in a mortar

½ tsp Thai fish sauce

2 g / ½ tsp granulated sugar

Pinch of finely ground Asian white pepper

THE DISH

2½ tbsp Naam Man Muu (Rendered Pork Fat; page 226, or use store-bought) or neutral oil, such as canola, soybean, or rice bran

12 g / 1 tbsp drained, peeled pickled garlic cloves

2 oz / 4 cherry tomatoes, halved

2 tbsp Naam Sup Muu (Pork Stock; page 111) or water

28 g / ½ cup roughly chopped (1½ inches) green onions, plus a large pinch

1 egg, at room temperature, lightly beaten

1 tbsp Thai thin soy sauce

Pinch of finely ground Asian white pepper

Suggested khruang phrung

Soak the Noodles and Marinate the Pork

In a medium bowl, combine the noodles and enough lukewarm (about 100°F) water to cover by an inch or so. Let soak until they're very pliable, about 8 minutes. Drain them well, then snip them into about 6-inch lengths. Set aside.

In a small bowl, combine the pork, 1 tbsp of the pounded garlic, the fish sauce, sugar, and pepper. Mix well with your hands, then let marinate for 5 minutes or so.

Make the Dish

Set a flat-bottomed wok over very high heat and heat until it begins to smoke lightly. Add 2 tbsp of the fat and swirl the wok to coat the sides. Add the pork mixture and cook, flipping the pork occasionally, until it's nearly cooked, about 30 seconds.

Add the noodles and pickled garlic, stir well, then add the tomatoes. Stir-fry, constantly stirring, scooping, and flipping the ingredients, for 20 seconds. Add the pork stock and stir-fry for 15 seconds. Add the 8 g / ½ cup green onion, stir-fry very briefly, then turn the heat to medium.

Push the mixture up the far side of the wok, add the remaining ½ tbsp fat to the empty space, and wait 5 seconds or so for the fat to get hot. Add the egg to the hot fat, tilt and turn the wok so the egg coats the empty space, and cook until about half of the egg is set, about 15 seconds. Stir the egg, breaking it into several pieces, then stir everything together. Add the soy sauce and pepper and stir-fry for 30 seconds so the flavors come together.

Transfer to a plate. Serve with the khruang phrung alongside.

Phat Si Ew Wun Sen

STIR-FRIED GLASS NOODLES WITH SOY SAUCE, PORK, AND CHINESE BROCCOLI

ผัดซีอิ๊ววุ้นเส้น

Made with glass noodles (aka bean thread noodles) rather than the more typical fresh, wide rice noodles, this common, slight variation on the classic stir-fry is a boon for home cooks in the US. The latter noodle is easier to find than you might expect, but if you live far from a good Chinese market or are otherwise disinclined to seek one out, the shelf-stable, readily available variety made from mung bean starch makes an equally compelling result. The thinner, more delicate strands are the only difference. Otherwise, it's business as usual—a mess of noodles, egg, pork, and Chinese broccoli charred in a hot wok and seasoned with two types of soy sauce, including the so-called black kind that gives the dish a sweet, bitter edge. (If you do want to use fresh wide rice noodles, substitute 6 ounces / 1½ cups *sen yai*, about 1½ inches wide, for the glass noodles in this recipe, skipping the soaking step and adding them along with the pork.)

Makes 1 plate (1 serving)

»

Note

I like *phat si ew* best with the young, thin-stemmed Chinese broccoli, sometimes called *gai lan miew* (essentially, "little Chinese broccoli"). If you can't find this type, buy standard Chinese broccoli (*gai lan*), then cut the stems on the diagonal into ⅛-inch-thick, 2-inch-long slices and roughly chop the leaves to yield 2 oz / 1 cup, tightly packed.

FLAVOR PROFILE

Fatty, salty

SUGGESTED KHRUANG PHRUNG

Phrik Naam Plaa (Fish Sauce–Soaked Chiles)
PAGE 236

Phrik Naam Som (Vinegar-Soaked Chiles)
PAGE 235

Phrik Pon Khua (Toasted-Chile Powder)
PAGE 240

Sugar (preferably raw cane sugar)

SUGGESTED UTENSILS

Make the Sauce

In an airtight container, combine the thin soy sauce, black soy sauce, water, and simple syrup and stir well. You'll have about 1 1/2 cups. Reserve 2 tbsp for this dish. The remaining sauce will keep, covered, in the fridge for up to 6 months.

Soak the Noodles and Cook the Pork

In a medium bowl, combine the noodles and enough lukewarm (about 100°F) water to cover by an inch or so. Let soak until they're very pliable, about 8 minutes. Drain them well, then snip into irregular 4- to 6-inch lengths and set aside.

Meanwhile, set a flat-bottomed wok over very high heat and heat until it begins to smoke lightly. Add the oil and swirl the wok to coat the sides. Add the garlic and cook, stirring often, until it's fragrant but not colored, 5 to 10 seconds.

Put the wok back on the heat, add the pork, and stir well. Add the fish sauce and sugar and stir-fry, constantly stirring, scooping, and flipping the ingredients, until the pork is just cooked through, about 1 minute. Transfer the pork to a small bowl.

Make the Dish

Wipe out the wok, if necessary, then set it over very high heat and heat until it begins to smoke lightly. Add the fried garlic oil and swirl the wok to coat the sides. Crack in the egg. It should spit and sizzle violently and the white should bubble and puff. Cook, without messing with it, until the edges turn light golden brown, about 30 seconds. Flip the egg, break it up slightly, and push it to one side of the wok (up the far wall of the wok is fine).

Add the Chinese broccoli to the center of the wok and spread it out slightly, then add the noodles, cooked pork, and pepper. Cook, without stirring, for 10 seconds, then stir-fry, breaking up the egg a bit more as you do, until the noodles and broccoli leaves have wilted slightly, about 15 seconds. Add the reserved 2 tbsp phat si ew sauce and stir-fry until the sauce is fully absorbed, the noodles are cooked, the pork is hot, and the flavors have come together, 30 seconds to 1 minute more.

Transfer to a plate and serve with the khruang phrung alongside.

Spaghetti Phat Khii Mao

DRUNKARD'S STIR-FRY WITH NOODLES

สปาเก็ตตี้ผัดขี้เมา

If you can rely on anything in this world, it's that your local Thai restaurant will serve *phat khii mao*. Translated on so many menus as "drunken noodles," the dish has joined green curry, *phat thai*, and satay on the seemingly unshakable roster of items on American Thai restaurant menus.

These dishes do exist in Thailand, but they're far less common and, at least outside restaurants geared toward tourists, made very differently than they are in the States. *Phat khii mao*, though, is an odd case. In the US, an order will typically get you a plate of wide rice noodles tossed in a wok with spicy sauce, the protein of your choosing, vegetables such as bell peppers and broccoli, and perhaps some Thai basil. While the specifics vary, the presence of noodles is a constant. Yet according to my research, the original dish doesn't contain noodles at all.

No one is sure whether the name, which translates to "drunkard's stir-fry" and has no explicit mention of noodles, refers to the dish's heat level (perhaps the intense spiciness was initially intended to revive a palate dulled by booze, or maybe it made one feel as if he were intoxicated) or its purportedly slapdash composition (as if it were thrown together by a cook who's off his trolley). Whatever the reason, the dish is indeed fiercely spicy and contains many ingredients that include, vitally, if you ask me, several varieties of chile and such additional aromatics as *phrik thai awn* (herbaceous, astringent fresh green peppercorns), *krachai* (an earthy, peppery ginger relative), and *bai kaphrao* (piquant, fragrant holy basil)—few of which, by the way, typically appear in American renditions.

There is no correct version of any food, of course, and it should be no surprise that a dish made on the other side of the world and cooked to satisfy a different audience has undergone metamorphosis. Still, the gulf between these two dishes with the same name is striking. To further complicate matters, recently in Thailand, the noodle-less original has given way to, go figure, *spaghetti phat khii mao*, which, as you have may have guessed, is made with spaghetti. (To appease the gluten-free and because I like the texture, I typically use spaghetti-shaped rice noodles.) Despite the innovation, it still shares more with the Thai original than its American counterpart. And lo and behold, noodles don't make it less delicious.

Makes 1 plate (1 serving)

»

FLAVOR PROFILE

Hot, salty, herbaceous

SUGGESTED KHRUANG PHRUNG

Thai fish sauce

Sugar (preferably raw cane sugar)

SUGGESTED UTENSILS

THE SAUCE

6 tbsp Thai oyster sauce

2 tbsp Thai fish sauce

2 tbsp Thai thin soy sauce

2 tbsp dry rice liquor, such as Shaoxing wine or shochu

1 tbsp Naam Cheuam (Simple Syrup; page 239)

THE PREP

4 oz bun (dried spaghetti-shaped rice noodles), or 50 g dried spaghetti

Splash of neutral oil, such as canola, soybean, or rice bran

42 g / 1/3 cup thinly sliced (1/4 inch; with the grain) yellow onion

28 g / 1/3 cup chopped (1 1/2 inches) long beans

28 g / 1/4 cup diagonally sliced (1/4 inch) fresh or thawed frozen baby corn

8 g / generous 1 tbsp fresh or drained jarred Thai green peppercorns, picked into 1-inch bunches

8 g / 2 tbsp fresh or thawed frozen shredded Chinese keys (see page 13)

6 g / 2 tbsp diagonally sliced (1/8 inch) moderately spicy fresh long green chiles, such as goat horn or Hungarian wax

6 g / 2 tbsp diagonally sliced (1/8 inch) moderately spicy fresh long red chiles, such as Fresno

4 g / 2 stemmed fresh or frozen green Thai chiles, bruised

14 g / 4 garlic cloves, peeled and halved lengthwise

6 g / 4 stemmed fresh or frozen red Thai chiles

THE DISH

2 tbsp Naam Man Muu (Rendered Pork Fat; page 226, or use store-bought) or neutral oil, such as canola, soybean, or rice bran

3 1/2 oz flank steak or beef chuck flap, cut against the grain into 2 by 1 by 1/8-inch strips

1/4 cup Naam Sup Muu (Pork Stock; page 111) or water

12 g / 1/2 cup packed holy basil leaves

Suggested khruang phrung

Make the Sauce

In an airtight container, combine the oyster sauce, fish sauce, thin soy sauce, rice liquor, and simple syrup and stir well. You'll have about 3/4 cup. Reserve 3 tbsp for this dish. The remaining sauce will keep, covered, in the fridge for up to 3 months.

Prep the Dish

Fill a large, tall pot with enough water to submerge a long-handled noodle basket and bring to a boil over high heat. Put the noodles in the basket, submerge them in the boiling water, and cook until the noodles are tender, 10 to 15 minutes. Remove the basket, rinse the noodles under cold running water, then firmly shake the basket to drain well. Reserve the pot of water. To prevent clumping, add a splash of oil to the noodles in the basket and toss to coat them.

In a medium bowl, combine the onion, long beans, baby corn, green peppercorns, Chinese keys, long green chiles, long red chiles, and bruised green Thai chiles and set the bowl near the stove.

In a mortar, combine the garlic and red Thai chiles and pound just until the garlic and chiles are in small pieces and you have a slightly wet-looking mixture (not a paste), about 30 seconds. Set aside.

Make the Dish

Return the pot of water to a boil over high heat.

Set a flat-bottomed wok over very high heat and heat until it begins to smoke lightly. Add the pork fat and swirl the wok to coat the sides. Add 8 g / 1 tbsp (or more to taste) of the garlic-chile mixture and cook, stirring constantly and quickly, until the mixture is fragrant but has not taken on color, 5 to 10 seconds. Do yourself a favor and avoid taking too deep or too close a sniff.

Add the steak and stir-fry, constantly stirring, scooping, and flipping the ingredients, until the exterior of the meat no longer looks raw, 20 to 30 seconds. Add the onion mixture and stir-fry until the onions just begin to wilt, about 20 seconds.

Meanwhile, dunk the noodle basket in the water just to warm up the noodles, 10 to 20 seconds. Remove the basket, firmly shake it to drain the noodles well, and add the noodles to the wok. Stir-fry very briefly, then add the reserved 3 tbsp of sauce, stir-fry very briefly, and add the pork stock. Stir-fry until the noodles have absorbed some of the liquid, about 30 seconds more. Turn off the heat, add the basil, and stir until it wilts.

Transfer to a plate and serve with the khruang phrung alongside.

MAMA Phat

STIR-FRIED INSTANT RAMEN NOODLES WITH PORK AND CABBAGE

มาม่าผัด

I was meeting my friend Ajaan Sunee for lunch at Chiang Mai University when I first encountered this unassuming stir-fry. Ajaan Sunee, the college's home ec professor at the time, took me to the school's cafeteria, which students swarmed between classes. In particular, they crowded around a vendor renowned for her MAMA *phat*. The dish is typical college-kid fare—economical, simple, filling. It was a testament to this cook's talent that she could inspire such enthusiasm for what is essentially a collection of the least expensive ingredients available— cabbage, carrot, onion, and briefly boiled instant noodles—tossed for a spell in a hot wok. Made with care, though, the dish transcends its status to become something I'd gladly eat any time.

Compared to most versions, this recipe calls for a goddamn panoply of vegetables, all of which count as suggestions that you can take or leave. One of the great things about MAMA *phat* is that it's a delicious fridge-clearer. Virtually any vegetable is welcome. The pork, too, can be swapped at will for shrimp, chicken, or tofu. Just don't get fancy with the noodles.

Makes 1 plate (1 serving)

»

FLAVOR PROFILE

Umami-rich, salty

SUGGESTED KHRUANG PHRUNG

Phrik Naam Plaa
(Fish Sauce–
Soaked Chiles)
PAGE 236

Phrik Naam Som
(Vinegar-Soaked
Chiles)
PAGE 235

Phrik Pon Khua
(Toasted-Chile Powder)
PAGE 240

Sugar (preferably
raw cane sugar)

SUGGESTED UTENSILS

THE PORK

2½ oz pork loin, cut into 2 by ½ by ⅛-inch strips

12 g / 4 garlic cloves, peeled and crushed into small pieces in a mortar

A few dashes of Thai seasoning sauce

Dash of Thai fish sauce

Pinch of finely ground Asian white pepper

THE DISH

42 g / ½ cup roughly sliced (½-inch half-moons) napa cabbage

28 g / ½ cup bean sprouts

25 g / ¼ cup julienned (about 3 by ⅛ inch) peeled carrot

25 g / ¼ cup thinly sliced (¼ inch; with the grain) yellow onion

20 g / ¼ cup roughly chopped (2 inches) yu choy (stems and leaves)

1 (60 g) package Thai instant ramen (such as MAMA brand), seasoning powder and seasoning paste discarded

1 tbsp neutral oil, such as canola, soybean, or rice bran

1 egg, at room temperature

¼ cup Naam Sup Muu (Pork Stock; page 111)

1 tbsp Thai seasoning sauce

1 tbsp Thai oyster sauce

5 g / 1 tsp granulated sugar

Generous pinch of finely ground Asian white pepper

8 g / 2 tbsp sliced (¼ inch) green onion

Suggested khruang phrung

Prep the Pork

In a small bowl, combine the pork, garlic, seasoning sauce, fish sauce, and pepper. Mix well with your hands, then let marinate for 5 minutes or so.

Make the Dish

In a small bowl, combine the cabbage, bean sprouts, carrot, onion, and yu choy and set aside.

Fill a large, tall pot with enough water to submerge a long-handled noodle basket and bring to a boil over high heat. Put instant ramen noodles in the basket (breaking the noodles slightly to fit if need be) and submerge the noodles in the boiling water. Cook, stirring occasionally with chopsticks to separate, until the noodles are tender, about 2 minutes. Firmly shake the basket to drain well and set aside.

Set a flat-bottomed wok over very high heat and heat until it begins to smoke lightly. Add the oil and swirl the wok to coat the sides. Add the pork mixture and stir-fry, constantly stirring, scooping, and flipping the ingredients, until the outsides of the pork are no longer raw, 5 to 10 seconds. Push to one side of the wok, then crack the egg onto the other side and cook until the white is nearly set, about 15 seconds. Flip the egg (it's okay if the yolk breaks) and stir-fry, breaking up the egg slightly, until it's just about fully cooked, about 10 seconds more.

Add the noodles and cabbage mixture and stir-fry until the vegetables are wilted and just tender, about 45 seconds. Add the pork stock, seasoning sauce, and oyster sauce and stir well. Add the sugar and pepper, stir-fry for 10 seconds, and turn off the heat.

Transfer to a plate and sprinkle with the green onion. Serve with the khruang phrung alongside.

Phat Mii Khorat

STIR-FRIED RICE NOODLES WITH PORK, EGG, AND TAMARIND

ผัดหมี่โคราช

Almost a decade before I opened Pok Pok, I took an interminable trip on a train from Bangkok to Isaan. Historically, the food of Isaan, the northeast region of Thailand, shares at least as much with that of Laos, its neighbor to the north, as it does with the rest of Thailand, the local palate favoring acidity, heat, and the umami and fierce funk of *plaa raa* (a sort of unrefined, unfiltered fish sauce). Sweetness occasionally cropped up, but most often sugar was just there to temper tartness. Indeed, on that trip I ate plate upon plate of *som tam* (papaya salad), *laap* (minced meat seasoned with dried chiles, toasted rice powder, and lime), and *tom saep* (spicy, sour soup). Then I got to Nakhon Ratchasima.

Nicknamed Khorat, the city is one of the largest in Isaan. It was the last stop on that diesel train's return trip south, the closest of Isaan's hubs to Bangkok and therefore one of the first to get a train station, about a century ago. That's my best guess for how Khorat's eponymous dish came to be so unlike the typical food of Isaan; the ingredients and flavor profile were likely imported from the cosmopolitan capital. When I exited the train to sample *phat mii khorat*, I found a stir-fry of noodles, egg, and pork belly made with a disconcerting amount of sugar but enough tangy tamarind and chile powder to keep the sweetness in check, barely. Similar in composition to *phat thai*—the bean sprouts and garlic chives, the egg and tamarind and noodle type—it tasted, funny enough, a bit like the versions of *phat thai* you see in the US. In other words, you'll like it.

This recipe calls for a range of palm sugar. The full 3 tablespoons will get you close to the noodles I've enjoyed in Khorat, though 2 tablespoons better matches my personal preference.

Makes 1 plate (1 serving)

»

Fried Noodles

FLAVOR PROFILE

Sweet, umami-rich

SUGGESTED KHRUANG PHRUNG

Phrik Naam Plaa
(Fish Sauce–
Soaked Chiles)
PAGE 236

Phrik Naam Som
(Vinegar-Soaked
Chiles)
PAGE 235

Phrik Pon Khua
(Toasted-Chile Powder)
PAGE 240

Sugar (preferably
raw cane sugar)

SUGGESTED UTENSILS

4¾ oz / 2 cups wide sen lek (semidried thin, flat rice noodles; similar in shape to fettuccine)

2½ oz skinless pork belly, cut into 2 by 1 by ¼-inch slices

1 g / ½ tsp kosher salt

2 tbsp neutral oil, such as canola, soybean, or rice bran

14 g / 2 tbsp thinly sliced (with the grain) small Asian shallots

40 to 60 g / 2 to 3 tbsp packed Naam Taan Piip (Softened Palm Sugar; page 239; preferably Thai)

2 tbsp Naam Makham Piak (Tamarind Water; page 238)

1 tsp Thai sweet soy sauce

1 tsp yellow bean sauce

1 g / ½ tsp Phrik Pon Khua (Toasted-Chile Powder; page 240)

2 tbsp Naam Sup Muu (Pork Stock; page 111) or water

2 oz / 1 cup bean sprouts, plus a large pinch

15 g / ¼ cup chopped (1½ inches) garlic chives, plus a large pinch

ACCOMPANIMENTS

Halved Key limes or regular (Persian) lime wedges

Bean sprouts

Whole garlic chives

Fresh banana blossom, trimmed and cut into ½-inch wedges (see page 8)

Suggested khruang phrung

Snip the noodles into approximately 8-inch lengths. In a medium bowl, combine the noodles and enough lukewarm (about 100°F) water to cover by an inch or so. Let soak until they're very pliable, about 30 minutes. Drain them well and set aside.

Season the pork belly all over with the salt. Set a flat-bottomed wok over medium heat and heat until it begins to smoke lightly. Add 1 tbsp of the oil and swirl the wok to coat the sides. Add the pork belly and cook, flipping once or twice, until it's golden brown on both sides, 4 to 5 minutes. Using a slotted spoon, transfer the pork belly to a plate, leaving the oil in the wok.

Add the remaining 1 tbsp oil to the wok, turn the heat to very high, and wait 5 seconds or so. Add the shallots and cook, stirring, until they've softened, about 15 seconds. Add the palm sugar and cook, stirring and breaking up any clumps, until melted, about 30 seconds. Add the tamarind water, sweet soy sauce, yellow bean sauce, and toasted-chile powder and stir well.

Add the noodles and pork belly and stir-fry, constantly stirring, scooping, and flipping the ingredients, until the noodles have absorbed most of the liquid, about 1 minute. Add the pork stock and stir-fry briefly, then add the 2 oz / 1 cup bean sprouts and stir-fry until there's no liquid remaining in the wok, about 30 seconds. Turn off the heat, add the 20 g / ¼ cup garlic chives, and stir-fry briefly.

Transfer to a plate and top with the remaining pinches of bean sprouts and chives. Serve with the accompaniments and khruang phrung alongside.

Phat Thai Ruam Mit

PHAT THAI WITH PORK AND SHRIMP

ผัดไทยรวมมิตร

Rarely can you pin down the origin of a Thai dish, or any dish for that matter, with much precision. In Thailand, as everywhere, food is always changing, cooks are constantly innovating (whether from a place of creativity, convenience, or necessity), and who can say for sure when the first bowl of *khao soi* was born or what sage first paired wide rice noodles with duck and cuttlefish?

Phat thai is different. We can pin down the decade and inspiration, if not the date and the person so inspired. Most accounts agree that the dish was born, with much fanfare, during a competition masterminded by Prime Minister Plaek Phibunsongkhram. Although the details in various historical accounts do blur a bit, the contest seems to have taken place in the 1940s, while nationalism was on the rise, with the goal of identifying a noodle dish that was resolutely Thai. As you're surely tired of hearing by now, most noodle dishes in Thailand are Chinese in origin, and only after the passage of time and some minor tweaks did they make the unofficial transition from foreign dish to part of the local repertoire.

Whether the winning creation, whose name literally means "Thai stir-fry," met the standard set by the prime minister is up for discussion. Many of its reported components—rice noodles, tofu, bean sprouts, preserved radish, and garlic chives—are imports from the Chinese kitchen. The fish sauce, tamarind, and palm sugar, however, do make it taste Thai.

What isn't up for debate is the appeal of the dish, which has become a sort of unofficial ambassador for Thai cuisine throughout the world. While I can't tell you what the original version looked like, it's clear that in the intervening years, one dish has forked into two. There's the dish as it's served to Thais in Thailand, the end to which the following recipe means to lead you. It's beloved, to be sure, though I must mention that it is also just one great noodle stir-fry among many, rather than the main attraction it might seem to be from the view stateside. And then there's the dish as it's typically served at Thai restaurants in America, which is attuned, quite successfully, to local tastes. It often lacks the elements that might challenge American diners, such as salty, funky radish and chewy dried shrimp, and plays up those that entice, such as sweetness, sauciness, and portion size.

I have nothing against that preparation, but I do prefer the one you see here. It's a composite of the *phat thai* from some of my favorite vendors, and like those versions, it's rich and flavorful, cooked (more slowly than most stir-fries) in pork fat, and meant to be doled out in

FLAVOR PROFILE

Rich, fatty, salty, sour, sweet

SUGGESTED KHRUANG PHRUNG

Phrik Pon Khua (Toasted-Chile Powder)
PAGE 240

Thai fish sauce

Sugar (preferably raw cane sugar)

SUGGESTED UTENSILS

»

relatively small allotments. (To reward the home cook, this recipe yields a larger portion than the old-school Thai standard.) Still, it comes to the table tamely seasoned along with *khruang phrung* for adjusting the flavors. Seek out the herb pennywort and fresh banana blossom and serve them alongside, to be eaten between bites.

Makes 1 plate (1 serving)

THE SAUCE

1 cup Naam Makham Piak (Tamarind Water; page 238)

3/4 cup Naam Cheuam Naam Taan Piip (Palm Sugar Simple Syrup; page 240)

1/2 cup Thai fish sauce

THE DISH

4 oz / 2 cups semidried sen lek (thin, flat rice noodles; similar in shape to fettuccine)

2 tbsp Naam Man Muu (Rendered Pork Fat; page 226, or use store-bought) or neutral oil, such as canola, soybean, or rice bran

2 oz / 4 medium-size shrimp, peeled and deveined

42 g ground pork

1 egg, at room temperature

35 g / 1/4 cup sliced (1 by 1/4 by 1/4 inch) unflavored pressed tofu

14 g / 1 tbsp shredded Thai salted radish (soaked in cold water for 10 minutes, rinsed, and drained well)

6 g / 1 tbsp Kung Haeng Khua (Dry-Fried Dried Shrimp; page 242)

2 oz / 1 cup bean sprouts

15 g / 1/4 cup roughly chopped (1 1/2 inches) garlic chives, plus a large pinch

20 g / 2 tbsp roughly chopped unsalted roasted peanuts

ACCOMPANIMENTS

Halved Key limes or regular (Persian) lime wedges

Roughly chopped unsalted roasted peanuts

Bean sprouts

Whole garlic chives and/or fresh pennywort

Fresh banana blossom, trimmed and cut into 1/2-inch wedges (see page 8)

Suggested khruang phrung

Make the Sauce

In an airtight container, combine the tamarind water, palm sugar simple syrup, and fish sauce and stir well. You'll have about 2 1/4 cups. Reserve 1/4 cup plus 2 tbsp for this dish. The remaining sauce will keep, covered, in the fridge for up to 3 months.

Make the Dish

Snip the noodles into approximately 8-inch lengths. In a medium bowl, combine the noodles and enough lukewarm (about 100°F) water to cover by an inch or so. Let soak until they're very pliable, about 30 minutes. Drain them well and set aside.

Set a heavy, well-seasoned 12-inch skillet over medium-high heat (or a flat-bottomed wok over high heat) and heat until it begins to smoke lightly. Add the pork fat and swirl the skillet to coat the bottom (or swirl the wok to coat the sides). Add the fresh shrimp and pork and cook, stirring and breaking up the pork, for 15 seconds. Push them to one side of the skillet.

Crack the egg into the empty area of the skillet and turn the heat to medium (if you're using a wok, keep the heat high). Cook, without messing with the egg, until the edges of the egg are lightly golden, about 30 seconds.

Add the tofu, radish, and dry-fried dried shrimp to an empty area of the skillet. Flip the egg (it's okay if the yolk breaks) and cook, without stirring, for 1 minute, then break it into several pieces with the spatula. Stir well and cook for 1 minute more.

Add the noodles on top of the ingredients in the skillet and cook, without stirring, for 45 seconds. Stir everything together, add the reserved 1/4 cup plus 2 tbsp sauce, and stir again. Add the bean sprouts and cook, stir-frying occasionally, until the noodles are fully tender and have absorbed the sauce and the bean sprouts are tender but still crunchy, 1 to 1 1/2 minutes.

Add the 20 g / 1/4 cup chives and 10 g / 1 tbsp of the peanuts, stir-fry briefly, then transfer it all to a plate. Sprinkle on the remaining peanuts and chives. Serve with the accompaniments and khruang phrung alongside.

Phat Thai Haw Khai

PHAT THAI IN AN OMELET

ผัดไทยห่อไข่

1 recipe phat thai
(see pages 137 and 141)

2 eggs, at room temperature

Splash of water

Dash of Thai fish sauce

Pinch of finely ground Asian white pepper

1 tbsp neutral oil, such as canola, soybean, or rice bran

The first time I ate *phat thai haw khai*, the noodle stir-fry wrapped and served in a thin omelet, was at the famous night market in Hua Hin, a former fishing village in the south turned beachside retreat for the Thai royal family turned resort town for the hoi polloi. When it gets dark, the main drag transforms into a street market with food vendors ranging from guy-with-a-wok to full-blown seafood restaurants. I approached a busy stall where a man was making *phat thai* with evident care. He didn't use precooked noodles, he wasn't using Sriracha, and he cooked each portion one by one, in contrast to the typical busy vendors who stir-fry ten portions at a go.

Most of his customers, I noticed, were digging into *phat thai* that had been neatly wrapped in a layer of cooked egg, a dash of showmanship and a good reason to charge them an extra fifteen *baht* per order. I ponied up, and the richness of the extra egg was as welcome as you'd expect.

Makes 1 plate (1 serving)

As soon as the phat thai is done, in a small bowl, combine the eggs, water, fish sauce, and pepper and beat well.

Set a medium nonstick skillet (or flat-bottomed wok) over medium-high heat and heat until it just begins to smoke. Add the oil and swirl the skillet to coat the bottom (or swirl the wok to coat the sides). When the oil shimmers, add the egg mixture and start swirling the pan to coat the bottom and an inch or so up the sides with an even, fairly thin layer of egg. When the egg is almost set, about 15 seconds, turn off the heat and let the egg cook in the residual heat until it's just set, about 30 seconds more.

Scoop the phat thai onto the omelet in the pan, fold one side over, and slide it all onto a plate.

Phat Thai Wun Sen

PHAT THAI WITH GLASS NOODLES AND CRAB

ผัดไทยวุ้นเส้นปู

Like most noodle dishes, *phat thai* has its variations. Often, these are a matter of which proteins enter the mix, be it fresh shrimp, ground pork, both, or neither. There's also *phat thai jay*, a version that omits animal products such as egg, fish sauce, and dried shrimp as well as garlic chives. The word *jay* technically refers to a Buddhist way of eating that's not just vegan but also cleansing of both body and spirit. For instance, strict adherents avoid the consumption of pungent ingredients (such as members of the garlic and onion families) as well as those thought to, as I've been told, inflame passions (hello, chiles). Notice that I did not mention chicken, which as far as I can tell appears only on plates destined for tourists and expats.

This version provides the familiar tart, sweet pleasures but strays from the more usual composition with both crab, as either picked meat or a hacked whole, and thinner, translucent noodles made from mung bean instead of the typical flat, thin ones made from rice.

Makes 1 plate (1 serving)

»

Note

Using a whole crab requires little more effort than tossing in lump crabmeat, but I also like to use whole crab for this dish. Any fresh small crab (about 6 oz) will do, though the blue crabs sold in Chinatown have especially sweet meat. Extracting it is a pleasure, at least if you're into sucking at shells. Buy it live, then kill it humanely and clean it as instructed on page 164. Boil the crab in generously salted water just until it turns red, then drain and quarter it. Add the crab to the pan with the tofu and proceed with the recipe as written.

FLAVOR PROFILE

Rich, fatty, salty, sour, sweet

SUGGESTED KHRUANG PHRUNG

Phrik Pon Khua (Toasted-Chile Powder) **PAGE 240**

Thai fish sauce

Sugar (preferably raw cane sugar)

SUGGESTED UTENSILS

THE SAUCE

1 cup Naam Makham Piak (Tamarind Water; page 238)

¾ cup Naam Cheuam Naam Taan Piip (Palm Sugar Simple Syrup; page 240)

½ cup Thai fish sauce

THE DISH

2¾ oz wun sen (dried glass noodles)

2 tbsp Naam Man Muu (Rendered Pork Fat; page 226, or use store-bought) or neutral oil, such as canola, soybean, or rice bran

1 egg, at room temperature

35 g / ¼ cup sliced (1 by ½ by ¼ inch) unflavored pressed tofu

14 g / 1 tbsp shredded Thai salted radish (soaked in cold water for 10 minutes, rinsed, and drained well)

6 g / 1 tbsp Kung Haeng Khua (Dry-Fried Dried Shrimp; page 242)

2 oz / 1 cup bean sprouts

42 g / ⅓ cup picked lump crabmeat

18 g / ¼ cup roughly chopped (1½ inches) garlic chives, plus a large pinch

20 g / 2 tbsp roughly chopped unsalted roasted peanuts

ACCOMPANIMENTS

Halved Key limes or regular (Persian) lime wedges

Roughly chopped unsalted roasted peanuts

Bean sprouts

Whole garlic chives and/or fresh pennywort

Fresh banana blossom, trimmed and cut into ½-inch wedges (see page 8)

Suggested khruang phrung

Make the Sauce

In an airtight container, combine the tamarind water, palm sugar simple syrup, and fish sauce and stir well. You'll have about 2¼ cups. Reserve ¼ cup plus 2 tbsp for this dish. The remaining sauce will keep, covered, in the fridge for up to 3 months.

Make the Dish

In a medium bowl, combine the noodles and enough lukewarm (about 100°F) water to cover by an inch or so. Let soak until they're very pliable, about 8 minutes. Drain them well, then snip into about 8-inch lengths. Set aside.

Set a heavy, well-seasoned 12-inch skillet over medium-high heat (or a flat-bottomed wok over high heat) and heat until it begins to smoke lightly. Add the pork fat and swirl the skillet to coat the bottom (or swirl the wok to coat the sides). Crack the egg into the pan (the white will bubble and puff), then turn the heat to medium (if you're using a wok, keep the heat high). Cook, without messing with the egg, until the edges of the egg are lightly golden, about 30 seconds.

Put the tofu, radish, and dry-fried dried shrimp to an empty area of the skillet. Flip the egg (it's okay if the yolk breaks) and cook, without stirring, for 1 minute, then break it into several pieces with the spatula. Stir everything together well.

Add the noodles on top of the ingredients in the skillet and cook, without stirring, for 45 seconds. Stir everything together, add the reserved ¼ cup plus 2 tbsp sauce, and stir again. Add the bean sprouts and cook, stir-frying occasionally, until the noodles are fully tender and have absorbed the sauce and the bean sprouts are tender but still crunchy, about 1½ minutes.

Add the crab, 20 g / ¼ cup garlic chives, and 10 g / 1 tbsp of the peanuts; stir-fry briefly, then transfer it all to a plate. Sprinkle on the remaining peanuts and garlic chives. Serve with the accompaniments and khruang phrung alongside.

Phat Macaroni

STIR-FRIED MACARONI WITH SHRIMP, VEGETABLES, AND KETCHUP

ผัดมะกะโรนี

Sometimes when I'm in a new city, I'll head to its Chinatown and find a diner. If I'm in San Francisco, Sydney, or another metropolis with a significant Cantonese or Teochew population, there will probably be a restaurant with weathered booths, mostly Chinese customers, and a menu of Western standards made by Chinese cooks. From what I can tell, the trend started with cooks formerly employed in Western households and consulates who eventually struck out on their own. I love these places because of the simplicity of their offerings, the time-warp interiors, and the low prices. The menus at these establishments don't necessarily betray the ancestry of their cooks. You certainly wouldn't know it from typical stuff such as eggs and toast, fried chicken, and pork chops with french fries. Soup with egg, ham, and macaroni, however, might give you a clue that you're not at Waffle House.

I also seek out these diners in Thailand, where the menus are similar, with occasional items that reflect overt Chinese Thai influence. One of those is *kuaytiaw neua sap* (see page 173). Another is *phat macaroni*, pasta elbows stir-fried with ketchup and vegetables. The ingredients may be Western, but the execution—wok as the cooking vessel, ketchup as sauce rather than condiment—is not. Kids love it. Adults, too—even this one, at least when the spirit moves me.

The specifics in the recipe are up to you. If you want a little spice, use *sauce phrik* (sweet chile sauce that's similar to ketchup in texture, if not flavor, and is sold by Thai brands and Heinz alike) in the place of some or all of the ketchup. Swap the shrimp for the same amount of ground beef or pork. Switch up the vegetables, though for a truly authentic experience, make sure the medley has been either frozen or extracted from a can.

Makes 1 plate (1 serving)

»

FLAVOR PROFILE

Sweet, salty, rich

SUGGESTED KHRUANG PHRUNG

Phrik Naam Plaa (Fish Sauce–Soaked Chiles)
PAGE 236

Phrik Naam Som (Vinegar-Soaked Chiles)
PAGE 235

Phrik Pon Khua (Toasted-Chile Powder)
PAGE 240

Sugar (preferably raw cane sugar)

SUGGESTED UTENSILS

2½ oz / ½ cup dried elbow macaroni

2 tbsp neutral oil, such as canola, soybean, or rice bran, plus a splash

2 oz / 4 cherry tomatoes, halved

28 g / ¼ cup sliced (¼ inch; with the grain) yellow onion

42 g / ¼ cup drained canned peas

42 g / ¼ cup diced mixed vegetables (fresh or thawed frozen medley)

2 tbsp ketchup

1 tbsp Thai thin soy sauce

13 g / 1 tbsp granulated sugar

3 oz / 6 medium-size shrimp, peeled and deveined

Suggested khruang phrung

Fill a large, tall pot with enough water to submerge a long-handled noodle basket, generously salt the water, and bring to a boil over high heat. Put the macaroni in the basket and submerge the noodles in the boiling water. Cook, stirring occasionally with chopsticks to prevent clumping, until fully cooked (not al dente), according to the package instructions. Remove the basket from the pot, rinse the noodles under cold running water, and firmly shake the basket to drain well. Dump the macaroni into a medium bowl and toss with the splash of oil.

Add the tomatoes, onion, peas, and mixed vegetables to the bowl with the macaroni. In a small bowl, combine the ketchup, thin soy sauce, and sugar and stir well. Set both bowls near the stove. Have the shrimp handy.

Set a flat-bottomed wok over very high heat and heat until it begins to smoke lightly. Add the remaining 2 tbsp oil and swirl the wok to coat the sides. Add the shrimp and cook, flipping once, until pink on both sides, about 10 seconds.

Add the tomato-macaroni mixture and stir-fry, constantly stirring, scooping, and flipping the ingredients, until the onion begins to wilt, about 30 seconds. Add the ketchup mixture and stir-fry until the tomatoes have softened and the macaroni has absorbed the flavor of the sauce, 45 seconds to 1 minute. Transfer it all to a plate and serve with the khruang phrung alongside.

Sukii Haeng

This stir-fry will not win plaudits for its beauty. Not that you'll care. A mess of glass noodles, egg, and protein, maybe with a sprinkle of sesame seeds, happens to be as delicious as it is homely—especially after you apply its mandatory condiment, a sauce that's sour, sweet, and spicy, with undercurrents of sesame oil and fermented tofu. The dish is beloved in Thailand, where it's available at street stalls, ancient shophouses, and mall food courts.

Halfway through a plate of brothless noodles, you might find yourself wondering what it has to do with its apparent namesake, the Japanese hot pot called *sukiyaki*. The first clue is the *haeng* in the Thai title, which indicates a dry riff on an otherwise brothy dish. The default form, *sukii naam,* is essentially the same ingredients in soup. This gets the gastronomic gumshoe a bit closer to *sukiyaki*, which also shares a few details with Thai *sukii*: thin slices of meat, a variety of vegetables, and noodles (in the Japanese dish, they're fashioned from the konjac plant rather than mung bean flour). The Japanese dish often comes with egg, beaten but uncooked, for dunking whatever you pluck from the broth with chopsticks.

Throwing a wrench in the mix are those who claim that the Chinese hot pot is the true forebear of the Thai dish—a reasonable hypothesis since so many Thai noodle dishes have Chinese origins. The name *sukii*, this theory goes, comes from a Japanese pop song, "Sukiyaki," that was a hit throughout Asia around the time the dish popped up in Bangkok. Some clever customer made a crack, the moniker caught on, and the rest is history.

You might meditate on these minutiae as you eat. Then again, you might just eat.

Makes 1 plate (1 serving)

≫

FLAVOR PROFILE

Rich, salty, umami-rich

SUGGESTED KHRUANG PHRUNG

Phrik Naam Plaa
(Fish Sauce–
Soaked Chiles)
PAGE 236

Phrik Naam Som
(Vinegar-Soaked
Chiles)
PAGE 235

Phrik Pon Khua
(Toasted-Chile Powder)
PAGE 240

Sugar (preferably
raw cane sugar)

SUGGESTED UTENSILS

THE SUKII SAUCE

1 cup Thai Sriracha sauce, such as Shark brand

½ cup boiling water

1 tbsp plus ½ tsp toasted sesame oil

1 tbsp plus ½ tsp distilled white vinegar

56 g / 3 tbsp plus 1 tsp packed red fermented bean curd, plus 1 tsp liquid from the jar

22 g / 1 pickled garlic head, drained and thinly sliced crosswise

15 g / 1 tbsp plus ½ tsp granulated sugar

THE PREP

50 g wun sen (dried glass noodles)

16 g / 1 cup roughly sliced (1-inch half-moons) napa cabbage

28 g / ½ cup bean sprouts

28 g / ¼ cup julienned (about 3 by ⅛ inch) carrot

28 g / ¼ cup thinly sliced (¼ inch; with the grain) yellow onion

7 g / ¼ cup chopped water spinach (bottoms trimmed by 2 inches), stems and leaves in 2-inch pieces

4 g / 2 tbsp very roughly chopped Chinese celery (thin stems and leaves)

8 g / 2 tbsp sliced (¼ inch) green onion

2 oz / 3 store-bought tofu puffs

15 g / 5 garlic cloves, peeled and halved lengthwise

THE DISH

2 tbsp neutral oil, such as canola, soybean, or rice bran

1 tbsp Thai oyster sauce

¼ cup Naam Sup Muu (Pork Stock; page 111)

2 oz / 4 medium-size shrimp, peeled and deveined

1 egg, at room temperature, lightly beaten with a splash of water

2 g / 1 tbsp very roughly chopped Chinese celery (thin stems and leaves)

2 g / 1 tbsp very roughly chopped cilantro (thin stems and leaves)

Suggested khruang phrung

Make the Sukii Sauce

In a blender, combine the Sriracha, boiling water, sesame oil, vinegar, bean curd, pickled garlic, and sugar and blend until smooth, then transfer to an airtight container. You'll have about 1⅔ cups. The sukii sauce will keep, covered, in the fridge for up to 3 months.

Prep the Dish

In a medium bowl, combine the noodles and enough lukewarm (about 100°F) water to cover by an inch or so. Let soak until they're very pliable, about 8 minutes. Drain them well, then snip into about 12-inch lengths. Set aside.

In a medium bowl, combine the cabbage, bean sprouts, carrot, yellow onion, water spinach, Chinese celery, green onion, and tofu puffs. Set aside.

Pound the garlic in a mortar just until the garlic is in small pieces and you have a slightly wet-looking mixture (not a paste), about 15 seconds. Set aside 12 g / 1 tbsp for this dish. Discard the rest.

Make the Dish

Set a large nonstick or well-seasoned flat-bottomed wok over very high heat and heat until it begins to smoke lightly. Add 1 tbsp of the oil and swirl the wok to coat the sides. Add the garlic and cook, stirring constantly and quickly, until the mixture is fragrant but has not taken on color, 5 to 10 seconds. Add the cabbage mixture and stir well, then add the noodles and stir well. Add 3 tbsp of the sukii sauce and the oyster sauce and stir-fry, constantly stirring, scooping, and flipping the ingredients, until the ingredients are evenly coated with the sauce and the vegetables just begin to wilt, about 20 seconds.

Add the pork stock and shrimp and stir-fry until the shrimp are cooked and the noodles are tender and have absorbed all of the liquid, 1 to 2 minutes.

Push the mixture up the far side of the wok, add the remaining 1 tbsp oil to the empty space, and wait 5 seconds or so. Add the egg to the hot oil and tilt and turn the wok so the egg coats the empty part of the wok, then cook until the egg is nearly set but still slightly runny on top, about 30 seconds. As the egg cooks, occasionally run the spatula along its edges to release them from the wok.

Scoop the noodle mixture onto the egg, then flip it all, egg-side up, onto a plate. Sprinkle with the Chinese celery and cilantro. Serve with the remaining sukii sauce and khruang phrung alongside.

Phat Khanom Jiin

STIR-FRIED RICE VERMICELLI

ผัดขนมจีน

A top-notch snack and a great way to use leftover *khanom jiin*, this simple stir-fry is often served on celebratory occasions. Long and tinted golden from soy and oyster sauces, the noodles represent longevity and wealth, hence their presence at New Year's get-togethers and housewarmings, which, in the company of my friend and mentor Sunny Chailert, is where I first tried the dish. The shallot oil in which the dish is cooked and the fried shallot and garlic sprinkled on before serving give it a luxurious flavor.

Makes 1 plate (2 to 4 servings, as part of a meal)

»

FLAVOR PROFILE

Salty, sweet, umami-rich

SUGGESTED KHRUANG PHRUNG

Phrik Pon Khua (Toasted-Chile Powder)
PAGE 240

Thai fish sauce

SUGGESTED UTENSILS

THE SAUCE

¾ cup Naam Cheuam
(Simple Syrup; page 239)

½ cup Thai black
soy sauce

¼ cup Thai
oyster sauce

¼ cup Thai thin
soy sauce

THE DISH

5¼ oz dried thin,
round rice noodles
(page 44)

2 tbsp Naam Man Hom
Jiaw (Fried Shallots in
Shallot Oil; page 236),
2 tbsp oil and 3 tbsp
solids

2 tbsp Naam Man
Krathiam Jiaw (Fried
Garlic in Garlic Oil; page
237), solids only

Suggested khruang
phrung

Make the Sauce

In an airtight container, combine the simple syrup,
black soy sauce, oyster sauce, thin soy sauce and
stir well. You'll have about 1¾ cups. Reserve 5 tbsp
for this dish. The remaining sauce will keep, covered,
in the fridge for up to 3 months.

Make the Dish

Bring a large pot of unsalted water to a boil. Add
the noodles, immediately stir and toss with tongs to
prevent clumping, and cook, stirring frequently and
separating any clumps, until they're fully soft—
you're not shooting for al dente—but not cooked so
long that they turn to mush. The timing varies by
brand, but expect 7 to 9 minutes.

Meanwhile, fill a large bowl with cold water and
ice cubes.

When the noodles are ready, drain them in a large
colander and rinse well under lukewarm running
water, gently stirring and tossing, for about 1 minute
to wash off the starch. Shake the colander to drain
the noodles well, then transfer the colander with
the noodles to the bowl of ice water. Gently stir
with your hands until the noodles have fully cooled.
Drain well once more.

In a medium bowl, combine the cooked noodles,
5 tbsp sauce, and 1 tbsp of the fried shallot oil and
toss well. Let the noodles sit for 10 minutes or so to
absorb some of the sauce.

Set a flat-bottomed wok over very high heat and
heat until it begins to smoke lightly. Add the remaining 1 tbsp shallot oil and swirl the wok to coat the
sides. Add the noodles and stir-fry, constantly
stirring, scooping, and flipping the ingredients, for
45 seconds. Add 1 tbsp of both the fried shallots
and fried garlic and continue to stir-fry until the
noodles are hot through and have completely
absorbed the sauce, about 30 seconds more. It's
fine if the noodles break as you stir.

Transfer to a plate, let cool slightly, and sprinkle on
the remaining 1 tbsp fried garlic and 2 tbsp fried
shallots. Serve with the khruang phrung alongside.
Toss well before you eat.

Kuaytiaw Sut Eun Eun

OTHER NOODLE DISHES

ก๋วยเตี๋ยวสูตรอื่นๆ

A simple dough is rolled into long sheets by a machine like the one you might use at home for pasta, only much bigger.

2
The sheets are then run through a machine wit a cutting die to make long, continuous strands and coiled into large piles.

How Ba Mii is Made

Ba mii are wheat noodles usually made with egg, as in this case at this hundred-year-old shophouse in Bangkok's Chinatown. The process, essentially the same as that of Italian pasta, has been perfected over generations by the family who runs this factory and makes *ba mii* fresh every day.

4
The portions are put into bags and weighed.

3 The long strands are portioned into small coils by simply breaking the strands by hand at the appropriate length.

5 The bags of finished noodles are sorted into boxes for delivery.

Yam MAMA

Instant noodles wind up practically everywhere regular noodles do, and even occasionally where they don't. For instance, I've seen people crunch into them straight from the bag. It's no shocker, then, that the beloved product—called MAMA in Thai, in reference to the best-known brand—makes great fodder for *yam*. *Yam* is often translated as "salad," and while the English word does the trick, it doesn't do much justice in describing the room-temperature jumbles of vegetables, herbs, and proteins dressed with lime juice, fish sauce, and chiles. When MAMA enters the fray, *yam* becomes a hearty snack to share while you booze, the heat and salt compelling another swig, and then another.

FLAVOR PROFILE

Hot, sour, salty, a little sweet

SUGGESTED UTENSILS

Makes 1 plate (2 to 4 servings, as part of a meal)

Fill a large, tall pot with enough water to submerge a long-handled noodle basket and bring to a boil over high heat. Meanwhile, pound the garlic and chiles in a mortar to a very coarse paste, about 1 minute. Transfer 12 g / 1 tbsp of the mixture (or more to taste) to a medium saucepan, add the lime juice, fish sauce, and palm sugar simple syrup and stir well.

When the water comes to a boil, put the instant ramen, shrimp, and pork roll in the noodle basket and submerge the contents in the boiling water. Cook, stirring occasionally with chopsticks to separate the noodles, until the shrimp are cooked and the noodles are fully tender (not al dente), about 2 minutes. Firmly shake the basket to drain well and set aside.

Set the saucepan with the garlic-chile mixture over medium heat and heat until the mixture is just warm to the touch, 15 seconds or so. Turn off the heat and add the noodles, shrimp, and pork roll to the saucepan, then the yellow onion, tomato, mint, green onion, Chinese celery, and cilantro. Toss well and transfer the salad (including all of the dressing) to a plate in a low heap. Serve right away.

14 g / 4 garlic cloves, peeled and halved lengthwise

6 g / 4 stemmed fresh or frozen Thai chiles (preferably green)

2 tbsp fresh lime juice (preferably from Key limes or from regular [Persian] limes with a squeeze of Meyer lemon juice)

2 tbsp Thai fish sauce

2 tbsp Naam Cheuam Naam Taan Piip (Palm Sugar Simple Syrup; page 240)

1 (60 g) package Thai instant ramen (such as MAMA brand), seasoning powder and seasoning paste discarded

2 oz / 4 medium-size shrimp, peeled and deveined

2 oz Vietnamese pork roll, halved lengthwise and cut crosswise into 1/8-inch-thick slices

2 oz / 1/4 cup thinly sliced (1/4 inch; with the grain) yellow onion

2 oz / 5 (1-inch) cored tomato wedges

3 g / 1/4 cup small mint leaves

8 g / 2 tbsp sliced (1/4 inch) green onion

4 g / 2 tbsp very roughly chopped Chinese celery (thin stems and leaves)

2 g / 1 tbsp very roughly chopped cilantro (thin stems and leaves)

Yam Kuay Chap

When you go to a place specializing in *yam*, you have options. Arrayed in front of the vendor are containers filled with the components used to make this category of Central Thai dish. Sometimes, customers select from a litany of standards, including *yam* fronted by poached squid, pomelo segments, or glass noodles. Sometimes, with the vendor's tacit blessing, they go their own route, selecting various components and rebuffing others until they've essentially invented a new *yam* on the spot.

My recipe for *yam kuay chap* shares this spirit of creation. It follows the formula for classic *yam*—the thrilling dressing, the vibrant mixture of vegetables, like tomatoes and shallots, and herbs, like cilantro and Chinese celery—but welcomes as its main ingredient a noodle better known for its presence in *kuay chap* (see page 97), a peppery offal soup found in Bangkok's Chinatown. Made from mung bean starch or rice flour and cut into squares, the noodles curl into tubes when soaked, which helps them hold on to the fiery, tart, sweet dressing. When cooked, they have a slick, chewy quality that makes for good eating.

Makes 1 plate (2 to 4 servings, as part of a meal)

FLAVOR PROFILE

Hot, sour, salty

SUGGESTED UTENSILS

»

THE PREP

2¼ oz / 3 cups sen kuay chap (dried bean sheet noodles)

1½ tsp neutral oil, such as canola, soybean, or rice bran

2 oz ground pork

3 oz / 6 medium-size shrimp, peeled and deveined

14 g / 4 garlic cloves, peeled and halved lengthwise

6 g / 4 stemmed fresh or frozen Thai chiles (preferably green)

2 tbsp fresh lime juice (preferably from Key limes or from regular [Persian] limes with a squeeze of Meyer lemon juice)

2 tbsp Thai fish sauce

2 tbsp Naam Cheuam Naam Taan Piip (Palm Sugar Simple Syrup; page 240)

THE DISH

28 g / 2 cherry tomatoes, halved

8 g / ½ cup lightly packed torn (2-inch pieces) green-leaf or iceberg lettuce

18 g / 2 tbsp thinly sliced (with the grain) shallot (preferably Asian)

8 g / ¼ cup very roughly chopped Chinese celery (thin stems and leaves)

4 g / 1 tbsp sliced (¼ inch) green onion

2 g / 1 tbsp very roughly chopped cilantro (thin stems and leaves)

Prep the Dish

In a large bowl, combine the noodles and enough lukewarm (about 100°F) water to cover by an inch or so. Let soak for 5 minutes, occasionally using your hands to make sure the noodles don't stick together. The noodles will curl to form a tubular shape. Drain well.

Meanwhile, line a plate with paper towels and set it near the stove.

Set a flat-bottomed wok over high heat and heat until it begins to smoke lightly. Add the oil and swirl the wok to coat the sides. Add the pork and shrimp and cook, flipping and breaking up the pork and flipping the shrimp, until just cooked through, about 2 minutes. Transfer to the prepared plate.

Fill a large, tall pot with enough water to submerge a long-handled noodle basket and bring to a boil over high heat. Meanwhile, pound the garlic and chiles in a mortar to a very coarse paste, about 1 minute. Transfer 12 g / 1 tbsp of the mixture (or more to taste) to a medium saucepan, then add the pork, shrimp, lime juice, fish sauce, and palm sugar simple syrup.

Put the soaked noodles in the noodle basket and submerge them in the boiling water. Cook, stirring occasionally with chopsticks, until the noodles are fully cooked (they'll still be chewy), about 1 minute. Firmly shake the basket to drain well and set aside.

Make the Dish

Set the saucepan with the garlic-chile paste and other ingredients over medium heat and heat, stirring once or twice, just until warm to the touch, 15 to 30 seconds. Turn off the heat, add the tomatoes, and briefly but firmly press on them with a wok spatula to release some of their juice.

Add the noodles, lettuce, shallot, Chinese celery, and green onion. Toss well and transfer the salad (including all of the dressing) to a plate in a low heap. Top with the cilantro. Serve right away.

Buu Op Wun Sen

CRAB AND GLASS NOODLES IN A CLAY POT

ปูอบวุ้นเส้น

Unlike many noodle dishes, this is not street-stall fare. It's the kind of dish you'll find in the Chinese seafood restaurants of Thailand, primarily those in urban centers or near beaches. Sharing space on tables with grilled prawns, steamed whole fish, and curry powder–tinted jumbles of shell-on crustaceans stir-fried with egg, you'll often find *buu op wun sen*, relatively unassuming in a covered pot.

Raise the lid at the table and you're hit with the fragrance of Chinese celery or green onion, black or Sichuan peppercorns, and *buu* (crab) or *kung* (shrimp). Inside the pot are layers—sea creature, then glass noodles stained from soy and oyster sauces, then slices of pork belly that cling to the scalding bottom of the pot. There are often some Thai elements, too, like cilantro root among the aromatics and tart, fiery dipping sauce for the seafood. After all, while this might essentially be Chinese food, it's often tweaked for the local palate.

The noodles in this dish are neither stir-fried nor boiled. Essentially, they're baked—cooked in a covered vessel over glowing coals whose heat envelops its bottom and sides. The belly browns, the noodles absorb flavorful liquid, and the seafood steams. If you've found a first-rate practitioner, the vessel is likely made of porous clay and the flame comes from charcoal, so some of its smoky character seeps in as the dish cooks.

This is neither here nor there, but technically speaking, if I were to stick to the transliteration regimen I use throughout this book, the Thai word for "crab" would be rendered phonetically with Roman characters not as *buu* but as *puu* (indicating an unaspirated "p" sound). Here, however, I made an exception to head off an unfortunate corollary for English speakers both unfamiliar with the particulars of the Royal Thai General System of Transcription and in possession of juvenile minds.

Makes 1 plate (2 to 4 servings, as part of a meal)

Note

This dish tastes best cooked on a charcoal *tao thaan* (see page 31). Prepare a medium fire in the *tao* as you would in a charcoal grill. (You can get away with cooking it on a gas stovetop over medium heat, as long as you use a cheap diffuser plate, which will give you a more even, radiant heat.)

FLAVOR PROFILE

Rich, salty, peppery

SUGGESTED UTENSILS

»

THE SAUCE

3 tbsp Naam Cheuam (Simple Syrup; page 239)

3 tbsp Thai thin soy sauce

1½ tbsp Thai oyster sauce

1½ tbsp Thai seasoning sauce

1½ tbsp Shaoxing wine

1½ tbsp water

1½ tsp toasted sesame oil

THE DISH

3½ oz wun sen (dried glass noodles)

½ tsp Thai black soy sauce

9 g / 9 cilantro roots

1 g / ½ tsp whole black peppercorns, plus ¼ tsp coarsely cracked

¼ tsp kosher salt

1 tbsp plus 1 tsp neutral oil, such as canola, soybean, or rice bran

4 oz / 1 cup thinly sliced (⅛ inch; with the grain) yellow onion

4 oz / 5 green onions, whites cut into 1½-inch lengths, greens cut into 2½-inch lengths

14 g / 2 tbsp julienned ginger

9 g / 3 garlic cloves, thinly sliced

2 oz skinless pork belly, cut against the grain into 2½ by ¼-inch-thick slices

1 small (about 6 oz) live crab, such as blue crab

Naam Jim Seafood (Spicy, Tart Dipping Sauce for Seafood; page 246)

Make the Sauce

In an airtight container, combine the simple syrup, thin soy sauce, oyster sauce, seasoning sauce, wine, water, and sesame oil and stir well. You'll have about ¾ cup. Reserve 3 tbsp plus 1 tsp for this dish. The remaining sauce will keep, covered, in the fridge for up to 6 months.

Make the Dish

In a medium bowl, combine the noodles and enough lukewarm (about 100°F) water to cover by an inch or so. Let soak until they're very pliable, about 8 min-utes. Drain them well, then snip into about 4-inch lengths. In a medium bowl, toss the noodles with the black soy sauce until the noodles are an even amber color.

In a mortar, pound the cilantro roots, whole peppercorns, and salt to a coarse paste, about 30 seconds. In a flat-bottomed wok or skillet over medium-high heat, warm 1 tbsp of the oil until it shimmers, turn the heat to medium, and add the yellow onion, the white parts of the green onions, the ginger, garlic, and cilantro root paste. Cook, stirring frequently, until the yellow onion has wilted slightly, about 1½ minutes. Turn off the heat.

Pour the remaining 1 tsp oil into a 1-quart clay pot and rub to coat the bottom and sides. Line the bottom of the pot with the pork belly in a single layer, then add the onion mixture in an even layer.

Kill the crab quickly by putting it shell-side down on a cutting board, with the eyes facing you, and, aiming between the eyes, firmly whack it with the top 2 inches or so of the blade of a meat cleaver. Now it's dead. Yank off the triangular flap from the bottom of the crab. Pry off the top shell, then pull off and discard the feathery gills. Cut the crab in half through the head and use the back of the cleaver or a pestle to strike the thick legs and claws to crack them slightly. Rinse the crab halves under cold running water, shake to drain, then add them to the clay pot in a single layer.

Add the noodles to the pot in an even layer and drizzle on the reserved 3 tbsp plus 1 tsp sauce. Top with the green parts of the green onions and sprinkle on the cracked peppercorns. Cover the pot with the lid.

Put the clay pot, covered, onto the tao (or stovetop) and cook, preferably without lifting the lid, until the noodles and the crab are completely cooked, 10 to 12 minutes. You won't be able to tell until you stir, but the pork belly should be slightly caramelized. If it's not, then use a slightly higher heat the next time you make the dish. Remove the lid at the table to release the aroma. Stir well, then serve with the spicy, tart dipping sauce for seafood alongside.

Ba Mii Yok Haeng

JADE NOODLES WITH PORK AND CHINESE BROCCOLI

บะหมี่หยกแห้ง

If you're Thai or if you have whiled away much of your thirties and forties in Thailand, these striking noodles probably bring to mind MK Restaurants, an international chain with more than two hundred locations in Bangkok alone. While MK is best known for *sukii* (see page 147), the Thai riff on the Japanese cook-it-yourself hot pot, you'll also find its tables covered with bowls of thin green noodles topped with roast duck. The noodles—once stained green with pandan leaf but nowadays typically dyed with food coloring—provide an alternative to the rice offered by most Chinese restaurants specializing in barbecued meats. At its best, this dish features a soy sauce slick for the noodles and a lardy mixture of fried garlic and pork cracklings on top.

Roasted duck does make a fine topping, but I couldn't adequately guide you through the process of making it. I do, however, have a grasp on two porcine preparations—the ruddy lacquered *muu daeng* (roasted pork) and the crunchy *muu krob* (fried pork)—that are also served to great effect on jade noodles. So here you are. For the pork, there's no shame in leaning on your local Chinatown's preeminent meat-hanging-in-the-window joint. For the noodles, there's no harm in using standard-issue *ba mii* (fresh thin wheat noodles), if you can't find the green stuff nearby in the fridge section.

Makes 1 bowl (1 serving)

»

FLAVOR PROFILE

Fatty, umami-rich, salty

SUGGESTED
KHRUANG PHRUNG

Phrik Naam Plaa
(Fish Sauce-
Soaked Chiles)
PAGE 236

Phrik Naam Som
(Vinegar-Soaked
Chiles)
PAGE 235

Phrik Pon Khua
(Toasted-Chile Powder)
PAGE 240

Sugar (preferably
raw cane sugar)

SUGGESTED UTENSILS

THE GARLICKY LARD

½ cup Naam Man Muu (Rendered Pork Fat; page 226, or use store-bought)

1¼ oz/ ¼ cup finely chopped (⅛ inch) garlic

8 g / ¼ cup crumbled (about ¼ inch) Khaep Muu (Pork Cracklings; page 225, or use store-bought)

THE BOWL

1 tbsp Thai thin soy sauce

2 g / ½ tsp granulated sugar

2 g / ½ tsp MSG (optional)

Generous pinch of finely ground Asian white pepper

THE DISH

2½ oz / 1 cup lightly packed ba mii yok (fresh jade noodles)

2 oz / 1 cup packed diagonally sliced Chinese broccoli, stems in long (2-inch), thin (⅛-inch) pieces, leaves whole

2½ oz / 4 to 6 slices (¼ inch thick; against the grain) Muu Daeng (Chinese-Style BBQ Pork; page 218), at room temperature

2½ oz / 4 to 6 slices (¼ inch thick; against the grain) Muu Krob (Crispy Pork Belly; page 220), at room temperature

Generous pinch of finely ground Asian white pepper

4 g / 1 tbsp sliced (¼ inch) green onions

Naam Jim Si Ew Dam Phrik Sot (Black Soy–Chile Dipping Sauce; page 234)

Suggested khruang phrung

Make the Garlicky Lard

Put the pork fat in a small saucepan and set over high heat. When it's hot, add the garlic, turn the heat to medium-low, and cook, stirring once or twice, until the garlic is light golden brown, 3 to 4 minutes. Turn off the heat, stir in the pork cracklings, and set aside. The garlicky lard will keep in an airtight container in the fridge for up to 2 weeks. Gently reheat to liquefy the lard before using.

Prep the Bowl

In a wide soup bowl, combine the soy sauce, sugar, MSG, and pepper and stir well.

Make the Dish

Fill a large, tall pot with enough water to submerge a long-handled noodle basket and bring to a boil over high heat. Put the noodles in the basket and submerge them in the boiling water. Cook, stirring occasionally with chopsticks, until the noodles are tender, 2 to 3 minutes. Firmly shake the basket to drain well and dump the contents into the prepared bowl.

Put the Chinese broccoli in the noodle basket and submerge the broccoli in the water. Cook until tender but still crunchy, about 30 seconds. Firmly shake the basket to drain well and dump the broccoli into the prepared bowl.

Top the bowl with 1 tbsp of the fried garlicky lard solids, 1 tbsp of the garlicky lard liquid, and the pepper. Add the Chinese-style bbq pork and crispy pork belly, and sprinkle on the green onions, Serve with the black soy–chile dipping sauce and suggested khruang phrung alongside. Stir very well before eating.

Kuaytiaw Lat Na

I ate this version of *lat na* the first time my friend Lakhana invited me over for lunch. She is responsible for many of my early eating epiphanies in Thailand, but, until then, these had been confined to markets and restaurants that served food I had never seen at the beach resorts down south, let alone the Thai restaurants back home.

She had talked up her rendition of *lat na*, and I was eager to try it, though I had eaten enough versions of the dish by then to be skeptical. Common in homes and at dedicated purveyors, as well from vendors who specialize in *phat si ew* (which shares several raw ingredients with *lat na*), the dish never captured my attention like so many other noodles dishes had. The average street-vendor version was noodles, strips of pork, and a piece or two of *yu choy* topped with a clear, viscous gravy whose only seasoning seemed to be MSG.

My impression changed after I made the drive from Chiang Mai to the Northern Thailand countryside to join Lakhana and her family at their sixty-year-old teak house in the sleepy village of Ban Saluang Nai. While Lakhana's *lat na* took the familiar form, it was full of flavor, seasoned robustly with soy sauce, rich from pork stock and egg, and generous with the vegetable matter. She served hers with fresh, wide rice noodles that she tossed with black soy sauce and then charred in a wok with a little pork fat for added texture and flavor.

This *lat na* recipe lets you forgo some of the fuss of the other recipes in this book, which attempt to adapt restaurant methods to work in a home kitchen. Whenever I make it for friends, I serve it as Lakhana did that day in Saluang: a plate of noodles for each guest and a pot of gravy on the table so people can help themselves.

If you wish, you can switch up the noodles as some vendors do, swapping in *mii krob* (thin wheat noodles deep-fried to a crunch) and, less common but no less delicious, fresh wide rice noodles deep-fried in pork fat until they bubble, puff, and crisp. They all have their pleasures, so I provide them all here.

Makes 6 bowls (6 servings)

FLAVOR PROFILE

Rich, umami-forward, salty

SUGGESTED KHRUANG PHRUNG

Phrik Naam Plaa (Fish Sauce–Soaked Chiles)
PAGE 236

Phrik Naam Som (Vinegar-Soaked Chiles)
PAGE 235

Phrik Pon Khua (Toasted-Chile Powder)
PAGE 240

Sugar (preferably raw cane sugar)

SUGGESTED UTENSILS

»

THE GRAVY

3 tbsp thin soy sauce

1 tbsp fish sauce

14 g / 1 tbsp drained salted yellow beans, rinsed

13 g / 1 tbsp granulated sugar

5 g / 1 tsp MSG (optional)

1/4 tsp finely ground Asian white pepper

2 tbsp Naam Man Muu (Rendered Pork Fat; page 226, or use store-bought) or neutral oil, such as canola, soybean, or rice bran

36 g / 1/4 cup thinly sliced small Asian shallots

24 g / 8 garlic cloves, peeled and crushed into small pieces in a mortar

1 lb boneless pork shoulder, cut into 2 by 3/4 by 1/8-inch strips

6 oz / 3 cups packed roughly chopped (2 inches) yu choy

3 cups Naam Sup Muu (Pork Stock; page 111)

30 g / 1/4 cup tapioca starch

2 tbsp water

2 eggs, at room temperature

THE BOWLS (SEN YAI VERSION)

36 oz / 9 cups sen yai (fresh wide rice noodles; 1½ inch wide)

2 tbsp Thai black soy sauce

3 tbsp Naam Man Muu (Rendered Pork Fat; page 226, or use store-bought) or neutral oil, such as canola, soybean, or rice bran

THE BOWLS (MII KROB VERSION)

Neutral oil, such as canola, soybean, or rice bran, for deep-frying

9 oz / 2¼ cups packed thin ba mii (fresh yellow Chinese wheat noodles)

THE BOWLS ("SINGAPORE-STYLE" VERSION)

Neutral oil, such as canola, soybean, or rice bran, for deep-frying

18 oz / 4½ cups sen yai (fresh wide rice noodles; 1½ inches wide)

TO SERVE

6 tbsp Naam Man Krathiam Jiaw (Fried Garlic in Garlic Oil; page 237), solids only, or Naam Man Hom Jiaw (Fried Shallots in Shallot Oil; page 236), solids only

Suggested khruang phrung

Make the Gravy

In a small bowl, combine the thin soy sauce, fish sauce, yellow beans, sugar, MSG, and pepper. Stir well and set aside.

In a medium pot over medium-low heat, heat the pork fat until it shimmers. Add the shallots and garlic and cook, stirring occasionally, until soft and light brown in spots, 5 to 8 minutes. Turn the heat to very high, then add the pork and cook, stirring and flipping frequently, until the pork is light brown in spots, about 2 minutes. Add the soy sauce mixture and stir well, then add the yu choy and stir well. Add the pork stock, let it come to a boil, and cook, stirring, until the yu choy stems are tender, about 1 minute.

In a small bowl, combine the tapioca starch and water and stir until smooth. Slowly drizzle the mixture into the pot, whisking while you do. The sauce will thicken to a viscous gravy. Lower the heat to low and simmer gently for 30 seconds, then turn off the heat. Keep warm.

Right before you serve, bring the gravy to a simmer. Lightly beat the eggs in a small bowl. Very slowly drizzle the eggs into the bubbling liquid in a circular motion, wait until the eggs set, about 30 seconds, then gently and briefly stir. Cover to keep warm.

For the Sen Yai Version

In a medium bowl, combine the noodles and black soy sauce and toss to coat well.

Cook the noodles in three batches. For each batch, set a flat-bottomed wok over very high heat and heat until it begins to smoke lightly. Add 1 tbsp of the pork fat or oil and swirl the wok to coat the sides. Add 12 oz / 3 cups noodles to the wok, spread them out slightly, and cook, stirring but not flipping, until they begin to char on the bottom, about 30 seconds. Flip the noodles and stir-fry, constantly stirring, scooping, and flipping them, until they're slightly charred in spots, about 45 seconds more. Split the noodles between two serving bowls and cook the rest.

For the Mii Krob and "Singapore-Style" Versions

Line a large sheet pan with fresh paper towels or newspaper and set it near the stove.

Pour 3 inches of oil into a medium pot, set the pot over high heat, and bring the oil to 375°F. Use a thermometer to take the temperature, measuring the oil at the center of the vessel and carefully stirring occasionally to ensure a consistent temperature.

Working in 42 g / ⅓-cup batches of the thin wheat noodles or 3 oz / ¾-cup batches of the wide rice noodles, carefully add the noodles to the oil and cook, using a spider to gently flip the cluster once or twice, until the noodles are puffed and crunchy all the way through, about 25 seconds for the wheat noodles and 1 to 1½ minutes for the rice noodles. (If the noodles don't puff up almost immediately, increase the oil temperature slightly before frying the next batch.)

Transfer the cluster to the prepared sheet pan. Repeat with the remaining noodles, letting the oil return to 375°F between batches. Transfer the noodles to serving bowls.

Serve the Dish

Bring the bowls of noodles and pot of gravy to the table. Divide the gravy over the noodles in each bowl and top with the fried garlic in garlic oil. Serve with the khruang phrung alongside.

Kuaytiaw Neua Sap

RICE NOODLES WITH GROUND BEEF, TOMATO, AND ONION "GRAVY"

ก๋วยเตี๋ยวเนื้อสับ

Nowadays, you don't often see *kuaytiaw neua sap*, wide rice noodles covered in a gravy-like mixture of ground beef, onion, and tomatoes, in Thailand. Odds are you won't spot it in the pots at the corner noodle shops, with their squat plastic stools and folding tables spilling onto the sidewalk, or among the clusters of night-market vendors, with their woks set over propane-fueled burners. In fact, I've only seen it in one genre of restaurant: the increasingly scarce diner run by Chinese cooks who once worked in the homes of Brits living abroad.

More typical in former British colonies, which Thailand is not, these restaurants were once fairly common in Bangkok. They're places where your meal might come with sliced white bread and butter. Where tables might sport bottles of Worcestershire rather than fish sauce. Where you can order the kind of food these cooks might have made for their old employers—pork chops with tinned peas, stewed tongue in gravy (also with tinned peas), and *phat macaroni* (see page 143).

Like these dishes, *kuaytiaw neua sap* reflects a sort of fusion, a delicious melding of East and West born of practicality. It features a slurried texture thickened with starch, the umami bump from fish and soy sauces, and rice noodles—all familiar to fans of Chinese and Thai cookery—but also a subdued flavor, curry powder (the British approximation of a South Asian spice blend), and, yes, the occasional addition of tinned peas. Note that these noodles, like those for *kuaytiaw khua pet* (see page 119) and *phat macaroni*, are served over lettuce. While it might seem strange to the uninitiated, the addition of uncooked lettuce, typically iceberg, is common to many noodle dishes served in Thailand's Chinatowns. And while lettuce isn't typically eaten raw in China, the vegetable has been cultivated there for well over a thousand years. Whatever the reason, the addition is good, not mere garnish, and should not be omitted.

Makes 6 plates (6 servings)

FLAVOR PROFILE

Rich, umami-forward, salty, slightly tart

SUGGESTED KHRUANG PHRUNG

Phrik Naam Plaa
(Fish Sauce-
Soaked Chiles)
PAGE 236

Phrik Naam Som
(Vinegar-Soaked
Chiles)
PAGE 235

Phrik Pon Khua
(Toasted-Chile Powder)
PAGE 240

Sugar (preferably
raw cane sugar)

SUGGESTED UTENSILS

»

THE GRAVY

2 tbsp neutral oil, such as canola, soybean, or rice bran

42 g / 14 garlic cloves, peeled and crushed into small pieces in a mortar

12 oz lean ground beef

5 oz / 1 cup diced (1/2 inch) yellow onion

1 lb / 2 cups roughly chopped (1/2 to 3/4 inch) cored tomatoes

4 cups Naam Sup Muu (Pork Stock; page 111), warm

3 tbsp Thai oyster sauce

1 1/2 tbsp Thai fish sauce

1 tbsp Thai thin soy sauce

1 tbsp Thai seasoning sauce

13 g / 1 tbsp granulated sugar

1 g / 1/2 tsp finely ground Asian white pepper

1 g / 1/2 tsp curry powder

1 g / 1/4 tsp MSG (optional)

2 1/4 oz / 1/2 cup tapioca starch

1/4 cup water

THE DISH

36 oz / 9 cups sen yai (fresh wide rice noodles; about 1 1/2 inches wide)

2 tbsp Thai black soy sauce

12 oz / 6 cups lightly packed torn (2-inch pieces) green-leaf or iceberg lettuce

3 tbsp neutral oil, such as canola, soybean, or rice bran

12 g / 6 tbsp very roughly chopped cilantro (thin stems and leaves)

Suggested khruang phrung

Make the Gravy

In a medium pot over medium-high heat, heat the oil until it shimmers. Add the garlic and cook, stirring frequently, until it's golden brown and fragrant, about 2 minutes. Turn the heat to high, add the beef, and cook, stirring and breaking up any clumps, until it's more or less cooked through, 1 to 2 minutes. Add the onions and cook, stirring occasionally, until the onions are translucent, 2 to 3 minutes.

Add the tomatoes, pork stock, oyster sauce, fish sauce, thin soy sauce, seasoning sauce, sugar, pepper, curry powder, and MSG to the pot. Bring everything to a boil and boil until the tomatoes have begun to break down and the liquid has reduced by about one-third, about 20 minutes.

In a small bowl, combine the tapioca starch and water and stir until smooth. While whisking, slowly drizzle about half of the mixture into the pot. The sauce will thicken to a viscous gravy. Gradually add more of the tapioca starch mixture if need be. Cook, stirring frequently, for 1 minute more, then turn off the heat. Cover to keep warm.

Make the Dish

In a large mixing bowl, combine the noodles and black soy sauce and toss to coat well. Put 2 oz / 1 cup lettuce on each of six serving plates.

Cook the noodles in three batches. Set a flat-bottomed wok over very high heat and heat until it smokes lightly. Add 1 tbsp of the oil and swirl the wok to coat the sides. Add 12 oz / 3 cups noodles to the wok, spread them out slightly, and cook, stirring but not flipping, until they begin to char on the bottom, about 30 seconds. Flip the noodles and cook, stirring but not flipping, until they're charred in spots, about 45 seconds more. Split the noodles between two of the prepared plates and cook the rest.

Bring the plates of noodles and pot of gravy to the table. Invite guests to ladle 3/4 to 1 cup of the gravy over the noodles in each plate and top with 2 g / 1 tbsp cilantro. Serve with the khruang phrung alongside.

Khao Soi Neua

ข้าวซอยเนื้อ

Khao soi has been having something of a moment in the US of late. The coconut milk–spiked curry with egg noodles, both boiled and fried, is perhaps the first Northern Thai dish to break the hegemony of Central and Isaan food in stateside Thai restaurants. Now, not only can plenty of American diners pick the once-obscure regional dish out of a lineup, but they can also recommend several nearby restaurants that serve it. This is good news for any fan of food. Here's more: There's another killer category of *khao soi* you may not have encountered.

In fact, the bowl that got me hooked on the dish in the first place belongs to this category. Twenty-five years ago, when I was an itinerant line cook and musician with a travel bug and a bit more hair on my head, a trip to Chiang Mai to visit my friends Chris and Lakhana brought me face-to-face with a bowl of beige broth dappled with globules of ruddy oil and topped with crunchy noodles. As I explored with my chopsticks, I found, submerged, egg noodles and bone-in chicken. As I saw Chris and Lakhana supplement their bowls with a squeeze of lime, pieces of raw shallots, chopped pickled greens, and ominously dark chile paste, I followed their lead. In minutes, our bowls were empty except for a layer of grit clinging to the sides—the remains of ground spices and onion—an attribute I'd later aspire to once I learned to make the dish myself.

Only after I'd sampled many bowls over many years did I realize that my first *khao soi* was distinct from those turned out by most *khao soi* operations in Chiang Mai and beyond. The prevailing version, or what I like to think of as the Thai version, is made from a paste of aromatics that conjures the fusion of flavors particular to the north of the country. It contains ingredients associated with Thai cooking, like lemongrass and galangal; Chinese cooking, like ginger and black cardamom; and Burmese cooking, like curry powder and turmeric. Fried in oil, then simmered in coconut milk and topped with coconut cream, however, the paste results in a concoction reminiscent of a Central Thai curry in form, if not entirely in flavor. It's the version I originally aimed to replicate at Pok Pok, in part because it was the version my culinary mentors knew best and the one I thought would most appeal to Westerners new to the dish.

Yet while my first bowl contained many of the same elements, the curry was decidedly different—its flavor defined more by dried spices and onions than by galangal and lemongrass, the meat stewed without

FLAVOR PROFILE

Rich, a little salty, warm-dry-spice-forward

SUGGESTED KHRUANG PHRUNG

Thai fish sauce

SUGGESTED UTENSILS

»

coconut milk. Those differences might seem subtle on paper but they're dramatic on the spoon.

Over the years, I began to recognize that these features were common to bowls made by Muslim cooks in Chiang Mai. At their shops throughout the city, their denomination is often discernable by signage bearing a star and crescent, employees wearing headscarves or beards, or, occasionally, in the case of Khao Soi Islam, thought to be the oldest restaurant in the city to serve the dish, the name of the establishment itself. And by the food on the menus, too, which, besides *khao soi*, often includes *kaeng neua* (essentially "beef curry") and *khao mok kai*, a plate of spiced rice that looks unmistakably like biryani. A few of these operations cluster along the street nicknamed Soi Islam, a bustling stretch near one of the city's four mosques and a stroll away from a market known for its concentration of vendors of Jiin Haw descent.

The Jiin Haw are Muslims originally from Yunnan who traveled as merchants to Thailand centuries ago. Incidentally, most theories have it that the Jiin Haw brought *khao soi* to Chiang Mai by way of the caravan routes that cut through present-day Burma. The details are, as usual, lost to time. No one can be sure whether the dish originated in China (in Thai, *khao soi* literally means "sliced rice" and may refer to the rice noodles once peddled by Jiin Haw vendors); was picked up en route (there's a similar Burmese dish called *ohn-hno hkauk hswe*; the final two words are a generic term for noodles and, rendered in Thai phonetics, sound like *khao soi*); or was hatched in Chiang Mai.

Even after all this time, my preferred bowl of *khao soi* comes from the same restaurant where I first tried the dish: Khao Soi Prince, once located in front of Prince Royal College and now located near Maejo University in San Sai, Chiang Mai. Worakarn "Keng" and Busarin "Amm" Yu Yang Thai run the modest place. Their *khao soi* is a marvel, the curry subtly spiced and barely sweet, the noodles made on the premises and excellent, each bowl finished at the last minute with a spoonful of warm coconut cream. Today, my choice of meat there, and at most Muslim-run joints, is beef, in this case shin simmered until its flavor melds with the curry and the chunks are tender with a slight chew.

The recipe in this book is modeled on this type of *khao soi* in general and theirs in particular. It is the product of extensive and perhaps excessive consumption of the dish. It is informed by conversations in spice shops and at markets and among opinionated friends in Chiang Mai. Compared to the flawless rendition at Khao Soi Prince, mine is a bit more liberal with the dried spices and less delicate in flavor, but otherwise similar and quite good to eat. It takes time and effort to make, no doubt. So get to it.

Makes 4 bowls (4 servings)

»

THE PREP

8 g coriander seeds (preferably Asian)

4 g fennel seeds

2 g cumin seeds

3 g black peppercorns

1 g whole cloves

1 g whole star anise

1 blade mace

1 pod black cardamom, smashed, pod discarded, and seeds reserved

1 pod white cardamom (preferably from China or Thailand), smashed, pod discarded, and seeds reserved

2 g cinnamon (cassia) stick

1 g finely grated whole nutmeg

2 g ground turmeric

12 oz yellow onion, chopped into 1-inch pieces

50 g garlic cloves, peeled

2 g dried puya chiles, split open, seeded, and soaked in hot tap water until fully soft, about 20 minutes

20 g peeled fresh or thawed frozen galangal, thinly sliced against the grain

15 g peeled ginger, thinly sliced against the grain

20 g kosher salt

28 g thinly sliced lemongrass, tender parts only (from about 4 large stalks)

THE CURRY

1/4 cup neutral oil, such as canola, soybean, or rice bran

1½ lb boneless beef shank or chuck, silver skin removed, cut against the grain into pieces 2 inches long, 1 inch wide, and 1/4 inch thick (for shank) or 1/2 inch thick (for chuck)

40 g / 2 tbsp packed Naam Taan Piip (Softened Palm Sugar; page 239; preferably Thai)

2 tbsp Thai fish sauce

2 tbsp Thai thin soy sauce

2¾ cups water

THE DISH

Neutral oil, such as canola, soybean, or rice bran, for deep-frying

11 oz / 6 cups flat, ba mii (fresh, yellow Chinese wheat noodles)

3/4 cup unsweetened coconut cream (preferably boxed), gently warmed

ACCOMPANIMENTS

Drained, chopped (1/2 inch) Phak Dong (Pickled Mustard Greens; page 247; stems preferred for their crunch; if store-bought, soak in cold water for 10 minutes, then drain well)

Small shallot wedges (1/4 inch; preferably Asian)

Naam Phrik Phao (Roasted-Chile Paste; page 233)

Halved Key limes or regular (Persian) lime wedges

Very roughly chopped cilantro (thin stems and leaves)

Suggested khruang phrung

Prep the Curry

In a small pan, combine the coriander seeds, fennel seeds, cumin seeds, peppercorns, cloves, star anise, mace, black cardamom, white cardamom, cinnamon, and nutmeg. Set the pan over medium-low heat and cook, stirring and tossing often, until the spices are very fragrant, about 3 minutes. Let the spices cool slightly, then grind them in a spice grinder to a fine powder. Scoop the powder into a bowl, stir in the turmeric, and set aside.

In a blender or food processor, combine the onion and garlic and process to a fine, thick sludge. Set aside.

Drain the chiles well, then wrap them in paper towels and gently wring out the water. Pound the chiles to a fairly smooth paste in a mortar, about 2 minutes. Add the galangal, ginger, and salt and pound to a fairly smooth paste, 1 to 2 minutes. Add the lemongrass and pound until you have a fairly smooth, slightly fibrous paste, 3 to 5 minutes. Set aside.

Make the Curry

In a 3- to 4-quart pot over medium heat, heat the oil until it shimmers. Add the ground spice mixture and cook, stirring frequently, until very aromatic, about 30 seconds. Add the galangal paste and cook, stirring frequently, until it loses its raw smell, about 5 minutes. Turn the heat to medium-high, add the beef, and cook, stirring to coat it well, for 3 minutes. Add the palm sugar, fish sauce, and thin soy sauce and cook, stirring, until the sugar has dissolved, about 3 minutes. Add the onion sludge and cook, stirring frequently, until it loses its raw taste and smell, about 5 minutes.

Lower the heat to medium. Add the water, stir, and let the mixture come to a simmer. Cover the pot, lower the heat to maintain a gentle simmer, and cook, stirring occasionally, until the beef is fairly tender, about 1 hour for shank and 30 to 40 minutes for chuck.

You can cover the curry and keep it warm on the stove for up to 2 hours, or you can let it cool and store it in an airtight container in the fridge for up to 3 days. (It'll get even better if you store it, as the flavors will meld and the meat will soak up some of the curry.) Bring it to a very gentle simmer right before serving to make sure the beef is heated through.

Finish the Dish

Line a large plate with paper towels or newspaper and set it near the stove.

Pour 3 inches of oil into a wide, large pot, set the pot over medium-high heat, and heat the oil to 350°F. Use a thermometer to take the temperature, measuring the oil at the center of the vessel and carefully stirring the oil occasionally to ensure a consistent temperature. Put 2 oz / 1 cup of the noodles on a plate and gently toss them so there are no clumps. In four 14 g / ¼-cup batches, transfer the noodles to the pot and fry, turning them once, just until they are golden brown and crunchy, 20 to 30 seconds per batch. Transfer the fried noodles to the prepared plate to drain and cool. They'll keep like this for a couple of hours or in an airtight container in a dry place for a few days.

When you're nearly ready to serve the curry, fill a large, tall pot with enough water to submerge a long-handled noodle basket and bring to a boil over high heat. Make one bowl at a time by putting 2¼ oz / 1¼ cups noodles in the basket and submerging the noodles in the boiling water. Cook, stirring occasionally with chopsticks, until the noodles are fully tender (not al dente), 2 to 3 minutes. Firmly shake the basket to drain well and dump the contents into a serving bowl. To the bowl, add 2¾ oz / 8 to 10 pieces of beef, ladle on about 1 cup of the curry, spoon on 3 tbsp of the warm coconut cream, and top with a nest of fried noodles. Repeat for the remaining bowls.

Serve with the accompaniments and khruang phrung alongside. Invite guests to add these ingredients to their bowls to taste and stir well before eating.

Khao Soi Naam Naa

TAI LEU–STYLE NOODLES WITH PORK, TOMATO, AND FERMENTED SOYBEAN

ข้าวซอยน้ำหน้า

In the US, as well as in and around Chiang Mai, *khao soi* has come to refer to a particular dish: coconut-spiked curry, marked by a complex paste made with myriad fresh and dried ingredients, and egg noodles, both boiled and fried. Yet when my wife, Kung, was growing up in Chiang Khong, in Chiang Rai Province, *khao soi* referred to the noodle soup you see here—a dish I've enjoyed primarily in the uppermost reaches of Thailand, including in Kung's hometown and other towns that abut the border with Burma and mostly from the pots of Tai Leu people, a Thai ethnic minority.

Compared with the version common in Chiang Mai, which people from Kung's neck of the woods call *khao soi kathi* (*khao soi* with coconut milk), *khao soi naam naa* is downright plain. Fresh medium-width rice noodles join stock flavored with a mixture of ground pork, tomato, dried chiles, and *thua nao khaep,* fermented soybeans sun-dried in disks (and adequately replaced in this recipe by a jarred product). These seasoning components, in case you're keeping track, essentially add up to *naam phrik ong*, the Northern Thai relish served with cracklings and vegetables. Sure, it's modest by contrast, but it's well worth your time.

Makes 6 bowls (6 servings)

»

FLAVOR PROFILE

Tart, salty

SUGGESTED KHRUANG PHRUNG

Phrik Naam Plaa
(Fish Sauce–
Soaked Chiles)
PAGE 236

Phrik Naam Som
(Vinegar-Soaked
Chiles)
PAGE 235

Phrik Pon Khua
(Toasted-Chile Powder)
PAGE 240

Sugar (preferably
raw cane sugar)

SUGGESTED UTENSILS

THE PREP

1 g dried Thai chiles

3 g kosher salt

3 g cilantro roots

16 g garlic cloves, peeled and halved lengthwise

16 g small Asian shallots, peeled and thinly sliced against the grain

3 tbsp yellow bean sauce

8 oz cherry tomatoes, halved

1 tbsp neutral oil, such as canola, soybean, or rice bran

8 oz ground pork

THE BOWLS

6 tbsp Thai fish sauce

12 g / 1 tbsp MSG (optional, but highly recommended)

16½ oz / 7½ cups tightly packed semi-dried sen lek (thin, flat rice noodles), snipped into approximately 8-inch lengths

6 oz / 3 cups bean sprouts

9 cups Naam Sup Muu (Pork Stock; page 111), hot

24 g / 6 tbsp sliced (¼ inch) green onion

12 g / 6 tbsp very roughly chopped cilantro (thin stems and leaves)

Suggested khruang phrung

Prep the Dish

In a mortar, combine the dried chiles and salt and pound firmly, scraping the mortar and stirring the mixture once or twice, until you have a fairly fine powder, about 3 minutes. Pound in the cilantro roots, occasionally stopping to scrape down the sides of the mortar, until you have a fairly smooth paste, about 2 minutes. Pound in the garlic, then the shallots, until you have a fairly coarse paste, about 5 minutes. Pound and stir in the yellow bean sauce to combine well. Transfer to a small bowl.

Pound the tomatoes briefly in the mortar so they give off some juice. Set aside.

In a medium saucepan over medium-low heat, heat the oil until it shimmers. Add all of the paste and cook, stirring frequently, until it is very fragrant and loses the smell of raw garlic and shallots, about 5 minutes. Add the pork, turn the heat to high, and cook, stirring constantly, until about half of the meat is just cooked (you're not trying to brown it), about 1 minute. Add the tomatoes and any juice in the mortar and cook, stirring and breaking up the meat as it cooks, for another minute. Cover the pot, adjust the heat to maintain a simmer, and cook, stirring occasionally to break up any meat clumps, until the tomatoes begin to break down and the mixture looks like a Bolognese sauce, very moist but still thick, 15 to 20 minutes. If it's watery, remove the lid and cook off some of the liquid. You'll have about 2 cups. (Fully cooled, it will keep in an airtight container in the fridge for up to 1 week.)

Assemble the Bowls

In each of six wide soup bowls, combine 1 tbsp fish sauce and 2 g / ½ tsp MSG.

Fill a large, tall pot with enough water to submerge a long-handled noodle basket and bring to a boil over high heat. Finish one bowl at a time (or two if you have two noodle baskets). Put 2¾ oz / 1¼ cups noodles and 1 oz / ½ cup bean sprouts in the basket and submerge the contents in the boiling water. Cook, stirring occasionally with chopsticks, until the noodles are tender, about 1 minute. Firmly shake the basket to drain well and dump the contents into one of the prepared bowls.

Spoon ¼ cup of the pork mixture onto the noodles, then ladle 1½ cups of the hot stock into the bowl (but not over the pork mixture). Sprinkle on 4 g / 1 tbsp green onion and 2 g / 1 tbsp cilantro. Serve with the khruang phrung alongside and get to work on the next bowl. Stir well before eating.

Kuaytiaw Haeng Neua Tuun

Once upon a time, I couldn't drive ten minutes in Northern Thailand without passing a stall on the side of the road selling these noodles topped with stewed beef. Nowadays, that's true of the sweet-sour noodle soup called *kuaytiaw tom yam*. *Kuaytiaw neua tuun*, particularly a good rendition, has become a dish that requires seeking out.

That's one reason why whenever I'm near the village of Ban Pong in the Mae Taeng District, where my friend and early culinary mentor Ajaan Sunee grew up, I make a detour for a bowl. I typically head straight to Kuaytiaw Pa Pai, where the *chao baan* (proprietor) runs the shop just as her mother did. Her version has no flourishes or innovations. It features the typical Thai way with stewed beef but has an exceptional subtlety of spice and a texture that hits the bull's-eye between chewy and falling apart. Hers served as my model when I developed this recipe, which reflects the *haeng* ("dry") style of serving. Rather than a lake of broth, just a splash moistens and flavors the noodles, along with fish sauce, sweet-bitter black soy sauce, and garlicky oil.

Scrupulous readers will note that this preparation is very similar to Kuaytiaw Kai Tuun (page 85), yet with beef's bolder flavor, and Kuaytiaw Reua Neua (page 81), yet without the last-minute additions of grilled-chile vinegar and blood.

Makes 12 bowls (12 servings)

Note

In the course of stewing the beef, you will end up with about 9 cups of broth. This recipe is for a so-called "dry" noodle soup, so you might wonder what to do with this liquid. It can be used, in the context of this book, to serve alongside or to make the *naam* version of this noodle soup. Just ladle in 1 cup per bowl. Otherwise, you can use the delicious stuff for whatever purpose you want.

FLAVOR PROFILE

Salty, umami, a bit sweet

SUGGESTED KHRUANG PHRUNG

Phrik Naam Plaa (Fish Sauce–Soaked Chiles)
PAGE 236

Phrik Naam Som (Vinegar-Soaked Chiles)
PAGE 235

Phrik Pon Khua (Toasted-Chile Powder)
PAGE 240

Sugar (preferably raw cane sugar)

SUGGESTED UTENSILS

THE STEWED BEEF

28 g / 1 cup lightly packed very roughly chopped (3 inches) Chinese celery (stems and leaves)

28 g / ¼ cup thinly sliced (⅛ inch; against the grain) unpeeled fresh or thawed frozen galangal

4 oz / 3 large stalks lemongrass (outer layer, bottom 1 inch, and top 9 inches removed), bruised and sliced ½ inch thick

10 g / 10 cilantro roots, bruised

3 g / 1½-inch cinnamon (cassia) stick

1 g / 4 dried bay leaves

9 g / 1 tbsp black peppercorns

2 g / 2 whole star anise

12 cups water

2½ lb boneless beef shank or chuck, silver skin removed, cut against the grain into 2 by 1 by ¼-inch strips

¾ cup Thai thin soy sauce

2 tbsp Thai black soy sauce

2 oz / ¼ cup Chinese rock sugar

14 g / 2 fresh or thawed frozen pandan leaves, folded to fit in pot and tied into a bundle

THE BOWLS

6 cups stewed-beef broth, hot

4 tbsp Thai fish sauce

12 g MSG (optional)

72 oz / 12 cups sen yai (fresh rice noodles; 1½ inches wide)

60 oz / 12 cups packed, diagonally sliced Chinese broccoli, stems in long (2-inch), thin (⅛-inch) pieces, leaves whole

36 fresh or thawed frozen Luuk Chin Neua (Beef Balls; page 215, or use store-bought), at room temperature

¾ cup Naam Man Krathiam Jiaw (Fried Garlic in Garlic Oil; page 237), about half solids and half oil

¼ cup Thai black soy sauce

12 generous pinches of finely ground Asian white pepper

12 generous pinches of very roughly chopped Chinese celery (thin stems and leaves)

12 generous pinches of very roughly chopped cilantro (thin stems and leaves)

12 generous pinches of thinly sliced (⅛ inch) sawtooth herb

Suggested khruang phrung

Make the Stewed Beef

On a large square of cheesecloth, combine the Chinese celery, galangal, lemongrass, cilantro roots, cinnamon, bay leaves, peppercorns, and star anise. Gather the edges around the ingredients, then twist and knot to secure the bundle.

In a large pot, combine the cheesecloth bundle, water, beef shank, thin soy sauce, black soy sauce, rock sugar, and pandan leaves and bring to a simmer over high heat. Immediately cover the pot, lower the heat to maintain a steady simmer, and cook, adjusting the heat as needed to maintain the simmer, until the beef is very tender but not falling apart, 1 to 1½ hours. Uncover the pot, adjust the heat to maintain a gentle simmer, and cook for 15 minutes more to concentrate the flavor slightly. Remove and discard the cheesecloth and pandan leaf bundles. (Fully cooled, the beef and broth will keep in an airtight container in the fridge for up to 1 week.)

Assemble the Bowls

Before you're ready to serve, bring the stewed beef to a bare simmer over medium-low heat.

In each of twelve wide soup bowls, combine 1 tbsp hot broth from the stewed beef, 1 tsp fish sauce, and 1 g MSG and stir well.

Fill a large, tall pot with enough water to submerge a long-handled noodle basket and bring to a boil over high heat. Finish one bowl at a time (or two if you have two noodle baskets). Put 5 oz / 1 cup noodles, 2 oz / 1 cup Chinese broccoli, and 3 beef balls in the basket and submerge the contents in the boiling water. Cook, gently swirling the basket occasionally, until the noodles are hot, about 30 seconds. Firmly shake the basket to drain well, dump the contents into the prepared bowl, and stir well.

To the bowl, add 3 oz / ½ cup stewed beef, 1 tbsp fried garlic in garlic oil, 1 tsp black soy sauce, a pinch of pepper, a pinch of Chinese celery, a pinch of cilantro, and a pinch of sawtooth herb. Serve the khruang phrung alongside the noodles, then get to work on the next bowl. Stir well before eating.

Ba Mii Tom Yam Haeng Muu

"DRY" SPICY, SWEET, TART WHEAT NOODLES WITH PORK, PEANUTS, AND HERBS

บะหมี่ต้มยำแห้งหมู

A bowl of these noodles offers the same spicy-sour-sweet interplay that characterizes the *tom yam* genre, the same flavors that make *tom yam kung* so beloved in the US and the noodle soup *kuaytiaw tom yam muu* (see page 79) so popular in Thailand. In this case, the latter is served *haeng* ("dry"—that is, without broth). You get the same noodles and sundry pork bits you'd find in the brothy version but with the full-strength flavor of the seasonings: grilled-chile vinegar and fish sauce, sugar and pickled radish, peanuts and lime. *Ba mii* (thin wheat noodles) are the preferred mode for this dish, though as always, all types are welcome. For those who miss broth, the dish often comes with some on the side, seasoned with fish sauce, pepper, and a pinch of herbs.

Makes 1 bowl (1 serving); to make more, double or quadruple the ingredients, but make each bowl separately

»

FLAVOR PROFILE

Salty, umami-rich

SUGGESTED KHRUANG PHRUNG

Phrik Naam Plaa (Fish Sauce–Soaked Chiles)
PAGE 236

Phrik Naam Som (Vinegar-Soaked Chiles)
PAGE 235

Phrik Pon Khua (Toasted-Chile Powder)
PAGE 240

Sugar (preferably raw cane sugar)

SUGGESTED UTENSILS

THE BOWL

28 g / ¼ cup Phat Muu Sap (Stir-Fried Ground Pork; page 228), hot or at room temperature

2 tbsp Naam Sup Muu (Pork Stock; page 111), hot

20 g / 2 tbsp coarsely pounded (⅛- to ¼-inch pieces) unsalted roasted peanuts

14 g / 1 tbsp shredded Thai salted radish (soaked in cold water for 10 minutes, rinsed, and drained well)

1 tbsp Thai fish sauce

10 g / 2 tsp granulated sugar

1 tsp Phrik Phao Naam Som (Grilled-Chile Vinegar; page 235)

2 g / 1 tsp Phrik Pon Khua (Toasted-Chile Powder; page 240)

1 tsp Naam Man Krathiam Jiaw (Fried Garlic in Garlic Oil; page 237), about half solids and half oil

THE DISH

28 g pork loin, sliced against the grain into 2 by ¾ by ⅛-inch strips

Splash of Thai fish sauce

Generous pinch of finely ground Asian white pepper

3 oz / 1 cup packed round ba mii (fresh, thin, yellow Chinese wheat noodles)

3 fresh or thawed frozen Luuk Chin Muu (Pork Balls; page 215, or use store-bought)

28 g / ½ cup bean sprouts

20 g / ¼ cup diagonally sliced (¼ inch thick, ¾ inch long) long beans

3 g / 1 tbsp crumbled Khaep Muu (Pork Cracklings; page 225, or use store-bought)

2 g / 1 tbsp very roughly chopped cilantro (thin stems and leaves)

4 g / 1 tbsp sliced (¼ inch) green onion

2 g / 1 tbsp thinly sliced (⅛ inch) sawtooth herb

2 triangles Kiaw Thawt (Fried Wonton Skins; page 243; optional)

ACCOMPANIMENTS

½ cup Naam Sup Muu (Pork Stock; page 111), hot

Pinch of very roughly chopped cilantro (thin stems and leaves)

Pinch of sliced (¼ inch) green onion

1 tsp Thai fish sauce

Pinch of finely ground Asian white pepper

Halved Key limes or regular (Persian) lime wedges

Suggested khruang phrung

Prep the Bowl

In a wide soup bowl, combine the stir-fried ground pork, pork stock, peanuts, salted radish, fish sauce, sugar, grilled-chile vinegar, toasted-chile powder, and fried garlic in garlic oil. Stir well.

Make the Dish

Put the pork loin in a small bowl and add the fish sauce and pepper. Mix with your hands, then let marinate while you continue.

Fill a large, tall pot with enough water to submerge a long-handled noodle basket and bring to a boil over high heat. Put the noodles, marinated pork loin, pork balls, bean sprouts, and long beans in the basket and submerge the contents in the boiling water. Cook, stirring occasionally with chopsticks, until the noodles are tender and the pork loin is cooked, about 2 minutes.

Firmly shake the basket to drain well and dump the contents into the prepared bowl. Stir well. Sprinkle on the pork cracklings, cilantro, green onion, and sawtooth herb, then garnish with the fried wonton skins.

For the accompaniments, stir together the hot pork stock, cilantro, green onion, fish sauce, and pepper in a small bowl and serve this hot soup, the lime halves, and the suggested khruang phrung alongside the noodles.

NOT NOODLES

Phat Phak Buung Muu Lat Khao

STIR-FRIED WATER SPINACH WITH GROUND PORK OVER RICE

ผัดผักบุ้งหมูราดข้าว

I've been coming to Thailand going on thirty years now, and on virtually every visit I eat something I've never had before. It's often the simpler stuff that escapes my notice. This dish is a good example. I ate it for the first time just a few years ago at Kuaytiaw Mae Yaa, a noodle shop next to the highway that leads from Ban Kua Moong, where I have a home, to the closest town, Mae Rim.

I'd eaten here many times before, but this time, my frequent lunch companion, Austin Bush, and I noticed a couple of woks had joined the familiar pots of broth and boiling water, long-handled baskets, and other components of a noodle-soup setup. Culinary specialization does tend to breed good food. Yet it isn't always a recipe for success. So nowadays, even single-minded restaurants diversify, expanding their menus to attract more customers, for better or worse. At Kuaytiaw Mae Yaa, it's arguably for the better. For as long as I've been coming, the owners made and sold excellent noodle soups. Now they have a *som tam* (papaya salad) station. In those new woks, they make *phat si ew* (see page 125), *kai phat kaphrao* (ground chicken stir-fried with chiles and hot basil), and *aahaan tham sang*, those dishes made using the various vegetables and proteins prepped and laid out on a nearby table. Because they're good cooks, their new offerings are worth eating.

Austin asked for *phat phak buung muu lat khao*. In what seemed like seconds, we were digging into a small heap of water spinach (a hollow-stemmed green called *on choy* in Cantonese and *phak buung* in Thai) and ground pork fragrant from garlic and fresh chile and propelled by the power of oyster sauce and fish sauce. It's straightforward and flavorful, and a satisfying meal with jasmine rice. Slide a fried egg onto the rice to make a good thing even better.

Makes 1 plate (1 serving)

FLAVOR PROFILE

Spicy, rich, salty

SUGGESTED KHRUANG PHRUNG

Phrik Naam Plaa
(Fish Sauce–
Soaked Chiles)
PAGE 236

SUGGESTED UTENSILS

»

THE SAUCE

¼ cup plus 2 tbsp Thai oyster sauce

¼ cup Thai fish sauce

¼ cup Naam Cheuam (Simple Syrup; page 239)

THE DISH

14 g / 4 garlic cloves, peeled and halved lengthwise

6 g / 4 stemmed fresh or frozen red Thai chiles

4½ oz / 3 cups packed chopped water spinach (bottoms trimmed by 2 inches), stems and leaves in 2-inch pieces

¼ cup Naam Sup Muu (Pork Stock; page 111) or water, at room temperature

4 g / 1 tsp drained salted yellow beans, rinsed

1 tbsp neutral oil, such as canola, soybean, or rice bran

3 oz ground pork

9 oz / 1½ cups Khao Hom Mali (Jasmine Rice; page 244), freshly cooked

Suggested khruang phrung

Make the Sauce

In an airtight container, combine the oyster sauce, fish sauce, and simple syrup and stir well. You'll have about ¾ cup. Reserve 2 tbsp for this dish. The remaining sauce will keep, covered, in the fridge for up to 3 months.

Make the Dish

In the mortar, combine the garlic and chiles and pound just until they are in small pieces and you have a slightly wet-looking mixture (not a paste), about 30 seconds. Set aside.

Combine the water spinach, pork stock, the reserved 2 tbsp sauce, 8 g / 1 tbsp (or more to taste) of the garlic-chile mixture, and the yellow beans in a medium bowl and put it near the stove.

Set a flat-bottomed wok over very high heat and heat until it begins to smoke lightly. Add the oil and swirl the wok to coat the sides. Add the pork and cook, quickly stirring and breaking up any clumps, until the pork is just cooked through, 30 to 45 seconds. Add the water spinach mixture and stir-fry, constantly stirring, scooping, and flipping the ingredients, until the stems are tender with a slight crunch, 1½ to 2 minutes.

Transfer to a plate and serve with the jasmine rice and the khruang phrung.

Khao Phat Naem

FRIED RICE WITH SOUR SAUSAGE

ข้าวผัดแหนม

Although it's a standard in Thailand, this take on fried rice doesn't show up much in the States. That's a shame, because it's excellent, the familiar pleasures of rice resurrected by heat, fat, and egg amplified by tart tomatoes and the sour tang of *naem*, a rustic fermented pork sausage flecked with chile and garlic. You'll find the sausage, typically thin logs wrapped in plastic, in many Asian markets with a robust Southeast selection. Better still, make it yourself.

Makes 1 plate (1 serving)

»

FLAVOR PROFILE

Umami-rich, sour, salty

**SUGGESTED
KHRUANG PHRUNG**

Phrik Naam Plaa
(Fish Sauce–
Soaked Chiles)
PAGE 236

SUGGESTED UTENSILS

THE SAUCE

¾ cup Thai fish sauce

½ cup Naam Cheuam
(Simple Syrup;
page 239)

¼ cup Thai thin
soy sauce

THE DISH

1 tbsp plus 1 tsp neutral
oil, such as canola,
soybean, or rice bran

2 oz / ½ cup sliced
(¼ inch) Naem
(Fermented Pork
Sausage; page 222, or
use store-bought)

1 egg, at room
temperature

28 g / ¼ cup thinly
sliced (with the grain)
yellow onion

12 g / 4 garlic cloves,
peeled and crushed into
small pieces in a mortar

12 oz / 2 cups Khao
Hom Mali (Jasmine Rice;
page 244; preferably a
day or two old)

2 oz cherry tomatoes,
halved

Generous pinch of
finely ground Asian
white pepper

8 g / 2 tbsp sliced
(¼ inch) green onion,
plus a pinch

2 g / 1 tbsp very roughly
chopped cilantro (thin
stems and leaves)

ACCOMPANIMENTS

½ cup Naam Sup
Muu (Pork Stock;
page 111), hot

Pinch of very roughly
chopped cilantro (thin
stems and leaves)

Pinch of sliced
(¼-inch) green onion

1 tsp Thai fish sauce

Pinch of finely ground
Asian white pepper

Sliced cucumber

Halved Key limes or
regular (Persian)
lime wedges

Suggested khruang
phrung

Make the Sauce

In an airtight container, combine the fish sauce,
simple syrup, and thin soy sauce and stir well. You'll
have about 1½ cups. Reserve 2 tbsp for this dish.
The remaining sauce will keep, covered, in the fridge
for up to 6 months.

Make the Dish

Set a flat-bottomed wok over very high heat and
heat until it begins to smoke lightly. Add 1 tbsp of
the oil and swirl the wok to coat the sides. Add the
sausage and cook, flipping once or twice, until hot
and very lightly browned, about 1 minute.

Push the sausage to one side of the wok, then
add the remaining 1 tsp oil to the other side. Crack
in the egg (the white will bubble and puff) and cook,
without messing with it, until all but the center of
the white has set, about 15 seconds. Flip the egg
(it's okay if the yolk breaks), break it up slightly, and
cook for 15 seconds more.

Add the onion and garlic and stir-fry, constantly
stirring, scooping, and flipping the ingredients, for
15 seconds. Add the jasmine rice and break up any
clumps, then add the tomatoes and stir-fry for
30 seconds. Add the reserved 2 tbsp sauce and
the pepper and stir-fry until the flavors have permeated the rice and the tomatoes have softened,
about 1 minute more.

Turn off the heat, stir in the 8 g / 2 tbsp green
onion, and transfer the rice to a plate. Top with
the cilantro and finish with the remaining pinch
of green onion.

For the accompaniments, stir together hot pork
stock, cilantro, green onion, fish sauce, and pepper
in a small bowl and serve the hot soup, cucumber
slices, lime halves, and suggested khruang phrung
alongside the noodles.

Khao Phat American

Many hotels and old-school cafés in Thailand serve something called ABF. The acronym stands for "American breakfast," though the plate of fried eggs with white bread, ham or bacon, and sometimes hot dogs won't strike a chord with most customers at Waffle House. As the story goes, this morning meal is a holdover from the Vietnam War era, fashioned to appeal to American troops stationed in Thailand. That it eventually morphed into fried rice is no big surprise to observers of Thai food.

The deftness with which Thai cooks welcome foreign foods into their repertoire is one of the defining features of the country's culinary evolution. It's evident in how thoroughly they've integrated chiles—introduced five centuries ago, a relatively recent import—into the cuisine, and in the recent popularity of pizzas topped with shrimp, crab, and pineapple. After all, even *phat thai*—perhaps the country's most famous export—is an amalgam of Chinese (the noodles, the stir-frying) and Thai (the tamarind, the fish sauce) influences.

Inevitably, then, Thai cooks turned ABF into something they'd eat themselves. A common sight at vendors who specialize in boxed lunches, the resulting fried rice fills Styrofoam clamshells and includes ketchup or *sauce phrik* (sweet chile sauce) as its most prominent seasoning, as well as peas (often) and raisins (almost always). It's typically accompanied by the components of the original breakfast, plus a piece of fried chicken. Despite the name, American fried rice isn't popular among Americans, at least if the blank stares I get when I bring it up with tourists and expats are any indication.

Makes 1 plate (1 serving)

FLAVOR PROFILE

Umami-rich, salty, sweet

SUGGESTED KHRUANG PHRUNG

Phrik Naam Plaa (Fish Sauce-Soaked Chiles)
PAGE 236

SUGGESTED UTENSILS

»

THE SAUCE

¾ cup Thai fish sauce

½ cup Naam Cheuam (Simple Syrup; page 239)

¼ cup Thai thin soy sauce

THE HOT DOG FLOWERS

Neutral oil, such as canola, soybean, or rice bran, for deep-frying

35 g / 3 mini hot dogs (aka cocktail franks)

THE DISH

2 tbsp neutral oil, such as canola, soybean, or rice bran

1 egg, at room temperature

42 g / ½ small Roma tomato

2 oz / 2 slices ham (⅛ inch thick)

6 oz / 1 cup Khao Hom Mali (Jasmine Rice; page 244; preferably a day or two old)

28 g / ¼ cup thinly sliced (with the grain) yellow onion

10 g / 1 tbsp thawed frozen or drained canned peas

12 g / 1 tbsp raisins, plus a few for garnish

6 g / 2 garlic cloves, peeled and crushed into small pieces in a mortar

1 tbsp ketchup

Generous pinch of finely ground Asian white pepper

1 fried chicken drumstick, warm or at room temperature (optional)

Sliced cucumbers

Suggested khruang phrung

Make the Sauce

In an airtight container, combine the fish sauce, simple syrup, and thin soy sauce and stir well. You'll have about 1½ cups. Reserve 2 tbsp for this dish. The remaining sauce will keep, covered, in the fridge for up to 6 months.

Make the Hot Dog Flowers

Line a sheet pan with paper towels or newspaper and set it near the stove.

Pour 2 inches of oil into a wide medium pot, set the pot over medium-high heat, and warm the oil to 275°F. Use a thermometer to take the temperature, measuring the oil at the center of the vessel and carefully stirring the oil occasionally to ensure a consistent temperature.

Meanwhile, working with one hot dog at a time, make a ½-inch-deep, X-shaped cut on each end. Add the hot dogs to the hot oil and cook, stirring occasionally, until the outsides darken a few shades and the ends blossom, about 3 minutes. Using a spider or other mesh strainer, transfer them to the prepared sheet pan. Set aside.

Make the Dish

Set a heavy medium skillet over high heat and heat until good and hot. Add 1 tbsp of the oil and swirl the pan to coat the bottom. Crack in the egg and cook for about 5 seconds; it should spit and sizzle violently and the white should bubble and puff. Turn the heat to medium and cook the egg, frequently tipping the pan slightly and basting the egg with the oil, just until the white has set and turned golden at the edges and the yolk is cooked the way you like it, about 1 minute for a slightly runny yolk. Turn off the heat. Transfer the egg to the prepared sheet pan to drain, leaving the oil in the skillet.

Return the heat to medium. Add the tomato, cut-side down, and ham to the skillet and cook, flipping once, until the tomato is lightly browned on the cut side and slightly softened and the ham is browned in spots but still soft, 2 to 3 minutes. Transfer to the prepared sheet pan.

Set a flat-bottomed wok over very high heat and heat until it begins to smoke lightly. Add the remaining 1 tbsp oil and swirl the wok to coat the sides. Add the jasmine rice, onion, peas, raisins, and garlic; break up any clumps of rice; and stir-fry, constantly stirring, scooping, and flipping the ingredients, for 30 seconds. Add the reserved 2 tbsp sauce, the ketchup, and the pepper and stir-fry until the flavors have permeated the rice, about 1 minute more.

Transfer the rice to a small rice bowl, pack it tightly, and overturn it onto a plate to make a neat mound. Add the fried chicken, cucumbers, ham, tomato, egg, and hot dog flowers, then garnish with raisins and serve with the khruang phrung alongside.

Khao Muu Daeng / Muu Krob

CHINESE-STYLE BBQ PORK / CRISPY PORK BELLY OVER RICE WITH CHINESE BROCCOLI AND SESAME GRAVY

ข้าวหมูแดง,หมูกรอบ

FLAVOR PROFILE

Meaty, umami rich,
a bit sweet

SUGGESTED UTENSILS

Familiar to visitors to Chinatowns all over the world, this dish is advertised by pork hanging from hooks in storefront windows. Two Cantonese preparations of pig—one lacquered and roasted to a glistening red, the other roasted or fried to a bubbly brown—end up sliced and perched on a bed of rice. It's straightforward, and, when the pork's good, it's near perfect—a meal only a vegetarian wouldn't love.

The dish happens to have legions of fans in Thailand, where dedicated vendors dispense the popular, quick lunch along with blanched Chinese broccoli. (It's quite similar to, but more common than, the pork-topped jade noodles on page 165.) The dish typically comes with sweet-salty sauce made significantly gloopy with tapioca or cornstarch, and while few versions will win awards for subtlety, the thick concoction is improved when vendors employ the pork's pan drippings. Most purveyors use plain white rice and there's no harm in that, though I prefer jasmine.

Makes 1 plate (1 serving)

»

THE GRAVY

1 cup Naam Sup Muu (Pork Stock; page 111)

¼ cup Thai thin soy sauce

3¼ oz / ¼ cup packed Naam Taan Piip (Softened Palm Sugar; page 239; preferably Thai)

2 tbsp Thai Sriracha sauce, such as Shark brand

2 tbsp toasted sesame oil

7 g / 2 tsp untoasted or toasted sesame seeds

14 g / 2 tbsp tapioca starch

1 tbsp water

THE DISH

9 oz / 1½ cups Khao Hom Mali (Jasmine Rice; page 244) or other steamed white rice, freshly cooked

3 oz / 1½ cups packed diagonally sliced Chinese broccoli, stems in long (2-inch), thin (⅛-inch) pieces, leaves whole

2 oz / 4 to 6 slices (¼ inch thick; against the grain) Muu Krob (Crispy Pork Belly; page 220), at room temperature

2 oz / 4 to 6 slices (¼ inch thick; against the grain) Muu Daeng (Chinese-Style BBQ Pork; page 218), at room temperature

4 g / 1 tbsp sliced (¼-inch) green onion

Naam Jim Si Ew Dam Phrik Sot (Black Soy–Chile Dipping Sauce; page 234) for serving

Make the Gravy

In a small saucepan, combine the pork stock, soy sauce, palm sugar, Sriracha, sesame oil, and sesame seeds and bring to a boil over high heat.

Meanwhile, in a small bowl, combine the tapioca starch and water and stir until smooth. While whisking, slowly drizzle the mixture into the pan. The mixture will thicken to a viscous sauce. Cook, stirring constantly, for 2 minutes, then turn off the heat. You'll have about 1½ cups. Reserve ¼ cup for this dish; keep warm until ready to use (if it develops a skin, just stir well). Fully cooled, the remaining gravy will keep in an airtight container in the fridge for up to 1 week.

Make the Dish

Fill a large, tall pot with enough water to submerge a long-handled noodle basket and bring to a boil over high heat.

When you're ready to serve, put the rice on a serving dish. Put the Chinese broccoli in the noodle basket and submerge the broccoli in the water. Cook until tender but still crunchy, about 30 seconds. Firmly shake the basket to drain well and add the broccoli to the serving dish. Add the crispy pork belly and Chinese-style BBQ pork, then spoon on the reserved ¼ cup gravy. Sprinkle with the green onions and serve with the dipping sauce.

Luuk Chin Thawt

In Thailand, a portable burner can become a sideline. Affix it to a cart, throw on a pot of oil, and you can do brisk business roving the bars and restaurants that spill onto the street. Merrymakers seated curbside know to look out for vendors selling grilled dried squid, skewers of beef and pineapple, and pork paste manifested in various shapes, from hot dog to sphere, and deep-fried. There's no rule against this sort of solicitation, so customers with a table full of drinks and snacks might well sidle up to a cart and bring back a plate of pork balls, pleasantly bloated with oil, to be dipped in emphatically sweet chile sauce. You see the same snack on offer at noodle shops, a no-brainer answer to diversifying the menu for an operation that already has hundreds of balls in stock. Now you can do the same in your kitchen.

Makes 4 to 6 servings

FLAVOR PROFILE

Meaty, savory

SUGGESTED UTENSILS

Line a large sheet pan with paper towels or news-paper and set it near the stove. Pat the balls dry.

Pour 3 inches of oil into a large pot or flat-bottomed wok, set over high heat, and heat the oil to 275°F. Use a thermometer to take the temperature, measuring the oil at the center of the vessel and carefully stirring the oil occasionally to ensure a consistent temperature.

Working in several batches to avoid crowding the pot, carefully add the balls to the hot oil and cook, adjusting the heat to maintain the temperature and occasionally turning over any balls that float, until hot through, puffed, and light golden brown, about 3 minutes. Using a spider or other mesh strainer, transfer them to the prepared sheet pan. They'll shrivel slightly soon after. That's okay.

Transfer to plate or bowl and serve with the sweet chile sauce alongside.

24 fresh or thawed frozen Luuk Chin Plaa (Fish Balls), Luuk Chin Neua (Beef Balls), or Luuk Chin Muu (Pork Balls); page 214, or use store-bought, at room temperature

Neutral oil, such as canola, soybean, or rice bran, for deep-frying

Naam Jim Kai (Sweet Chile Sauce; page 234)

Luuk Chin Ping

FLAVOR PROFILE

Meaty, savory

SUGGESTED UTENSILS

You can add a dish to your spread by making use of leftover fish, pork, or beef balls. Extras are good speared onto bamboo skewers and grilled using the same method you do for fish balls. Made yourself, the balls are especially flavorful—meat bound with a little starch, unlike the commercial product, which tastes as if it's mostly starch bound with a little meat. And made yourself, the dipping sauce is improved, quite sweet still but tempered by acidity and heat.

Makes 4 to 6 servings

24 fresh or thawed frozen Luuk Chin Plaa (Fish Balls), Luuk Chin Neua (Beef Balls), or Luuk Chin Muu (Pork Balls); page 214, or use store-bought, at room temperature

Neutral oil, such as canola, soybean, or rice bran, for rubbing

Naam Jim Kai (Sweet Chile Sauce; page 234)

Soak six to eight wooden skewers in tepid water for 30 minutes. Drain well. Prepare a grill, preferably charcoal, to cook with medium-high heat or preheat a heavy skillet over medium-high heat. Rub a little oil on the grill grates or skillet surface to prevent sticking.

Gently rub the meatballs with a thin slick of oil. Thread 3 or 4 balls onto each bamboo skewer, making sure to leave a couple of inches empty at the bottom of the skewer and making sure the tips aren't exposed (otherwise they'll burn).

Grill the skewers, turning them over occasionally, until the balls are browned in spots and hot through, 3 to 4 minutes. Transfer to a plate and serve with the sweet chile sauce on top or alongside.

Khai Mangkawn

ไข่มังกร

FLAVOR PROFILE

Salty, meaty

SUGGESTED UTENSILS

For a long stretch, whenever I was in Chiang Mai and craving boat noodles (see page 81), I made my way to Suthep Road to Kuaytiaw Tii Noi. The modest shop, which is now nowhere to be found, sold diminutive bowls of the rich, blood-spiked soup. It was so good you'd end up eating several. During one leisurely lunch, I spotted a photo depicting a menu item that resembled hard-boiled eggs that had been deep-fried, quartered, and served with a side of sweet chile sauce. I knew I'd order it even before I'd learned they were called, intriguingly, *khai mangkawn* (dragon eggs).

What I got was a nice surprise—something like a Scotch egg made from the Thai perspective. The egg white, it turned out, wasn't egg at all. It was a paste of pork and starch—the same mixture used to make *luuk chin muu* (see page 215)—that had been used to coat the yolk and then patted into an ovoid. Deep orange, highly seasoned, and with a slightly dry but still creamy texture, the yolks had clearly been extracted from *khai khem* (salted duck eggs). It's a clever creation, and not just because of the presentation. The salty yolks offset the fatty pork, and a dip in syrupy sauce does the same for the yolks. I haven't seen this preparation at a restaurant since, though I've made it often.

Makes 10 "eggs"

»

10 Khai Khem (Salted Duck Eggs; page 231)

1 lb 2 oz fatty ground pork

7 oz / 1½ cups crushed ice

14 g / 1 tbsp plus 2½ tsp Asian sweet potato starch

14 g / 2 tsp fine sea salt

1 g / ¾ tsp finely ground Asian white pepper

Neutral oil, such as canola, soybean, or rice bran, for deep-frying

Naam Jim Kai (Sweet Chile Sauce; page 234)

Form and Boil the Eggs

Peel the salted duck eggs. Carefully break open each one and remove the yolk, taking care to keep it intact. Transfer the yolks to a plate. Discard the whites.

In a food processor, combine the pork, ice, sweet potato starch, salt, and pepper (work in two batches if your machine isn't powerful) and process on high speed until the mixture is glossy and very smooth, stopping occasionally to stir and to prevent the processor from getting too hot and heating the mixture, about 6 minutes. Transfer the mixture to a large bowl. A handful at a time, pick up the mixture with one hand, steady the bowl with your free hand, and forcefully throw the mixture into the bowl a couple of times to force out some air and give the dragon eggs a pleasant, bouncy texture.

While the mixture is still cool, fill a large, wide bowl with 2 inches or so of warm (about 120°F) water. With wet hands, grab about 2½ oz / ⅓ cup of the pork mixture and form it into a very rough ball. Then, holding it on the fingers of an open hand, flatten it into a disk. Put an egg yolk in the center of the disk and ease the edges up and around the yolk to encase it completely. Very gently roll between your palms to make a smooth ball, then roll the ball into an egg shape. Put the egg in the warm water and repeat with the remaining pork mixture and yolks.

Bring a medium pot of water to a boil, then lower the heat to maintain a strong simmer (about 200°F, if you're counting). Working in three batches, cook the eggs in the simmering water, turning them over occasionally, until they're firm but still give slightly when squeezed, 2 to 3 minutes. As they're done, use a slotted spoon or spider to scoop them onto a plate in a single layer. (Fully cooled, the eggs will keep in an airtight container in the fridge for up to 1 week. Bring them to room temperature before frying.)

Fry and Serve the Eggs

Line a large sheet pan with paper towels or newspaper and set it near the stove. Pat the eggs dry.

Pour 3 inches of oil into a large pot, set over high heat, and bring the oil to 350°F. Use a thermometer to take the temperature, measuring the oil at the center of the vessel and carefully stirring the oil occasionally to ensure a consistent temperature.

Working in three or four batches, carefully add the eggs to the hot oil and cook, turning them over occasionally, until the outsides turn light golden brown, 3 to 5 minutes. Using the spider or another mesh strainer, transfer them to the prepared sheet pan.

Transfer to a plate, slice into quarters, and serve hot with the sweet chile sauce alongside.

บะหมี่ไข่-เกี๊ยวกุ้ง•
NOODLES EGG-CHINESE SOUP WITH MEAT
บะหมี่ 50.- ข้าวหน้าเป็ด 50.-
บะหมี่เป็ด 50.- เกี๊ยวกุ้ง 60.-

Suan Phasom
Eun Eun

SUNDRIES

ส่วนผสมอื่นๆ

Luuk Chin Muu / Neua / Plaa

ลูกชิ้นปลา,หมู,เนื้อ

Note

Depending on the strength of your food processor, consider pureeing the mixture in two batches to avoid overtaxing the machine. If it has to work too hard, it will heat up and you'll risk cooking the protein.

Plenty of exceptional noodle dishes, in Thailand and elsewhere, include mass-produced balls of fish, pork, or beef. A fine broth or intense hunger can lead you to forgive a bowl its minor faults. Still, when you happen upon a shop that makes its own, say, fish balls, it's tough to go back to the typical leaden orbs that lack any discernible flavor. Produced without lots of starch, oil, and additives, the balls actually taste like the fish or meat from which they're made and have an appealing light texture, even though they're still pleasantly springy and dense by design.

No question, fashioning them at home is a hassle. Getting it right takes practice. Yet even the imperfect orbs you turn out early on, before you've got a grip on the fine points of the process, will sell you on the merits of the undertaking. The mixture itself is easy enough: you blitz protein, along with a little starch and ice (which both provides liquid to bind with the starch and keeps the protein from cooking as the food processor labors), to a glossy, emulsified sludge.

The true test of your mettle comes when it's time to form the balls themselves, a task that master practitioners do with such speed and assurance that it is encouraging to watch and then, after your clumsy first attempt, baffling. Since the mixture is too loose to form using the conventional between-the-palms methods, you must grab some of the mixture with your hand and squeeze gingerly to coax out small, rough spheres, depositing them in warm water as you work so they hold their shape until they're later boiled. If this customary process, provided in the method of this recipe, proves too challenging, just use a spoon to scoop and then drop little lumps into the warm water.

Luuk Chin Muu / Neua

PORK / BEEF BALLS

ลูกชิ้นหมู,เนื้อ

Makes about forty 1-inch balls

1 lb 2 oz fatty ground pork or fatty ground beef, such as chuck, cold

7 oz / 1½ cups crushed ice

14 g / 1 tbsp plus 2½ tsp Asian sweet potato starch

14 g / 2 tsp fine sea salt

1 g / ¾ tsp finely ground Asian white pepper

In a food processor, combine the meat, ice, sweet potato starch, salt, and pepper (work in two batches if your machine isn't powerful enough) and process on high speed until glossy and very smooth, stopping occasionally to stir and to prevent the processor from getting too hot and heating the mixture, about 6 minutes. Transfer the mixture to a large bowl. A handful at a time, pick up the mixture, steady the bowl with your free hand, and forcefully throw the mixture against the bowl hard enough that you hear a good thwack. Do this for the remaining mixture, then repeat the process three or four times. This gets rid of the air incorporated by the food processor and gives the balls a pleasant bouncy texture.

While the mixture is still cool, fill a large, wide bowl with 2 inches or so of warm (about 120°F) water. Grab a small handful of the mixture, hold your hand upright, and gently squeeze to force a scant 1 tbsp or so of the mixture out of the space between your thumb and forefinger. Gently squeeze several more times, subtly sweeping the middle of your forefinger under the mixture as you squeeze to rotate the mixture and help form a rough 1-inch ball. Once you have a rough ball, hold it in place by tucking your forefinger under the ball so the finger overlaps your thumb, then, with your other hand, use a small spoon to transfer the ball to the warm water. Repeat with the remaining mixture.

Bring a medium pot of water to a boil, then lower the heat to maintain a gentle simmer (about 200°F, if you're counting). Working in two batches, transfer the balls to the simmering water and cook, turning them over occasionally, until they're fully cooked, about 3 minutes. To determine when they're done, scoop out and halve one and check that the center is firm. As they're done, use a slotted spoon or spider to scoop them onto a plate in a single layer.

Fully cooled, the balls will keep in an airtight container in the fridge for up to 3 days or in the freezer for up to 3 months.

Luuk Chin Plaa

FISH BALLS

ลูกชิ้นปลา

Makes about forty 1-inch balls

1¼ lb fresh or thawed frozen skinless firm white-fleshed fish fillets, such as basa, tilapia, or striped bass, cold

2 oz / 4 fresh or thawed frozen medium-size shrimp, peeled, deveined, and chopped into small pieces, cold

3½ oz / ⅔ cup crushed ice

18 g / 2 tbsp plus 1 tsp Asian sweet potato starch

11 g / 1½ tsp fine sea salt

6 g / 1½ tsp superfine sugar

¼ tsp finely ground Asian white pepper

Cut the fish fillets lengthwise along the line that runs down the center. Trim off any dark bits or connective tissue and remove any straggling bones, then chop the flesh into 1-inch pieces.

In a food processor, combine the fish, shrimp, ice, sweet potato starch, salt, sugar, and pepper (work in two batches if your machine isn't powerful enough) and process on high speed until glossy and very smooth, stopping occasionally to stir and to prevent the processor from getting too hot and heating the mixture, 4 to 5 minutes. Transfer the mixture to a large bowl. A handful at a time, pick up the mixture, steady the bowl with your free hand, and forcefully throw the mixture against the bowl hard enough that you hear a good thwack. Do this for the remaining mixture, then repeat the process three or four times. This gets rid of the air incorporated by the food processor and gives the balls a pleasant bouncy texture.

While the mixture is still cool, fill a large, wide bowl with 2 inches or so of warm (about 120°F) water. Grab a small handful of the mixture, hold your hand upright, and gently squeeze to force a scant 1 tbsp or so of the mixture out of the space between your thumb and forefinger. Gently squeeze several more times, subtly sweeping the middle of your forefinger under the mixture as you squeeze to rotate the mixture and help form a rough 1-inch ball. Once you have a rough ball, hold it in place by tucking your forefinger under it so the finger overlaps your thumb, then, with your other hand, use a small spoon to transfer the ball to the warm water. Repeat with the remaining mixture.

Bring a medium pot of water to a boil, then lower the heat to maintain a gentle simmer (about 200°F, if you're counting). Working in two batches, transfer the balls to the simmering water and cook, turning them over occasionally, until they're fully cooked, 2 to 3 minutes. To determine when they're done, scoop out and halve one; you're looking for uniform color all the way to the center. As they're done, use a slotted spoon or spider to scoop them onto a plate in a single layer.

Fully cooled, the balls will keep in an airtight container in the fridge for up to 3 days. They don't freeze well.

Other Shapes

Following the method instructions will guide you to making the more familiar spherical shape. In Thailand, you see other shapes as well, including these two.

To make an irregular elliptical shape: Instead of scooping the ball of fish mixture from your fist with a spoon, grab it with the fingers of your other hand and add it to the warm water.

To make *sen plaa* (fish noodles) for Yen Ta Fo (Sour-Sweet Noodle Soup with Seafood and Fermented Tofu; page 93) or fish cakes for Laksa Nyonya (Nyonya-Style Noodle Soup; page 103): Lay out an approximately 14 by 12-inch sheet of plastic wrap, with one of the long edges facing you. Transfer 1 cup of the fish mixture to the plastic wrap. Use your hands to form it into a rough log about 1½ inches in diameter. Roll the plastic wrap over the mixture to form it into a tight log, gently forcing any air out of the open ends as you roll. Twist the open ends in opposite directions and knot them to seal. Snip off the excess plastic.

Bring a medium pot of water to a rolling simmer, add the wrapped log, and cook just until firm, 2 to 3 minutes. Transfer the log to a plate, let sit until cool enough to handle, and unwrap.

For fish noodles, cut the log into long strips, about ⅛ by ¼ inch by 4 inches. For fish cakes, slice the log into ⅛-inch-thick rounds.

Muu Daeng

CHINESE-STYLE BBQ PORK

หมูแดง

The harried cook looking to whip up *khao muu daeng* (see page 201) or *ba mii yok haeng* (see page 165) could certainly take a trip to his or her local Chinatown and purchase this glistening red pork by the pound. *Muu daeng* is essentially *char siu*, the same Cantonese pork you find hanging in restaurant windows—next to the flock of ducks, deceased and delicious looking—in practically every Chinese enclave outside of China. But it's absolutely worth the effort to make it yourself.

This recipe clocks in somewhere between the proper way and the easy way. No, I don't demand that you hang the pork in a smoker, just that you use a kettle grill and some charcoal to add a subtle smokiness. I don't abandon the packaged seasoning powder, essentially just salt, sugar, and food coloring, but I do supplement it with a marinade that includes, among other things, fresh ginger, star anise, and *taohu yii* (a kind of fermented tofu). The result will make you glad you lit the coals, whether you opt for leaner tenderloin or a fattier cut, like shoulder or neck, that comes off the grill noticeably juicier. Or, for a change, try the recipe with whole turkey tails—a riff I learned in Hawaii.

Want to make extra? Double the marinade. Double the amount of pork, too, but cut it into two pieces of the same dimensions as those specified in the original recipe.

Makes 14 oz

6 g / 2 garlic cloves, peeled

6 g / ¾ by ¾-inch knob peeled ginger, thinly sliced against the grain

1 g / 1 whole star anise

11 g / 2 tsp packed fermented bean curd, plus 1 tsp liquid from the jar

2 tsp Thai thin soy sauce

10 g / 2 tsp Thai or Chinese roast red pork (char siu) seasoning mix, such as Lobo brand

1 tsp Thai fish sauce

1 tsp Shaoxing wine

1 tsp toasted sesame oil

5 g / 1 tsp granulated sugar

1 lb trimmed boneless, skinless pork shoulder or pork tenderloin (a 8 by 3-inch piece)

¼ cup honey or maltose syrup (facing page)

In a mortar, pound the garlic, ginger, and star anise to a very smooth paste, 1 to 2 minutes. Pound in the red bean curd until smooth, about 15 seconds. Add the thin soy sauce, pork seasoning mix, fish sauce, wine, sesame oil, and sugar and stir until well combined.

Put the pork in a resealable plastic bag, scrape in the seasoning mixture, and rub the pork to coat it well. Seal the bag, pushing out the air inside. Let the pork marinate in the fridge for 4 to 6 hours.

Prepare a charcoal grill to cook with medium heat (about 400°F), or preheat the oven to 450°F and set a rack over a sheet pan.

Put the pork on the grill grates away from the fire and cover the grill, or put it on the prepared sheet pan and put in the oven. Cook until fairly firm to the touch, 25 to 35 minutes.

Brush the top and sides of the pork with some of the honey, re-cover the grill or put it back in the oven, and cook for 5 minutes more. Flip the pork and repeat (glazing and flipping every 5 minutes) until the pork is cooked to medium to medium-well doneness (a thermometer inserted into the thickest part should register 145°F to 155°F), about 15 minutes. If using right away, transfer it to a cutting board, let rest for 5 to 10 minutes, then slice against the grain into ¼-inch-thick pieces. Otherwise, leave the cooked pork whole, let cool to room temperature, then store, tightly wrapped, in the fridge for up to 1 week.

Maltose Syrup

This thick syrup, made by fermenting grains such as wheat and rice to extract the type of sugar called maltose, makes the preferred baste for Chinese-style roasted pork. Available in small tubs at Chinese markets and often labeled "maltose," it is more neutral in flavor and significantly less sweet than honey, though honey is an acceptable substitute.

Because maltose syrup is so thick, it adheres especially well to the pork, even after the dilution with water prescribed here.

Makes about 1/3 cup

1/4 cup maltose syrup	2 tbsp hot water

In a small pan over medium-high heat, combine the maltose syrup and hot water and bring to a boil, stirring frequently. Turn off the heat and let cool slightly before using.

Muu Krob

CRISPY PORK BELLY

หมูกรอบ

Count this as one of several recipes inspired by a visit to the cafeteria at Chiang Mai University, where a collection of independent vendors hawk some pretty legit food to the students and faculty. When I would come here to meet my friend Ajaan Sunee, who worked for the college, I'd make a beeline to the *muu krob* guy. For twenty years, he'd been making the juicy pork belly capped with crackling skin, a preparation pioneered in China and adopted enthusiastically by cooks in Thailand. His was so good that I asked if he'd show me how he made it. With his approval, I showed up the next afternoon with a bottle of whiskey to repay his generosity.

When I arrived, he and his son were preparing bellies for the next day. They scored the meat, pricked the skin, and rubbed on salt and vinegar. They then hung the bellies to dry in a fridge, where they would remain until the evening, when they would hang them again, this time inside an enclosed fifty-five-gallon barrel with a little clay stove holding smoldering charcoal sitting at the bottom. Father and son would head home for the night, leaving the pork to cook as the coals burned to ash. By then, the father told me, the bellies would be done.

The morning I was there, after they had hung the next day's bellies to dry, I watched them retrieve the bellies that had been slow-roasted the night before, now tender and slightly smoky. The father and son built a new fire in the barrel, cooked the bellies until hot through, and then dunked them one by one into a large wok full of bubbling oil so the skin puffed.

Were I running a dedicated *muu krob* outfit, I'd want to make mine the same way. Since I'm not, I choose the way practiced by Thai cooks who make small batches of the stuff. This way requires no special equipment and achieves a similar end product. You won't achieve the smoky brilliance of the original, but the results are still delicious.

In this book, slices of *muu krob* wind up on *ba mii yok* (see page 165), but they're excellent laid on top of garlicky stir-fried Chinese broccoli.

Makes about 15 oz

Kosher salt	Neutral oil, such as canola, soybean, or rice bran, for deep-frying
2 lb skin-on boneless pork belly, cut against the grain into 2½- to 3-inch-wide pieces	

Set a cooling rack on a sheet pan.

Pour 4 to 5 inches of water into a large, tall pot, bring to a boil over high heat, and salt the water as if you were cooking pasta. Lower the heat to maintain a gentle simmer, add the pork, and cook until the meat gives easily when prodded with a finger but before it's fork-tender, about 1 hour.

Transfer the pork belly to a cutting board, discarding the liquid. Use a fork to poke the skin all over, spending 30 seconds or so per piece of pork. Transfer the pieces to the prepared rack. Leave uncovered in the fridge to dry further, at least 4 hours or up to 24 hours.

Line a sheet pan with a cooling rack and set it and a large plate near the stove.

Once the pork has dried sufficiently, pour 3 inches of oil into a large pot, set over high heat, and bring the oil to 320°F. Use a thermometer to take the temperature, measuring the oil at the center of the vessel and carefully stirring the oil occasionally to ensure a consistent temperature.

Add the pork belly to the hot oil, cover with a lid, and cook until the oil stops popping and spitting loudly, about 5 minutes. Carefully remove the lid, set a splatter guard on the pot, and cook until the pork is golden brown all over and the skin has started to bubble, about 6 minutes more. Using a spider or tongs, transfer the pork to the large plate.

Now bring the oil to 400°F. Working in batches if necessary to avoid crowding the oil, add the pork belly pieces to the hot oil and fry until the skin puffs up like chicharrón, 30 to 45 seconds. Using the spider or a slotted spoon, transfer them to the prepared sheet pan to drain.

The fried pork is best eaten within a couple of hours.

Naem

FERMENTED PORK SAUSAGE

แหนม

This sour sausage is one of several delicious fermented-meat products made in Thailand. Like *sai khrawk isaan* (a sour pork and rice sausage from the Northeast region) and *jin som* (a coarse mixture of pork meat and skin grilled in banana leaf packages), *naem* likely originated as a way to preserve meat. As refrigeration became more common and the flavor of *naem* caught on, it evolved, as so many foods do, from necessity to indulgence. Yet unlike its brethren, *naem* can be either main event or pantry ingredient—eaten uncooked as a snack with peanuts and fresh chiles alongside or added to scrambled eggs, spicy *yam* ("salads," to translate feebly), and *khao phat* (see page 195).

The process by which it's made is essentially the same as that used to make salami, though instead of the relatively long, low-temperature bacterial encouragement of Western charcuterie, *naem* is fermented quickly at a higher temperature and with a boost from cooked rice. Salt keeps the harmful stuff in check, and the salt along with the acidity created through fermentation preserves the meat.

Naem is readily available for sale in the US, often made by operations that distribute locally to Southeast Asian markets. These renditions will do in a pinch. Making it yourself, however, produces a more crumbly (and less rubbery), sour, and vibrant sausage.

Makes about 15 oz

56 g / ¼ cup packed freshly cooked Khao Niaw (Sticky Rice; page 245)

4 oz pork skin, stray hairs removed with a razor

14 g / 1 tbsp plus 1½ tsp kosher salt

10 oz fatty ground pork, at room temperature

20 g / 3 tbsp chopped (¼ to ⅛ inch) garlic cloves

4 g / 2 tsp thinly sliced (⅛ inch) fresh or frozen red or green Thai chiles

3 g / ¾ tsp MSG

1 g / ¼ tsp granulated sugar

Rinse the sticky rice in a medium bowl filled with tap water to cool it down to room temperature, breaking up any clumps with your fingers, then drain it well.

Put the pork skin in a small pot and add water to cover by about 1 inch. Set the pot over high heat and bring to a strong simmer. Lower the heat to maintain a gentle but steady simmer and cook, skimming off any surface scum, until the skin is translucent and soft enough to slice easily but not falling apart, about 30 minutes. Drain well and let sit just until cool enough to handle. Trim off and discard any stray meat or fat from the skin. Slice the skin into 1 by ¹⁄₁₆-inch slivers. Reserve 28 g / ¼ cup of the warm skin for this recipe.

In a medium bowl, combine the drained rice, reserved 28 g / ¼ cup skin, the salt, the ground pork, garlic, chiles, MSG, and sugar and mix very well with your hands.

Lay out an approximately 12 by 14-inch sheet of plastic wrap, with one of the long edges facing you. Transfer about one-fourth of the meat mixture to the plastic wrap. Use your hands to form a rough log about ¾ inch in diameter and 7½ inches long. Fold one end of the plastic over the log and roll the log forward one rotation. Use your hands to gently compact the log and force any air out of the open ends. Continue to roll the log tightly in plastic, gently forcing out more air as you roll. Lift the log by the loose plastic ends and whack it against the counter a dozen or so times, then gently force any air out the open ends once more. Twist the open ends in opposite directions and knot them to seal. Snip the excess plastic. Repeat with the remaining meat to make four logs total.

Set a cooling rack over a sheet pan. Put the logs on the rack with some space between them. Use a toothpick to pierce the plastic four or five times along the top of each log. Rotate the logs so the pierced side faces down.

Leave the sheet pan in a warm place until the meat has achieved the sourness you prefer, 24 to 48 hours, depending on the ambient temperature and your preference (see Note). Take a close sniff to assess the sourness. The meat will also firm up slightly and express a little liquid.

Naem tastes best just after curing, but it will keep wrapped in the fridge for up to 1 week.

Note

Making this sausage is a no-brainer in Thailand, where the climate cooperates. For cooks outside of Southeast Asia, however, achieving the temperature friendly to this kind of fermentation (95°F to 100°F, give or take) can require a little creativity. Unless you're in Los Angeles and Florida during the summer, consider fermenting indoors—say, in an oven with a pilot light, in a proofing box, or close to a strategically placed space heater. If you do ferment outside, make sure to keep the flies away, perhaps with an overturned colander draped with cheesecloth. Whatever you use, keep in mind that airflow is good and bugs are bad.

To gauge the *naem*'s progress, either sniff or taste the meat. The temperature will determine the speed of the fermentation. The level of sourness is up to you. I prefer it noticeably sour, which usually requires between 36 and 48 hours of fermentation, though even *naem* that's only slightly tart (after, say, 24 hours) is good. I don't recommend, however, fermenting longer than 48 hours, as to my taste the overall flavor will suffer and bacterial activity can begin to go sideways. A requisite caveat: If you spot any dramatic discoloration or smell rot, dump it, figure out what went wrong, and start again from scratch.

Muu Sap Sawng Khreuang

MINCED-PORK BALLS

หมูสับทรงเครื่อง

The MAMA *naam* at Mama Fah Thani (see page 87) contains these garlicky little meatballs. Unlike springy, emulsified *luuk chin muu* (see page 215), these have a coarse texture and are just a little denser than an Italian meatball. Also added to other dishes like *jok* (rice porridge) or *khao tom* (rice soup), they make a good lazy person's substitute for the slightly more complex version known as *muu deng* (bouncy pork).

Makes about 30 balls

28 g / 9 garlic cloves, peeled and halved lengthwise

12 oz fatty ground pork

15 g / 3 tbsp fairly finely chopped cilantro (thin stems and leaves)

1 tbsp Thai fish sauce

1 g / ¾ tsp finely ground Asian white pepper

Bring a large pot of water to a very gentle simmer and adjust the heat to maintain the simmer.

Meanwhile, in a mortar, pound the garlic to a fairly smooth paste, 2 to 3 minutes. Working in batches, if necessary, add the pork, cilantro, fish sauce, and pepper and pound until the mixture is well combined and slightly sticky (remember, you're not being gentle with the mixture as you would with Italian meatballs), about 1 minute.

In three or four batches, and working one by one, make about 1-inch balls—grab about 14 g / 2 tsp of the mixture and quickly form a rough ball—and carefully drop them into the simmering water as you form them. Cook until they float and are just cooked through, 2 to 3 minutes. As they're done, use a slotted spoon or spider to scoop them onto a plate in a single layer.

Fully cooled, the balls will keep in an airtight container in the fridge for up to 1 week or in the freezer for up to 6 months.

Khaep Muu

PORK CRACKLINGS

แคบหมู

These dense, crunchy pork skins—fried slowly to extract their fat and liquid, then again quickly so they puff—deliver texture, flavor, and richness to bowls of noodles, including Ba Mii Yok Haeng (page 165) and Kuaytiaw Tom Yam Muu Naam (page 79). Some Asian and Mexican markets sell fresh cracklings, either made in house or by local cooks, which will save you some effort. Avoid prepackaged cracklings that may have been sitting on the shelf for months, getting stale.

Makes about 4 cups

½ lb pork skin, stray hairs removed with a razor

25 g / 1 unpeeled small garlic head, halved crosswise

1½ tbsp distilled white vinegar

15 g / 1½ tbsp kosher salt

1 g / 1½ tsp finely ground Asian white pepper

Neutral oil, such as canola, soybean, or rice bran, for deep-frying

The day before you cook the cracklings, set cooling racks on as many sheet pans as needed to fit the skin in a single layer.

Use a meat tenderizer to prick the exterior side of the pork skin in rows ¼ to ½ inch apart. Rub the cut side of the garlic head on both sides of the skin. Sprinkle the vinegar on the exterior side of the skin and rub with your hands to distribute well. Sprinkle the salt and pepper on both sides of the skin. Lay the skin on the prepared racks and leave uncovered in the fridge to dry for at least 8 hours or up to 12 hours.

The next day, line a large sheet pan with paper towels or newspaper and set it and a large plate near the stove.

Select a large, tall pot that is at least 12 inches wide and pour in oil to a depth of 3 inches. Set the pot over high heat and heat the oil to 275°F. Use a thermometer to take the temperature, measuring the oil at the center of the vessel and carefully stirring the oil occasionally to ensure a consistent temperature.

While the oil is heating, use a sharp knife to cut the skin into strips about 2 inches long and ½ inch wide.

Add the pork skin to the hot oil and cook, stirring almost constantly for the first 5 minutes to prevent the pieces from sticking to one another and adjusting the heat as needed to maintain an oil temperature of 250°F to 260°F, then continue cooking, stirring occasionally after that, until the bubbling has mostly subsided and most of the pieces of skin are floating, 25 to 40 minutes. Using a spider or slotted spoon, transfer the skins to the large plate.

Now bring the oil to 400°F. Working in small batches to avoid crowding the oil, add the skin strips to the hot oil and fry until they puff and float to the surface, 10 to 15 seconds. Using the spider or slotted spoon, transfer them to the prepared sheet pan to drain. Let them cool.

The cracklings will keep in an airtight container in a cool, dark place (not the fridge) for up to 2 weeks.

Naam Man Muu

RENDERED PORK FAT

น้ำมันหมู

This frying medium (also known as lard) lends its porky flavor to *phat thai* (see page 137), Kuaytiaw Khua Pet (page 119), and other stir-fried noodles, for which it is highly recommended, though not mandatory. Like *khaep muu* (pork cracklings, see page 225), rendered pork fat can be purchased or made at home. The benefit of making it yourself is thrift—fatback is cheap and leftover scraps of belly and shoulder work just as well—and what the Thais call *gaek muu*, the crunchy bits that remain after all the fat has melted. Reserve them for snacking, sprinkling on *phat thai*, and adding to noodle soups. Know that the yield of both the liquid fat and *gaek muu* will vary depending on the cut of pork you use.

Makes 1 to 2½ cups, plus some gaek muu

1 to 2 lb fatty pork scraps, such as fatback, skin, belly, and shoulder, cut into about 1½-inch pieces

To ease the task of grinding, freeze the pork scraps on a plate in a single layer until the edges are frozen, about 15 minutes.

Grind the fat and scraps through a meat grinder fitted with a ⅜-inch die and transfer to a heavy medium pot. Pour in about ½ inch of water and set the pot over high heat. Bring the water to a boil, turn the heat to medium-low, and simmer, stirring occasionally, until the fat has melted, the water has evaporated, and the remaining bits of skin, flesh, and other protein are golden and crunchy, 30 to 40 minutes.

Strain through a fine-mesh strainer into a heat-proof container, reserving the crunchy pieces. To make sure there's no lingering water, return the liquid fat to the pot and cook over medium-low heat until it no longer pops and sizzles at all, about 3 minutes.

Fully cooled, the rendered fat and crunchy stuff will keep in an airtight container in the fridge for up to 3 months. To use, heat over medium heat until it no longer pops and sizzles (to get rid of any water that may have got in there due to condensation).

Khruang Nai

เครื่องใน

Skin and viscera are common additions to noodle soups, whether requested by the customer or definitional to a dish (*kuay chap*—see page 159—without guts is like pizza without crust). Here you'll find instructions that are more guidelines than recipe. The process is simple: Simmer the offal, along with aromatics that mitigate much of the bold fragrance, in enough water to cover by a couple of inches until the various innards are tender enough to eat but still have the chew that makes them satisfying. If you're using liver, it gets added near the end of the simmering and cooked until it's firm—just barely pink inside (my preference for pork liver) or fully gray brown (the Thai way). The recipe can be easily scaled up or down as needed. Tendons require longer cooking and should be prepared according to the instructions on page 82.

Makes 6 to 9 oz / 2 to 3 cups cooked and chopped, depending on the parts

2½ oz / 1 large stalk lemongrass, outer layer, bottom 1 inch, and top 9 inches removed

1 lb mixed pork offal (such as intestines, skin, heart, and liver), cut to fit in the pot if necessary

2 tbsp Thai fish sauce

25 g / 2 tbsp thinly sliced peeled fresh or thawed frozen galangal

9 g / 1 tbsp Asian white peppercorns

Bruise the lemongrass with a pestle, a pan, or the flat side of a knife, then cut the stalk crosswise into about 1-inch pieces.

In a medium pot, combine the lemongrass, offal (except any liver, which you will add later), fish sauce, galangal, peppercorns, and enough water to cover by about 2 inches. Set over high heat and bring the water to a strong simmer. Lower the heat to maintain a gentle simmer and cook, occasionally stirring and skimming off any surface scum, until the offal is pleasantly chewy, 45 minutes to 1 hour. A few minutes before the offal is ready, add the liver and simmer until firm but still barely pink in the center. Transfer the offal to a cutting board, discarding the cooking liquid, and chop into bite-size pieces.

The offal will keep in an airtight container in the fridge for up to 5 days or in the freezer for up to 3 months.

Phat Muu Sap

STIR-FRIED GROUND PORK

ผัดหมูสับ

Some recipes in this book called for ground pork cooked in a hot wok and seasoned with fish sauce.

Makes about 5 oz / 1 cup

1 tsp neutral oil, such as canola, soybean, or rice bran	7 oz ground pork
	A few dashes of Thai fish sauce

In a flat-bottomed wok or medium skillet over medium-high heat, heat the oil until it shimmers. Add the pork and cook, stirring, breaking up the meat, and adding the fish sauce about halfway through, just until it's cooked through, 3 to 5 minutes. Transfer the pork to a bowl.

Fully cooled, the pork will keep in an airtight container in the fridge for up to 1 week.

Muu Sap Luak

POACHED GROUND PORK

หมูสับลวก

Some recipes in this book call for ground pork cooked gently in salty water. Here's how to do it.

Makes about 5 oz / 1 cup

Kosher salt	7 oz ground pork

Bring a medium pot of water to a boil over high heat and salt the water as if you were cooking pasta. Add the pork to the water and turn off the heat. Immediately stir and break up the clumps of pork, then let it sit in the hot water until just cooked through, 1 to 2 minutes. Drain well.

Fully cooled, the pork will keep in an airtight container in the fridge for up to 1 week.

Neua Kai Chiik

SHREDDED POACHED CHICKEN

เนื้อไก่ฉีก

Some recipes in this book call for poached chicken. Here's how to do it.

Makes about 1 lb / 2 cups

2 boneless, skinless
chicken breast halves
(6 to 8 oz each)

Bring a large pot of water to a boil.

Put the chicken in a small pot, baking dish, or another heatproof container big enough to fit the breasts in a single layer with a little room to spare. Pour in enough of the boiling water to cover the chicken by about 2 inches, then cover and set aside until the water has cooled completely and the chicken is just cooked through, about 1 hour. Drain the chicken and pull the meat into bite-size shreds.

Fully cooled, the shredded chicken will keep in an airtight container in the fridge for up to 1 week.

Sambal Belacan

SPICY SHRIMP PASTE

Toasted *belacan*, the pungent fermented shrimp paste beloved in Malaysia and Indonesia, teams up with lime juice and a shitload of chiles to make a brutally spicy condiment for Laksa Nyonya (page 103).

Makes about 3/4 cup

2½ oz / ¼ cup packed Malaysian fermented shrimp paste

2¾ oz / 40 stemmed fresh or frozen red Thai chiles

2 g / 4 large fresh or frozen makrut lime leaves, center stem removed, very thinly sliced

26 g / 2 tbsp plus 2 tsp kosher salt

9 g / 2 tsp granulated sugar

¼ cup fresh lime juice (preferably from Key limes or from regular [Persian] limes with a squeeze of Meyer lemon juice)

Make a double layer of aluminum foil, put the shrimp paste on the center, and fold in the sides to make a packet. Set a heavy pan over medium heat (or better yet, grill it over a low charcoal fire) and add the packet. Cook, flipping the packet occasionally, until the shrimp paste is very fragrant, about 15 minutes.

Working in several batches, depending on the size of your mortar, combine the chiles, lime leaves, salt, and sugar in the mortar and pound to a fairly smooth paste, 10 to 15 minutes. Unwrap the foil packet, scoop the shrimp paste into the mortar, and pound until smooth and well combined. Add the lime juice and mix well.

The paste will keep in an airtight container in the fridge for up to 1 month.

Khai Tom

BOILED EGGS

ไข่ต้ม

A common accompaniment to saucy *khanom jiin* dishes (see pages 47 and 53 to 61) and Laksa Nyonya (page 103), boiled eggs are as easy to make as they sound. If you're making Kuaytiaw Kai Tuun (page 85), do yourself a favor and add some peeled boiled eggs to the pot of hot stewed chicken and let them chill out for an hour or two, so they absorb some of the sweet, aromatic broth.

Makes 10 eggs

10 eggs, at room temperature

Prepare a big bowl of ice and water.

Bring 4 quarts water to a boil in a large pot over high heat. Carefully add the eggs, set a timer, and cook them for 7 minutes (for yolks still molten in the center) or 8 minutes (for yolks that are set but not dry), then turn off the heat. Immediately use a slotted spoon or spider to transfer the eggs to the ice water. Once the eggs are fully cool, drain them well.

The eggs will keep in an airtight container in the fridge for up to 1 week.

Khai Khem

SALTED DUCK EGGS

ไข่เค็ม

These are a great argument for making this Thai pantry staple yourself. Yes, you can purchase them in most well-stocked Chinese or Southeast Asian supermarkets, where they're packaged in containers or set out in flats. (They're frequently dyed pink to distinguish the preparation from *balut*, the fertilized duck egg popular in the Philippines that is frequently on offer as well, thus sparing you quite a surprise.) But whatever bit of industrial food magic makes them shelf stable also renders the whites unpleasantly dry, the yolks unpleasantly grainy, and the flavor dramatically inferior.

Make them yourself and it's a different ballgame—the flavor cleaner, the texture better by a wide margin. Then you'll understand why *khai khem* are added to papaya salad; transformed into a *yam* (salad) via a sweet, salty, sour dressing; and served as an accompaniment to *khanom jiin kaeng khiaw waan* (see page 55). Sometimes just the yolks are used, encased in starchy pork paste for *khai mangkawn* (see page 209), or used to enrich the sauce for a stir-fry of squid.

And while the process of making them takes several weeks, the recipe might count as the dopiest of all time. You make a brine, add the eggs, and blammo! For the formula, I brazenly rip off chef David Thompson, who has been studying Thai food since I was bumming around Southern Thailand sporting fisherman pants and a rat-tail, and who over the years has conferred upon me

both friendship and culinary guidance. In an attempt to evade his ire (or perhaps to provoke it), I leave out his suggested addition of durian husk ash. I just don't know very many home cooks who have carbonized durian husk to spare.

Makes 12 eggs

8 cups water	12 duck eggs
8¾ oz / 1¾ cups kosher salt	

In a large saucepan, combine the water and salt and bring to a boil over high heat, stirring to help the salt dissolve. As soon as it reaches a boil, turn off the heat and let this brine cool to room temperature.

Put the eggs in a clean, tall, straight-sided container with an approximately 1-gallon capacity (such as a canning jar or Cambro) and pour in enough of the brine to submerge them by an inch or so. Use a plate to weigh down the eggs so they stay submerged. (Alternatively, fill a resealable bag with water, slip it inside another resealable bag to prevent leaks, and use it to weigh down the eggs.)

Keep the container in a cool, dry place (but not in the refrigerator) for 30 days, then drain the eggs well. They will keep in an airtight container in the fridge for up to 6 months.

When you're ready to cook the eggs, bring 3 quarts water to a boil in a large pot over high heat. Meanwhile, prepare a big bowl of ice and water.

Carefully add the eggs to the boiling water, set a timer, and cook for 9 minutes.

Use a slotted spoon or spider, transfer the eggs to the ice water. Once the eggs are fully cool, drain them.

They will keep in an airtight container in the fridge for up to 1 week.

Naam Phrik Phao

CHILE JAM

น้ำพริกเผา

Although it shares its Thai title with a simple roasted-chile condiment (see facing page) served with *khao soi*, this *naam phrik phao* is more ingredient than condiment. It's also more complex in both preparation and flavor. Mixed with dressings for *yam* (salads), stirred into soups, added to stir-fries, and spread like jam on the white toast that accompanies *sateh* (or satay, as it's spelled on American menus), it features more than just chiles. It's slightly spicy but also sweet, aromatic, toasty, and salty from a parade of ingredients— shallots and garlic and dried shrimp—that are fried in oil and then blended to a coarse paste along with palm sugar and a little tamarind for tang.

Each bowl of Kuaytiaw Tom Yam Plaa Naan Khon (page 73) requires just a couple teaspoons of the stuff, so you might give in and purchase the jarred version, often labeled "roasted chile paste" or "chile paste in oil." That's fine, as long as you buy a Thai brand, such as Pantainorasingh, Maepranom, or Nittaya, and check the ingredients to make sure they more or less match the ones listed here to confirm you have identified the right product. Freshly made *naam phrik phao*, however, tastes better, and since it keeps well in the fridge, you won't have to make it again for a long time.

Makes about 2 cups

50 g / ½ cup medium-size dried shrimp

Neutral oil, such as canola, soybean, or rice bran, for deep-frying

10 oz / 2 cups small Asian shallots, peeled and very thinly sliced against the grain

7 oz / 1⅓ cups garlic cloves, peeled and chopped into about ⅛-inch pieces

28 g / 14 dried puya chiles, stemmed, slit open, and seeded

3½ oz / ¼ cup plus 1 tbsp packed Naam Taan Piip (Softened Palm Sugar; page 239; preferably Thai)

2 tbsp Naam Makham Piak (Tamarind Water; page 238)

2 tbsp Thai thin soy sauce

2 g / ¾ tsp kosher salt

Soak the shrimp in a small bowl full of water for 10 minutes. Drain, briefly rinse, and pat them dry with paper towels.

Set a fine-mesh strainer over a heatproof container.

Set a medium flat-bottomed wok or saucepan over high heat. Pour in enough oil to reach a depth of 2 inches and heat the oil to 300°F to 325°F. Use a thermometer to take the temperature, measuring the oil at the center of the vessel and carefully stirring the oil occasionally to ensure a consistent temperature. Add the dried shrimp to the hot oil and fry, stirring frequently, until golden brown, 1 to 2 minutes. Scoop them out with a spider and transfer them to a small plate to cool.

Lower the heat to bring the oil for 275°F. Add the shallots to the hot oil, stir, and cook, stirring occasionally and adjusting the heat to maintain a temperature of 250°F to 275°F, until the shallots are deep golden brown and fully crisp, 10 to 20 minutes. Pour the contents of the wok through the prepared strainer and transfer the shallots to a large plate. Return the oil to the wok and the strainer to the heatproof container.

Bring the oil back to 275°F. Add the garlic to the hot oil, stir, and cook, stirring occasionally and adjusting the heat to maintain a temperature of 250°F to 275°F, until the garlic is light golden brown and fully crisp, 3 to 5 minutes. Pour the contents of the wok through the prepared strainer and add the garlic to the plate with the shallots. Return the oil to the wok and the strainer to the heatproof container.

Let the oil cool to 225°F to 250°F. Add the chiles and cook over low heat, stirring constantly, until the chiles are tobacco brown but not burnt, 3 to 5 minutes. Strain the contents of the wok into the heatproof container and transfer the chiles to the plate with the shallots and garlic. Let the oil cool to room temperature. Set aside ½ cup of the oil for this recipe. (Reserve the remaining oil to use as a flavorful cooking liquid; it will keep in an airtight container in the fridge for up to 1 month.)

In a small food processor, combine the fried shallots, garlic, and chiles and process to a coarse paste. Transfer to a medium mixing bowl. Combine the sugar, tamarind water, thin soy sauce, and salt in the processor and process just until smooth, 15 to 30 seconds. Add the sugar mixture to the bowl with the fried garlic mixture. Pound the dried shrimp in a mortar until completely shredded and add them to the bowl along with the reserved ½ cup oil. Stir well.

The chile jam will keep in an airtight container in the fridge for up to 3 months.

Naam Phrik Phao

ROASTED-CHILE PASTE

น้ำพริกเผา

Along with sliced raw shallots, pickled mustard greens, fish sauce, and lime wedges, bowls of *khao soi* (see page 175) come with a dark, oily paste of fried dried Thai chiles. It's fiery, aromatic, and slightly (pleasantly) bitter, to be stirred into bowls at each diner's preference.

Makes a generous ½ cup

½ cup neutral oil, such as canola, soybean, or rice bran	½ tsp toasted sesame oil
2 oz / 2 cups dried Thai chiles	

Set a flat-bottomed wok or large skillet over low heat. Pour in the oil and heat until it shimmers. Add the chiles and cook, stirring frequently, until they're evenly dark brown but not black, 10 to 15 minutes.

Using a slotted spoon, transfer the chiles to a food processor and let them cool; reserve the oil. Process the chiles to a coarse paste. (Alternatively, pound them in a mortar.) Stir in just enough of the reserved oil to saturate the paste but not so much that it's swimming in oil. (The consistency should be like that of chunky peanut butter.) Stir in the sesame oil.

The paste will keep in an airtight container at room temperature for up to 6 months.

Naam Jim Kai

SWEET CHILE SAUCE

น้ำจิ้มไก่

This condiment is familiar to most Americans only in the sickly sweet jarred form found often at Thai restaurants, as well as, for some reason, many American bento-box joints. Made yourself, however, the sauce is plenty sweet but tempered by enough tartness from vinegar and heat from chiles to provide balance and to make the dipping of Luuk Chin Thawt (page 205) and Khai Mangkawn (page 209) advisable.

Makes about 1 1/4 cups

7 oz / 1 cup granulated sugar	21 g / 14 stemmed fresh or drained pickled red Thai chiles, roughly sliced
1/4 cup plus 2 tbsp distilled white vinegar	35 g / 10 garlic cloves, peeled and halved lengthwise
1/2 cup water	3 g / 1 tsp kosher salt

In a small saucepan, combine the sugar, vinegar, and water, set over high heat, and bring to a vigorous simmer, whisking to dissolve the sugar. Cook for 5 minutes or so, whisking as needed.

Meanwhile, combine the chiles, garlic, and salt in a mortar and pound to a coarse paste. Add the chile mixture to the saucepan, lower the heat to maintain a steady simmer, and cook until the liquid thickens a bit and becomes slightly syrupy, about 12 minutes. Remove from the heat and let cool to room temperature.

The sauce will keep in an airtight container in the fridge for up to 2 months.

Naam Jim Si Ew Dam Phrik Sot

BLACK SOY–CHILE DIPPING SAUCE

ซีอิ๊วดำพริกสด

This is a dead-simple dipping sauce for cooked pig—for example, the ribs in Ba Mii Bak Kut Teh (page 107) or the roasted and fried pork in Ba Mii Yok Haeng (page 165). The pleasure comes from the heat and aroma of fresh chiles and bitter-edged sweetness of the black soy sauce.

Makes about 2/3 cup

42 g / 1/2 cup thinly sliced (1/4 inch) fresh or frozen red Thai chiles	1/2 cup Thai black soy sauce

In a small bowl or container, combine the chiles and soy sauce and stir. The sauce will keep in an airtight container in the fridge for up to 2 weeks.

Phrik Phao Naam Som

GRILLED-CHILE VINEGAR

พริกน้ำส้ม

Sharp, grassy green chiles pick up char and complexity from the grill. Pounded and then mixed with vinegar, they provide an essential seasoning for *kuaytiaw reua* (see page 81), Kuaytiaw Tom Yam Muu Naam (page 79), and Ba Mii Tom Yam Haeng Muu (page 187).

Makes about 1 cup

2 oz / 32 fresh or frozen green Thai chiles, or about 8 fresh serrano chiles, stemmed

¾ cup distilled white vinegar

Prepare a grill, preferably charcoal, to cook with medium-high heat or preheat a wide, heavy skillet over medium-high heat.

If using a grill, thread the chiles onto skewers. Put the chiles on the grill grate or in the skillet in a single layer and cook, turning them over occasionally, until they are completely blistered and almost completely blackened all over and the flesh is fully soft but not mushy, 5 to 10 minutes, depending on their size.

Remove the chiles from the skewers, if necessary, and roughly slice them (nope, don't peel them). Pound them in a mortar to a very coarse paste, then stir in the vinegar.

The chile vinegar will keep in an airtight container in the fridge for up to 5 days.

Phrik Naam Som

VINEGAR-SOAKED CHILES

พริกน้ำส้ม

Offered as part of the standard *khruang phrung* (see page 36), the condiments diners use to season noodle dishes, this combination of moderately spicy chiles and vinegar barely requires a recipe. Just thinly slice some chiles, put them in a jar or bowl, and pour in enough vinegar to cover them by an inch or so. Due to the quirks of the Thai language, this has a very similar name as the version made with grilled chiles.

Makes about ½ cup

21 g / 3 fresh serrano chiles, stemmed and cut into ⅛-inch-thick slices

½ cup distilled white vinegar

In a small bowl or container, combine the chiles and vinegar and stir.

The chiles will keep in an airtight container in the fridge for up to 4 days.

Phrik Naam Plaa

FISH SAUCE–SOAKED CHILES

พริกน้ำปลา

Like Phrik Naam Som (page 235), this common *khruang phrung* (see page 36) is just sliced chiles drowned in flavorful liquid—in this case, the chiles are fiery and the liquid is fish sauce, perfect for adding salt, umami, and heat to dishes such as noodles and fried rice. Consider adding some thinly sliced garlic to punch up the flavor.

Makes about ¹/₂ cup

21 g / about 14 fresh or frozen Thai chiles (preferably green), stemmed and cut into ¹/₄-inch-thick slices

¹/₂ cup Thai fish sauce

In a small bowl or container, combine the chiles and fish sauce and stir.

The chiles will keep in an airtight container in the fridge for up to 2 days.

Naam Man Hom Jiaw

FRIED SHALLOTS IN SHALLOT OIL

หอมเจียว,น้ำมันหอมเจียว

The recipe for fried shallots, like the one for fried garlic (at right), is a two-for-one deal. Not only do you get sweet, crisp slivers of shallots that put jarred products to shame, but you end up with sweet, aromatic oil that's great for stir-frying and seasoning.

Makes about 35 g / ¹/₂ cup fried shallots and about 1 cup shallot oil

Naam Man Muu (Rendered Pork Fat; page 226, or use store-bought), warmed, or neutral oil, such as canola, soybean, or rice bran, for deep-frying

3 oz / ³/₄ cup very thinly sliced Asian shallots

Set a fine-mesh strainer over a heatproof container. Line a plate with paper towels.

Pour 1 inch of pork fat or oil into a flat-bottomed wok or saucepan, set over high heat, and heat to 275°F. Use a thermometer to take the temperature, measuring the hot fat at the center of the vessel and carefully stirring the fat occasionally to ensure a consistent temperature.

When the fat is hot, add the shallots, stir well, and cook, stirring occasionally and adjusting the heat to maintain a temperature of 250°F to 275°F, until they are deep golden brown and fully crisp, about 10 minutes.

Pour through the prepared strainer, capturing the liquid in the container. Gently shake to drain well, then transfer the shallots to the prepared plate in a single layer. Let cool completely.

Combine the shallots and liquid in an airtight container and store in a cool, dry place—or, to avoid rankling most US departments of health, in the fridge—for up to 1 week. If necessary, gently reheat to liquefy just before using.

Naam Man Krathiam Jiaw

FRIED GARLIC IN GARLIC OIL

กระเทียมเจียว,น้ำมันกระเทียม

Crunchy fried garlic provides texture and flavor to countless noodle dishes. Unless your local Thai market sells the freshly fried product, as some do, you'll want to make it yourself, since jarred versions pale in comparison. Another reason? In addition to fried garlic, the process leaves you with oil infused with the garlic's sweetness and fragrance, another vital seasoning for many of the noodle dishes in this book and, more generally, a pleasure to have on hand.

Makes about 45 g / ½ cup fried garlic and about 1 cup garlic oil

Naam Man Muu (Rendered Pork Fat; page 226, or use store-bought), warmed, or neutral oil, such as canola, soybean, or rice bran, for deep-frying	3 oz / 30 garlic cloves, peeled and chopped into about ⅛-inch pieces

Set a fine-mesh strainer over a heatproof container. Line a plate with paper towels.

Pour 1 inch of pork fat or oil into a flat-bottomed wok or saucepan, set over high heat, and warm to 275°F. Use a thermometer to take the temperature, measuring the hot fat at the center of the vessel and carefully stirring the fat occasionally to ensure a consistent temperature.

When the fat is hot, add the garlic, stir well, and cook, stirring occasionally and adjusting the heat to maintain a temperature of 250°F to 275°F, until it is light golden brown and fully crisp, 3 to 5 minutes.

Pour through the prepared strainer, capturing the liquid in the container. Gently shake to drain well, then transfer the garlic to the prepared plate in a single layer. Let cool completely.

Combine the garlic and liquid in an airtight container and store in a cool, dry place—or, to avoid rankling most US departments of health, in the fridge—for up to 1 week. If necessary, gently reheat to liquefy just before using.

Naam Makham Piak

TAMARIND WATER

น้ำมะขามเปียก

To make the sauce for *phat thai* (see pages 137 and 141) and to season the broth for MAMA Naam (page 87), you'll need tamarind water, a tangy extract of the fruit. The process is too simple to settle for prepared concentrate, which lacks the bright flavor of the fresh stuff. Steep the pulp (sold in shelf-stable blocks at most Chinese or Southeast Asian markets) in boiling water, mash with a spoon, and strain. Because it keeps well, this yields more than you'll need for any one recipe in this book.

Makes about 1 2/3 cups

2 oz / 3 tbsp packed Vietnamese or Thai seedless tamarind pulp (also called tamarind paste)	1 3/4 cups water

In a medium saucepan, combine the tamarind pulp and the water and bring to a boil over high heat, breaking up the tamarind as it softens. Immediately turn off the heat, cover the pot, and let the mixture sit until the tamarind is very soft, about 30 minutes. There's no need to skim off any foam.

Set a medium-mesh strainer over a heatproof container.

Use a whisk or wooden spoon to mash and stir the tamarind mixture, breaking up any large clumps. Pour the contents of the pan into the strainer, stirring, pressing, and smashing the solids to extract as much liquid as possible. There may be pulp clinging to the outside of the strainer; add that to the container, too. Discard the remaining solids.

The tamarind water will keep in an airtight container in the fridge for up to 1 week and in the freezer for up to 3 months. Stir well before each use.

Kapi Kung

HOMEMADE SHRIMP PASTE

กะปิกุ้ง

Combining a little jarred *kapi* (Thai shrimp paste) with a lot of tiny salted shrimp (a Korean product) gives you a mellow but still salty, funky paste that's similar to what my friends in Northern Thailand favor in their cooking. In this book, you'll need it for Kaeng Khiaw Waan Luuk Chin Plaa (page 55) and Naam Ngiaw (page 47) served with *khanom jiin*. The process of making it requires little effort and the result keeps in the fridge for many months.

Thai shrimp paste is readily available online and at most Chinese or Southeast Asian supermarkets near the Thai products. Jars of tiny salted shrimp are available in the refrigerated case at Asian supermarkets with a Korean focus.

Makes about 9 oz / 1 cup

1 1/4 lb / 2 cups jarred Korean salted shrimp, such as Choripdong brand	25 g / 2 tbsp Thai shrimp paste

Have ready a double layer of cheesecloth.

Briefly rinse and drain the salted shrimp, put them on the cheesecloth, and gently squeeze out most of the liquid. Combine the salted shrimp and shrimp paste in the mortar and pound, stirring occasionally with a spoon, until you have a coarse paste that is more or less an even light brown, 3 to 5 minutes.

The paste will keep in an airtight container in the fridge for up to 6 months.

Naam Taan Piip

น้ำตาลปี๊ป

This is the process meant to approximate the soft palm sugar that is easily found in Thailand but not so in the States.

Makes 5¾ oz / ¼ cup plus 3 tbsp

6 oz palm sugar (preferably Thai)	1 tsp water

Put the palm sugar in a small microwavable bowl, sprinkle on the water, cover the bowl with plastic wrap, and microwave on low power in 10-second increments just until the sugar has softened (not liquefied), 30 seconds to 1 minute. Pound the mixture in a mortar to a smooth paste.

The sugar will stay soft in an airtight container at room temperature for up to 1 week.

Naam Cheuam

SIMPLE SYRUP

น้ำเชื่อม

Take a few minutes to dissolve sugar in water and you'll have simple syrup for making iced drinks, such as Naam Manao (page 252) and Cha Manao (page 254), and several sauces for noodle stir-fries (see pages 119, 125, and 127). Making the syrup ensures that the sugar fully dissolves and distributes in the drinks and other mixtures.

Makes about 3 cups

2 cups water	14 oz / 2 cups granulated sugar

In a medium saucepan, combine the water and sugar and bring to a boil over high heat. As soon as it reaches a boil, turn off the heat. Whisk until the sugar has completely dissolved. Let cool completely.

The syrup will keep in an airtight container in the fridge for up to 3 months.

Naam Cheuam Naam Taan Piip

PALM SUGAR SIMPLE SYRUP

น้ำเชื่อมน้ำตาลปี๊ป

To make the dressings for Yam Kuay Chap (page 159) and Yam MAMA (page 157), as well as the sauce for *phat thai* (see pages 137 and 141), you must dissolve palm sugar in water to make this syrup.

Makes about 1³/₄ cups

10 oz palm sugar (preferably Thai)	1¹/₄ cups water

In a small saucepan, combine the sugar and water and bring to a boil over high heat. As soon as it reaches a boil, turn off the heat. Let it sit, breaking up chunks, until the sugar has fully dissolved and the mixture has cooked completely.

The syrup will keep in an airtight container in the fridge for up to 3 months.

Phrik Pon Khua

TOASTED-CHILE POWDER

พริกป่นคั่ว

Mexican puya chiles make a solid stand-in for a type of Thai dried chile that's toasted slowly, seeds and all, and then ground into a coarse powder. It's a common seasoning and, in this book, an important member of *khruang phrung* (see page 36), the assortment of simple condiments served with noodle dishes so the diner can adjust the flavor to his or her liking. A burr grinder, even an inexpensive hand-crank kind, is ideal for grinding because it ensures an even grind, but a granite mortar and pestle paired with extra attentiveness works too.

Fair warning—depending on your kitchen's ventilation and your tolerance for discomfort, consider taking steps to protect yourself from the effects of vaporized capsaicin. At the very least, open a window and turn on your stove's exhaust fan before you begin. But consider wearing a dust mask or taking the whole operation outdoors.

Makes about 30 g /¹/₂ cup

2 oz / 30 stemmed dried puya chiles

Put the chiles in a large, dry skillet or flat-bottomed wok, turn the heat to high to get the pan hot, and then turn the heat to low. Toast the chiles, stirring almost constantly and flipping them occasionally so all sides make contact with the hot pan, until they're very brittle and very dark brown all over, 10 to 15 minutes. Remove the chiles from the pan as they are ready. Discard any seeds that escape from the chiles, as they will have burned and taste bitter.

Let the chiles cool, then, working in batches if necessary, grind them in a burr grinder or pound in a mortar, to a coarse powder that is about halfway between cayenne powder and store-bought red pepper flakes. Immediately transfer to an airtight container.

The powder will keep in a cool, dry place for several weeks.

Kung Haeng Khua

DRY-FRIED DRIED SHRIMP

กุ้งแห้งคั่ว

Before you use dried shrimp for *phat thai* (see pages 137 and 141) or papaya salad, you must first briefly soak and rinse the crustaceans and then slowly toast them in a dry pan until they're aromatic and dry once more, this time with a chewy-crisp texture.

Makes 35 g / ⅓ cup

50 g / ½ cup medium-size dried shrimp

Soak the shrimp in a small bowl full of water for 10 minutes. Drain, briefly rinse, and pat them dry.

Set a small dry skillet or flat-bottomed wok over medium heat. Add the shrimp and cook, stirring frequently, until they are dry all the way through and slightly crispy, 8 to 10 minutes. Set them aside to cool completely.

The shrimp will keep in an airtight container at room temperature for up to 1 week.

Phrik Haeng Thawt

DRIED THAI CHILES FRIED IN OIL

พริกแห้งทอด

Some dishes call for dried Thai chiles to be fried in a slick of oil until dark and fragrant. Here's how to do it.

Makes 7 g / 16 chiles

10 g / 16 stemmed dried Thai chiles	1 tbsp neutral oil, such as canola, soybean, or rice bran oil

---

Put the chiles in a dry small skillet or flat-bottomed wok, add the oil to coat, and set the pan over medium-low heat. Cook the chiles, stirring and tossing them almost constantly, until they're a deep, dark brown (but not black), 7 to 10 minutes. Keep in mind that the residual heat of the oil will continue cooking the chiles. As they're ready, use a slotted spoon to transfer the chiles to a paper towel to drain. Discard any seeds that escape from the chiles, as they will have burned and taste bitter.

The chiles will keep in an airtight container in a cool, dry place for up to 5 days.

Phrik Haeng Khua

PAN-TOASTED DRIED THAI CHILES

พริกแห้งคั่ว

Some dishes called for dried Thai chiles to be toasted in a dry pan until smoky and fragrant. They're often served alongside the dish, to be eaten or crumbled on to provide heat and flavor. For the impatient, toast the chiles *sai wep*—in the microwave. Put them on a plate in a single layer and microwave on high power until they're fragrant, crispy, and lightly browned, about 1 minute.

Makes 7 g / 16 chiles

10 g / 16 stemmed
dried Thai chiles

Set a small skillet dry or flat-bottomed wok over high heat to get hot, then turn the heat to low. Add the chiles and cook, stirring almost constantly and flipping them occasionally so all sides make contact with the hot pan, until they're very brittle and very dark brown all over, 10 to 15 minutes. Transfer the chiles to a plate as they are ready. Discard any seeds that escape from the chiles, as they will have burned and taste bitter.

The chiles will keep in an airtight container in a cool, dry place for up to 5 days.

Kiaw Thawt

FRIED WONTON SKINS

เกี๊ยวทอด

Deep-fried wonton skins are a common, crunchy garnish for noodle soups. The key is the right oil temperature, which you can gauge with a thermometer or a test run: The wonton skin should puff almost immediately after it hits the oil and get fully crunchy before it turns any darker than pale golden brown.

Makes 16 triangles

Neutral oil, such as canola, soybean, or rice bran, for deep-frying

8 fresh square, "thin" wonton skins, separated and halved diagonally

---

Line a large sheet pan with paper towels or newspaper and set it near the stove.

Pour 3 inches of oil into a medium pot, set it over high heat, and bring the oil to 375°F to 400°F. Use a thermometer to take the temperature, measuring the oil at the center of the vessel and carefully stirring the oil occasionally to ensure a consistent temperature.

Working in batches of two triangles, carefully add the wonton skins to the hot oil and cook, turning the triangles over once or twice, until puffed and light golden brown, 15 to 30 seconds. Using a spider or other mesh strainer, transfer them to the prepared sheet pan in a single layer.

Fully cooled, the skins will keep in an airtight container in a cool, dry place for up to 2 days.

Khao Hom Mali

JASMINE RICE

With a few exceptions, Thais don't typically eat rice with noodles. Noodles tend to fall in the category of *aahaan jaan diaw*, one-plate (or bowl) meals, while rice is the centerpiece of the category of *aahaan kap khao*, the proper meal of multiple dishes meant to be eaten with the pleasantly bland grains. Still, this book includes a handful of dishes that require jasmine rice, such as one-plate meals of fried rice and noodle-less stir-fries on offer at some noodle shops, as well as Khao Kan Jin (page 49), rice steamed with pig's blood that's served alongside Khanom Jiin Naam Ngiaw (page 47). And even if it didn't, you should know how to make jasmine rice well.

Makes about 2 lb / 6 cups

14 oz / 2 cups uncooked Thai jasmine rice	2 cups water

Set a fine-mesh strainer inside a large bowl. Add the rice and fill the bowl with enough cool tap water to cover the rice by an inch or so and use your hand to stir the rice gently. Lift the strainer, dump out the cloudy water, and repeat the process until the water is no longer cloudy, about three times. Drain the rice, gently shaking it occasionally, until it's fully dry to the touch, about 15 minutes.

Put the rice in a rice cooker in an even layer. Add the 2 cups water, cover with the lid, press the button, and let the cooker do its thing. Once it's done, let the rice sit in the cooker with the cover on for about 20 minutes. Don't skip this step. It allows some of the steam to dissipate and some to get absorbed into the rice. It keeps the rice from clumping and gives the grains a chance to cool slightly, so when you fluff the rice, the grains aren't so soft that they break.

Finally, fluff the rice, trying your best not to break or smash the grains. The rice will keep after fluffing for several hours in the rice cooker on its Warm setting until you're ready to eat. For fried rice, for which older rice is best, let it cool and then store in an airtight container in the fridge for up to 5 days.

Khao Niaw

ข้าวเหนียว

In this book, Thai sticky rice (also called glutinous rice or sweet rice) is required only for making Naem (page 222). Yet any cook up for my somewhat onerous recipes for noodle dishes will want to know how to make sticky rice as well. Commonly eaten in the North and Northeast of Thailand, the glutinous grains are used as a sort of edible eating implement to grab and dab the various dishes on the table. The best way to cook the rice is with a sticky rice steamer set—a bamboo basket and its partner pot (see page 31).

Makes about 17 oz / 2¾ cups

400 g / 2 cups uncooked
Thai sticky rice

Put the sticky rice in a large bowl, add tepid tap water to cover by an inch or so, and let soak for at least 4 hours or up to 10 hours. Alternatively, you can soak the rice in hot tap water for 2 hours.

Drain the rice in a fine-mesh strainer held over the sink, then set the strainer with the rice inside a large bowl. Fill the bowl with enough cool tap water to cover the rice by an inch or so and use your hand to stir the rice gently. Lift the strainer, dump out the cloudy water, and repeat the process until the water is no longer cloudy, about three times.

Pour enough water into a sticky-rice steamer pot to reach a depth of about 2 inches and bring to a boil over high heat. Line the steamer basket with a double layer of damp cheesecloth and transfer the rice to the basket. Fold the cheesecloth so it covers the rice, pat the bundle to flatten the top, and cover with a pot lid or a clean, damp kitchen cloth, tucking it around the bundle.

Lower the heat so the water in the steamer pot is at a steady but not furious boil and set the basket in the pot. Cook, carefully flipping the bundle after 15 minutes, until the grains in the center are fully tender but still chewy (almost springy) and not mushy, 25 to 35 minutes.

Transfer the rice to an insulated container, like a cooler, or to a large bowl covered with a plate. Wait for about 15 minutes before digging in. The sticky rice will stay warm for 30 minutes or so.

Naam Jim Seafood

SPICY, TART DIPPING SAUCE FOR SEAFOOD

น้ำจิ้มซีฟู๊ด

Hot from charred Thai chiles, tart from lime juice, pungent from garlic, herbaceous from cilantro root, and humming with umami from fish sauce, this sauce electrifies Buu Op Wun Sen (page 163). It goes great with grilled fish, squid, or shrimp and, despite the dip's moniker, virtually any protein you cook.

Makes about ¾ cup

21 g / 14 stemmed fresh or frozen green Thai chiles, or 21 g / 3 fresh serrano chiles

7 g / 7 cilantro roots

1 g / ½ tsp kosher salt

21 g / 7 garlic cloves, peeled and halved lengthwise

6 tbsp fresh lime juice (preferably from Key limes or from regular [Persian] limes with a squeeze of Meyer lemon juice)

¼ cup Thai fish sauce

22 g / 1 tbsp plus 2 tsp granulated sugar

4 g / 2 tbsp very roughly chopped cilantro (thin stems and leaves)

Soak three wooden skewers in tepid water for 30 minutes. Drain well.

Prepare a grill, preferably charcoal, to cook with medium-high heat or preheat a stovetop grill pan over medium-high heat.

If using a grill, thread the chiles onto the skewers. Put the chiles on the grill grate or in the grill pan and cook, turning them over once or twice, until they are completely blistered and almost completely blackened all over and the flesh is fully soft but not mushy, 5 to 10 minutes, depending on their size. Slide the chiles off the skewers if necessary. (Use a small knife to peel the serrano chiles—but not the Thai chiles—as best you can.)

In a mortar, combine the cilantro roots and salt and pound to a fairly smooth, slightly fibrous paste, about 30 seconds. Add the garlic and pound until fully incorporated, 1 to 2 minutes. Add the chiles and pound them until you have a fairly smooth paste (the seeds will still be visible), about 1 minute more.

Scrape the paste into a small bowl or other container, add the lime juice, fish sauce, and sugar, and stir well. Let the sauce sit for an hour or two. Just before serving, stir in the cilantro.

Phak Dong

PICKLED MUSTARD GREENS

ผักดอง

This sour, salty pickle is served with curried noodle dishes, like *khao soi* (see page 177) and *khanom jiin naam ngiaw* (see page 47), to be eaten alongside or added right to the bowl. It helps cut their richness and provides a slight crunch. Familiar to anyone who frequents Chinese and Southeast Asian markets, pickled mustard greens usually appear in vacuum-packed pouches. These packaged versions range in color from dark khaki to electric yellow. While many have an unwelcome sweetness, a Thai brand, after a good soak in water, makes a decent option for those who lack the inclination to pickle the greens themselves.

The determined cook, however, will end up with a more delicious product, even though my recipe skips the sun-drying step of the artisanal Chinese Thai version. The trade-off is a little fermented funk for a simpler process. The key is locating the right variety of leafy mustard, which is sold at supermarkets that cater to Chinese customers. Called *gai choy* and occasionally labeled, unhelpfully, "Chinese mustard green," the kind you're after has floppy, vivid green leaves (they resemble ruffled romaine lettuce) and wide, pale green stems (a bit like those of mature bok choy in shape) that curl to form a bulbous head. Don't confuse the right stuff with *gai choy sum*, which is a related, leafier vegetable with narrow stems.

Makes 4 quarts

5 lb Chinese mustard greens (gai choy), yellowed outer leaves removed, heads halved lengthwise, washed well

7 quarts water

4 oz / ¾ cup kosher salt

4 g / 1 tsp red or white limestone paste

4½ oz / ⅓ cup packed Naam Taan Piip (Softened Palm Sugar; page 239; preferably Thai)

2½ cups distilled white vinegar

In a 1½- to 2-gallon pot, crock, or other heatproof container narrow enough that the mustard greens will be comfortably crowded, arrange the greens, leaves up.

In a medium pot, combine 4 quarts of the water, 2 oz / ¼ cup plus 2 tbsp of the salt, and 2 g / ½ tsp of the limestone paste and set over high heat. Bring the water to a boil, whisking to be sure the salt and limestone paste dissolve, then immediately pour this brine over the mustard greens. Agitate slightly with tongs so the brine can seep into the spaces between the greens and to make sure they're submerged. Let the greens sit, uncovered, at room temperature for 4 hours, then cover and refrigerate overnight.

The next day, drain the mustard greens well. Wash and dry the container and return the mustard greens to it, leaves up again.

In a medium pot, combine the remaining 3 quarts water, 2 oz / ¼ cup plus 2 tbsp salt, and 2 g / ½ tsp limestone paste, the palm sugar, and the vinegar. Set over high heat and bring the water to a boil, whisking occasionally to be sure the sugar, salt, and limestone paste dissolve, then immediately pour this brine over the mustard greens.

Fill a large resealable bag with water, slip it inside another resealable bag to prevent leaks, and use it as a weight to keep the mustard greens submerged in the brine. Cover the container and let them pickle at room temperature overnight.

Transfer the mustard greens to smaller containers, if desired (distribute the brine among them to submerge the greens if you do), and store, covered in brine, in the fridge for up to 6 months.

Khreuang Deum
DRINKS

เครื่องดื่ม

Naam Krachiap

ICED HIBISCUS TEA

น้ำกระเจี๊ยบ

Steeped in water, dried hibiscus flowers leave the liquid a vivid red and impart a mouth-puckering tartness. Plenty of sugar balances this acidity and some salt keeps things interesting.

Makes 6 to 8 servings

10 cups water

45 g / 1¼ cups dried hibiscus flowers, briefly rinsed and drained

7 oz / 1 cup granulated sugar

7 g / 2 tsp kosher salt

Ice cubes, for serving

Pour the water into a medium pot and bring to a boil over high heat. Stir in the hibiscus, sugar, and salt. Cover, lower the heat to maintain a gentle simmer, and simmer for 20 minutes to extract the hibiscus flavor. Let cool to room temperature, strain into a pitcher, and refrigerate until chilled.

The tea will keep, covered, for up to 1 week. To serve, stir well and pour into ice-filled pint glasses.

Naam Lam Yai

DRIED-LONGAN DRINK

น้ำลำไย

Sweet with a floral, tropical flavor, the longan is similar to its cousin, the lychee, and grows like crazy in Thailand. This drink features the darker, slightly musky, honeyed quality of dried longan. Rehydrated in the course of making the drink, the fruit is added to the glasses and is pleasant to chew on.

Makes 6 to 8 servings

10 cups water

14 oz / 2 cups granulated sugar

3½ oz / 1¼ cups dried longans (preferably Thai)

5 g / 1½ tsp kosher salt

Ice cubes, for serving

In a medium pot, combine the water, sugar, longans, and salt and bring to a boil over high heat, stirring occasionally to dissolve the sugar. Turn the heat to medium-low and simmer for 5 minutes, then turn off the heat. Let cool to room temperature, then pour (including the longans) into a pitcher and refrigerate until chilled.

The drink will keep, covered, for up to 1 week. To serve, stir well and pour the liquid and some longans into ice-filled pint glasses.

Naam Manao

น้ำมะม่วง

Salt makes food taste better. In Thailand, this logic extends to drinks as well. There you'll find it in orange juice, pineapple juice, and this lime drink (pictured opposite, at left), where it tempers the sweetness of the sugar and bumps up the flavor of the citrus. Making the Salty Water takes no time at all and ensures that the salt will dissolve in the cold drink. A pinch of salt stirred in also does the trick, though not as reliably.

Makes 1 serving

Ice cubes, for serving

1/4 cup plus 2 tbsp Naam Cheuam (Simple Syrup; page 239)

2 tbsp fresh lime juice (preferably from Key limes or from regular [Persian] limes with squeeze of Meyer lemon juice), plus 1 lime wedge (preferably Key lime)

3 drops Salty Water (recipe follows), from an eyedropper or straw

Seltzer, chilled, for topping off

Fill a pint glass with ice and add the simple syrup, lime juice, and salty water. Top off with seltzer and stir well. Squeeze on the lime wedge and serve.

Salty Water

Makes about 1/2 cup

1/2 cup water

45 g / 2 tbsp plus 2 tsp fine sea salt

In a small pot, bring the water to a simmer, then turn off the heat, add the salt, and stir until dissolved. Let the mixture cool. It will keep in an airtight container in the fridge for up to 1 year.

Cha Manao

THAI ICED TEA WITH LIME

น้ำมะนาว

In the States, Thai tea typically gets mixed with a copious amount of sugar and half-and-half. In Thailand, it's often treated with a similar dose of sugar plus evaporated and sweetened condensed milks. Yet there you'll also find boldly sweetened Thai tea spiked with lime for a drink (pictured opposite, at right) that's lighter and more refreshing. Thai tea varies by brand. Some pair black tea with star anise and cardamom and others with lemongrass and pandan. Most contain artificial colors that tint the brewed tea orange. Results vary, but only slightly.

Makes 4 servings

6 cups water

4 oz / 1 1/3 cups Thai tea mix, such as Pantainorasingh or Number One Hand brand

1 1/4 cups plus 2 tbsp Naam Cheuam (Simple Syrup; page 239)

5 1/2 tbsp fresh lime juice (preferably from Key limes or from regular [Persian] limes with a squeeze of Meyer lemon juice), plus 4 lime wedges (preferably Key lime)

Ice cubes, for serving

In a medium pot, bring the water to a boil over high heat. Add the tea, stir well, let the water come back to a boil, then turn off the heat. Cover and let steep until the water has cooled to room temperature, 1 to 2 hours. Strain through a fine-mesh strainer into a pitcher, pressing lightly to extract the liquid, then stir in the simple syrup, and refrigerate until chilled.

The tea will keep, covered, for up to 1 week. To serve, add the lime juice and stir well. Pour the tea into four ice-filled pint glasses and stick a lime wedge on the rim of each glass.

Nước Mát

VIETNAMESE ICED ARTICHOKE TEA

ชาวติโชค

On hot days in Vietnam, I often seek out this popular drink made from fresh artichokes simmered until they infuse water with their vegetal, vaguely anise-like flavor. Pandan leaf, a common ingredient in Thailand as well, lends a welcome nutty, rice-like quality.

Makes 12 to 16 servings

5 oz / 1 small artichoke	4 g / ½ fresh or thawed frozen pandan leaf
4 quarts water	
1 lb 5 oz / 3 cups granulated sugar	Ice cubes, for serving

Halve the artichoke lengthwise and scoop out and discard the fuzzy choke from each half. In a medium pot, combine the artichoke and water and bring to a boil over high heat. Cover the pot, lower the heat to maintain a gentle simmer, and cook for 1 hour to extract the flavor from the artichoke.

Turn off the heat and remove the lid. Add the sugar and pandan leaf and stir until the sugar has fully dissolved. Let cool to room temperature, strain into a pitcher, and refrigerate until chilled.

The tea will keep, covered, for up to 1 week. To serve, stir well and pour into ice-filled pint glasses.

Naam Gek Hoi

ICED CHRYSANTHEMUM TEA

น้ำเก๊กฮวย

Dried chrysanthemum flowers make a floral, slightly sweet, and particularly refreshing iced tea.

Makes 6 to 8 servings

11 cups water	Ice cubes, for serving
28 g / 1½ cups dried chrysanthemum flowers	

Pour the water into a medium pot and bring to a boil over high heat. Stir in the chrysanthemums, cover, and turn off the heat. Let steep until cooled to room temperature, then strain into a pitcher and refrigerate until chilled.

The tea will keep, covered, for up to 1 day. To serve, stir well and pour into ice-filled pint glasses.

Naam Takrai Dawk Anchan

LEMONGRASS AND BUTTERFLY PEA FLOWER DRINK

น้ำตะไคร้อัญชัญ

Fresh lemongrass supplies the flavor and aroma, while dried butterfly pea flowers (all the rage at health-minded markets) provide the striking blue color. Squeeze in a lime wedge and watch blue become purple.

Makes 10 servings

10½ cups water	25 g / 1¼ cups dried butterfly pea flowers
10½ oz / 1½ cups granulated sugar	Ice cubes, for serving
3 g / 1 tsp kosher salt	10 lime wedges (preferably Key lime)
17 oz / 7 large stalks lemongrass	

Combine the water, sugar, and salt in a large saucepan and bring to a boil over high heat, stirring occasionally so the sugar and salt dissolve completely. When the water reaches a boil, lower the heat to maintain a rolling simmer.

Cut off the top 9 inches and the bottom 1 inch from the lemongrass and remove the outer layer. Bruise and then cut it into ¼-inch pieces.

Add the lemongrass to the pot. Let the water return to a simmer, then take the pan off the heat and stir in the butterfly pea flowers.

Cover the pan and steep for 15 minutes. Strain through a fine-mesh strainer into a heat-safe pitcher. Let cool to room temperature and then refrigerate until chilled.

The drink will keep, covered, for up to 1 week. To serve, stir well before pouring into ice-filled pint glasses. Stick a lime wedge on the rim of each glass.

Naam Bai Boa Bok

PENNYWORT DRINK

น้ำใบบัวบก

A relative of parsley, pennywort (*bai boa bok* in Thai) is an herb that's sometimes served raw alongside *phat thai* in Thailand. It's also blended with water and sugar to make this refreshing, vivid-green drink. Find bunches at Southeast Asian markets with a solid stock of herbs.

Makes 6 to 8 servings

3½ oz fresh pennywort, roots trimmed and discarded	8¾ oz / 1¼ cups granulated sugar
8½ cups water	Ice cubes, for serving

Combine the pennywort and 2 cups of the water in a blender and blend until smooth.

Drape a double layer of cheesecloth over a medium-mesh strainer and set the strainer over a large mixing bowl. Pour the pennywort mixture through the cheesecloth-lined strainer. Gather the edges of the cheesecloth around the solids and squeeze to extract as much liquid as possible. Discard the remaining solids in the cloth. Set the liquid aside.

Combine the remaining 6½ cups water and the sugar in a medium saucepan and bring to a boil over medium heat, stirring occasionally so the sugar dissolves completely. Take the pan off the heat, let the mixture cool for 5 minutes before adding it to the pennywort juice. Whisk well.

Let the mixture cool to room temperature and then refrigerate until chilled.

The drink will keep, covered, for up to 1 week. To serve, stir well and then pour into ice-filled pint glasses.

Acknowledgments

This book would never have seen the light of day if it were not for JJ Goode, who busted his butt to transcribe my mutterings into something cohesive. Many other folks shared the burden of carrying this one across the finish line: Emma Rudolph, Emily Timberlake, Doug Ogan, Betsy Stromberg, Serena Sigona, and all the other good folks at Ten Speed Press; Kimberly Witherspoon, my amazing agent and trustworthy adviser; Austin Bush for his intrepid photographic endeavors and indispensable translation services (shout out to his assistant on this project, Beer Thanet); Kat Craddock for her diligent recipe testing; and Natcha Butdee (Goong), my lovely partner, who graciously allowed the team to take over our house to test and shoot the recipes, washed dishes, hand modeled, kept the cats at bay, and tasted more noodles than anyone should have to in a two-week period. And, of course, all the noodle vendors I have met over the years who have shared their wisdom, skill, and pride in their craft!

This book is dedicated to the memory of Anthony Bourdain, a noodle man extraordinaire.

Index

Published in the United States by Ten Speed Press, an imprint of the Crown Publishing
Group, a division of Penguin Random House LLC, New York.
www.crownpublishing.com
www.tenspeed.com

Ten Speed Press and the Ten Speed Press colophon are registered trademarks
of Penguin Random House LLC.

Library of Congress Cataloging-in-Publication Data
Names: Ricker, Andy, author. | Goode, J. J., author.
Title: Pok Pok noodles : recipes from Thailand and beyond / Andy Ricker with JJ Goode.
Description: California : Ten Speed Press, [2019] | Includes index.
Identifiers: LCCN 2018046259
Subjects: LCSH: Cooking, Thai. | Pok Pok (Restaurant) | LCGFT: Cookbooks.
Classification: LCC TX724.5.T5 R5325 2019 | DDC 641.59593—dc23
LC record available at https://lccn.loc.gov/2018046259

Hardcover ISBN: 978-1-60774-775-8
eBook ISBN: 978-1-60774-776-5

Printed in China

Design by Betsy Stromberg

10 9 8 7 6 5 4 3 2 1

First Edition